N

Juneau

Vancouver

Seattle

Spokane

Portland

Butte

Boise

San Francisco

The Deserts of the Southwest
The Middle Atlantic Coast:
   Cape Hatteras to Cape Cod
The North Atlantic Coast:
   Cape Cod to Newfoundland
The North Woods of Michigan, Wisconsin,
   Minnesota and Southern Ontario
The Pacific Northwest
   Oregon, Washington, Idaho, Western Montana, and the
   Coastal Forests of Northern California, British Columbia,
   and Southeastern Alaska
The Piedmont of Eastern North America
The Sierra Nevada
Southern New England

A Sierra Club Naturalist's Guide to

THE PACIFIC NORTHWEST

Oregon, Washington, Idaho, Western Montana, and the Coastal Forests of Northern California, British Columbia, and Southeastern Alaska

by Stephen Whitney

ILLUSTRATIONS BY STEPHEN WHITNEY

SIERRA CLUB BOOKS   *San Francisco*

Copyright © 1989 by Stephen Whitney

All rights reserved under International and Pan-American Copyright Conventions. No part of this book may be reproduced in any form or by any electronic or mechanical means, including information storage and retrieval systems, without permission in writing from the publisher.

Library of Congress Cataloging in Publication Data

Whitney, Stephen, 1942-
    A Sierra Club naturalist's guide to the Pacific Northwest.

    Bibliography: p.
    Includes index.
    1. Natural history—Northwest, Pacific.   I. Sierra Club.
II. Title.
QH104.5.N6W47   1989   508.795   88-23937
ISBN 0-87156-743-1
ISBN 0-87156-696-6 (pbk.)

Production by Felicity Gorden
Book design by Robyn Brode, The Compleat Works,
    based on a series design by Klaus Gemming
Illustrations by Stephen Whitney

Printed in the United States of America

10   9   8   7   6   5   4   3   2   1

TABLE OF CONTENTS

PREFACE

THE PACIFIC NORTHWEST offers both residents and visitors a wealth of spectacular scenery, great diversity in climate, terrain, and vegetation, and some of the loneliest landscapes left in the United States. This book is meant to serve as a friendly guide to the natural treasures of the region, a source of general information about its forests, wetlands, steppes, deserts, and mountains.

Chapter 1, *The Lay of the Land,* introduces the Northwest's major landform regions, its mountain chains, coastal valleys, and high interior plateaus.

Chapter 2, *The Record in the Rocks,* summarizes the geologic history of the region—a story of colliding continents, advancing glaciers, catastrophic floods, and volcanic upheavals that make the 1980 eruption of Mount St. Helens seem trivial.

Chapter 3, *Wet Side, Dry Side,* examines how latitude, mountain ranges, and the Pacific Ocean contribute to the Northwest's enormous diversity of climate, which ranges from rain-forest wet along the coast to desert dry in the interior.

Chapter 4, *Patterns on the Land,* surveys the vegetation of the region and the factors determining the distribution of plants.

Chapter 5, *The Kingdom of Conifers,* discusses the history, ecology, and general features of conifer forests in general and those of the Pacific Northwest in particular.

Chapter 6, *Rain Forests,* focuses on the lush coastal forests extending from southern Alaska to northern California.

Chapter 7, *A Touch of California,* describes the vegetation of southwestern Oregon's mountains and valleys, whose forests, woodlands, and brush are northern extensions of widespread California communities. This chapter also discusses the redwood forest of northern California, which occurs intermittently southward down the coast to below Big Sur.

Chapter 8, *East to the Rockies,* features the montane conifer forests that mantle the interior mountain ranges of the Northwest, including the Northern Rockies, the eastern slope of the Cascades, Washington's Okanogan Highlands, and the Blue and Wallowa mountains of eastern Oregon.

Chapter 9, *Snow Forests,* describes the region's upper montane and subalpine forests, which range upslope to timberline.

Chapter 10, *Living with Conifers,* talks about conifer forests as wildlife habitat and the various ways in which animals have adapted to forest life.

Chapter 11, *High Country Parklands,* focuses on the parklands, meadows, and alpine fell fields that mantle the region's highest mountain ranges.

Chapter 12, *Life at the Top,* discusses the animals living at and above timberline and the ways in which they cope with their harsh environment.

Chapter 13, *Rainshadow Lands,* surveys the desertlike vegetation lying east of the Cascades, including the region's vast sagebrush steppes, the Palouse grasslands, the meadow steppes of northeastern Washington, and the desert communities of southeastern Oregon and southern Idaho.

Chapter 14, *At Water's Edge,* describes the plants, animals, and ecology of the Northwest's salt marshes, freshwater marshes, fens, bogs, and riparian woodlands.

As the preceding chapter outline indicates, this book focuses on terrestrial habitats, though Chapter 13 ventures far enough from dry land to include emergent and intertidal salt-marsh plants. Strictly marine and freshwater aquatic habitats are not included, mainly for reasons of space. A line 'had to be drawn somewhere and the water's edge seemed a logical boundary.

Although this book contains illustrations of a number of the more important plants found in the region, it is not meant to be used for identifying specimens in the field. For that purpose a number of fine guides already exist (see *Appendix B*). Rather, this book attempts to acquaint readers with the communities in which our plants and animals exist and to provide the information whereby those communities can be recognized and understood. The emphasis is on how plants adapt to their physical environment and on how animals respond to the habitats created by plants.

The book concentrates on Oregon, Washington, and Idaho, which form the heart of the region known as the Pacific Northwest. Attempting to draw firm boundaries for the region proved futile, however, on all but arbitrary grounds. Therefore, much of what is discussed here also applies in varying degree to adjacent sections of Montana, Wyoming, Utah, Nevada, British Columbia, and Alaska. As is usually the case, existing political borders only haphazardly correspond to the geologic, topographic, and ecologic boundaries by which natural regions are most sensibly defined.

This book departs from earlier volumes in the *Sierra Club Naturalist's Guide* series by listing scientific names for plants and animals in an appendix rather than including them in the main text of the book. This change in format was undertaken to improve the readability of the text without sacrificing the greater precision of scientific names or the sense of serious purpose conveyed by their use.

The information forming the bulk of this book is drawn partly from personal observations but mostly from the field work of hundreds of scientists whom space does not permit listing by name. Their findings, as reported in various professional publications, form the core of this book. I would particularly like to thank Jim Cohee of Sierra Club Books for initiating and supporting this project, Heath Silberfeld for her skillful editing of the manuscript, and Jerry Franklin of the University of Washington College of Forest Resources for reviewing the manuscript and suggesting ways of improving it. Finally, I am grateful to my family for putting up with my long working hours and frequent rendezvous with my word processor.

Stephen R. Whitney
Seattle, Washington

CHAPTER ONE

The Lay of the Land

THE PACIFIC NORTHWEST is a region of enormous diversity, where a traveler can easily visit coastal salt marshes, conifer forests, timberline meadows, and sagebrush plains all in a single day. This diversity results from the proximity of high, rugged mountains to the Pacific Ocean and the effect of that juxtaposition on climate and vegetation. The combined forces of wave, wind, ice, water, and volcanic fire have also created in the Pacific Northwest some of the most spectacular scenery on the continent.

The boundaries of the Pacific Northwest are unclear, except that however defined they must include the states of Washington, Oregon, and Idaho. Adjacent parts of British Columbia, Montana, and California are also included in this book because they are "northwestern" in geology, topography, and vegetation—in short, in everything that counts in a book such as this. On the other hand, parts of southern Oregon and Idaho have more in common with the vegetation and terrain of adjacent Nevada and Utah than they do with the rest of the Pacific Northwest. Even so, by virtue of their position north of the invisible line forming the southern boundary of Oregon and Idaho, these atypical areas are also discussed.

The Pacific Northwest is divided here into six distinct physiographic provinces—major landform regions characterized by more or less unified topography and geologic history. As a consequence of the interplay of these factors with regional climatic patterns, each province also tends to have more or less distinctive patterns of soil and vegetation. Physiographic provinces therefore provide a systematic way to survey the entire Pacific Northwest.

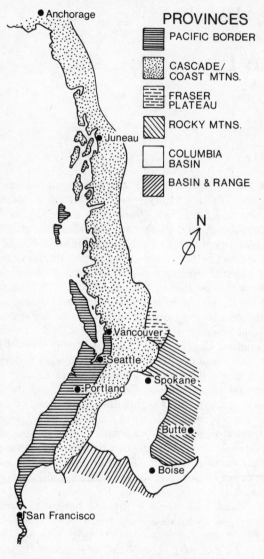

PROVINCES

▤	PACIFIC BORDER
▨	CASCADE/ COAST MTNS.
▤	FRASER PLATEAU
▨	ROCKY MTNS.
☐	COLUMBIA BASIN
▨	BASIN & RANGE

N

1. Physiographic provinces of the Pacific Northwest

Pacific Border Province

The Pacific Border Province comprises the immediate coast as well as the mountain ranges and interior valleys that lie between it and the Cascade Range to the east. The region includes British Columbia's Insular Range, the Olympic Peninsula, the Coast Range of Oregon and Washington, the Klamath Mountains, the California Coast Range, and the Puget–Willamette Lowlands.

Lush temperate rain forests dominated by Sitka spruce and western hemlock occur on the western side of the Olympic Peninsula and along the southwestern coast of Vancouver Island. At higher elevations montane and subalpine forests feature various mixtures of western hemlock, Douglas-fir, Pacific silver fir, western redcedar, Alaska-cedar, and mountain hemlock. A mosaic of prairies, oak woodlands, and Douglas-fir forests characterize southeastern Vancouver Island, including the Victoria area, and the northeastern Olympic Peninsula, across the Strait of Juan de Fuca. These areas lie in the rainshadow of the Olympic Mountains and therefore receive significantly less precipitation than the windward slopes.

Conifer forests dominated by Douglas-fir, western hemlock, and western redcedar are characteristic of typical habitats in the Puget Sound region. Atypical habitats support distinctive types of vegetation that are common nowhere else in western Washington. For example, oak woodlands and grasslands occur on gravelly soils from Tacoma southward as well as in rainshadow areas to the east and northeast of the Olympic Mountains. Rainshadow conifer forests often include large numbers of lodgepole (or shore) pine or western white pine, both of which are otherwise scarce in the region. Sitka spruce and redcedar dominate bottomland swamps.

The Willamette Valley lies in the rainshadow of the Oregon Coast Range and experiences hotter, drier summers than areas along the coast. As a result, the native vegetation is noticeably different from that of the rest of northwestern

Oregon. Conifer forests are mainly restricted to adjacent foothill areas. In these drier woods characteristic regional species such as western hemlock, which require more humid environments, may be scarce or absent. Woodlands of Oregon white oak, Douglas-fir, and Pacific madrone mingle with large areas of grassland. Deciduous woodlands of Oregon ash, black cottonwood, white alder, and assorted willows occur along the Willamette River and other waterways.

The Umpqua and Rogue valleys to the south are even drier than the Willamette. The conifer forests of these valleys feature trees such as ponderosa pine, incense-cedar, and sugar pine, which are characteristic of California's Sierra Nevada. On hot, dry slopes the forest often gives way to dense tracts of brush known as chaparral. Grasslands similar to those of the Willamette Valley occur on the valley floors. The mosaic of conifer forest, chaparral, and grassland occurs widely in northern California but nowhere else in the Pacific Northwest.

Spruce-hemlock forests occur along a narrow coastal strip northward to Alaska and southward through Oregon into northwestern California. The Oregon dunes, south of Florence, support drier forests in which Sitka spruce, shore pine, salal, Pacific rhododendron, and evergreen huckleberry are prominent. Forests of western hemlock and Douglas-fir mantle the Oregon Coast Range. Grassy balds crown numerous summits.

Redwood forests occur from extreme southwestern Oregon to south of Big Sur, California. Inland, on the western slopes of the Klamath Mountains and California North Coast Range, they are gradually replaced by mixed evergreen forests dominated by Douglas-fir, tanoak, and madrone. Similar forests occur at higher elevations on the eastern side of the Siskiyou Mountains and other ranges in the Klamath Mountains complex. Above the mixed evergreen forest, the Klamaths support extraordinarily riched mixed conifer forests featuring species drawn from Northwestern, Californian, and even Rocky Mountain sources. Distinctive, albeit scraggly, forests occur on the large areas of peridotite scattered through the Klamath Mountains. These areas feature trees such as Jeffrey pine and knobcone pine, which rarely occur on normal soils, as well as a host of shrubby and herbaceous species that are found nowhere else in the world.

Insular Range

British Columbia's Insular Range is a mostly drowned mountain range that rises above the sea most prominently in the form of Vancouver Island and the Queen Charlotte Islands. The Hecate Strait and Strait of Georgia lie between the islands of the Insular Range and the British Columbia mainland. The Strait of Juan de Fuca separates Vancouver Island from the Olympic Peninsula. The Insular Range consists of assorted sedimentary and volcanic rocks that have been intruded by bodies of granite. The range was heavily glaciated during the Ice Age and still features sizable alpine glaciers on the higher summits of Vancouver Island and the Queen Charlottes. The west coasts of the islands are deeply indented with fiords, the drowned valleys of former tidewater glaciers.

Olympic Peninsula

The Olympic Mountains take up most of western Washington's Olympic Peninsula. They consist of volcanic and sedimentary rocks that have been severely folded and thrust upward into steep, rugged ridges. The ridges radiate like spokes from a central knot of peaks, culminating in 7,900-foot Mount Olympus, and are separated by deep, relatively narrow river valleys. The Olympics were glaciated during the Ice Age and still bear substantial alpine glaciers on a number of the higher peaks. Evidence of glacial erosion and deposition is abundant. The Olympics are bordered on the west by a broad, forested coastal plain and beyond it the Pacific Ocean, on the north by the Strait of Juan de Fuca, on the east by Puget Sound, and on the south by the Chehalis River valley.

Oregon–Washington Coast Range

In Oregon the Coast Range parallels the coast from the Coquille River in the south to the Columbia River in the north. It is bordered on the west by the Willamette Valley. Elevations are modest: Summits on the highest ridges are generally between 1,500 and 2,500 feet high, with scattered higher peaks reaching as much as 4,100 feet elevation. The ridges are often quite steep, however, and their crests can be surprisingly sharp. The low, rounded Willapa Hills in southwestern Washington are the northernmost expressions of the Coast Range; the Olympic Mountains to the north are geologically related but are much higher and more rugged. The Coast Range of Washington and Oregon consists mainly of sandstones and shales derived from volcanic ash, along with basalts and related rocks. These more resistant igneous rocks make up the highest peaks in the range as well as the more prominent capes and headlands along the spectacular Oregon Coast.

Klamath Mountains

The Klamath Mountains are a complex assemblage of ranges and rocks that are sandwiched between the California Coast Range on the southwest, the Cascade Range on the northeast, and the Oregon Coast Range on the northwest. The Klamaths are extremely rugged, consisting of steep and rugged ridges separated by deep river gorges. The highest peaks are just over 7,000 feet. The Siskiyou Mountains constitute that portion of the Klamaths found in southwestern Oregon and adjacent parts of northwestern California. South of the Siskiyous, the other major Klamath ranges are the Salmon Mountains, Marble Mountains, Scott Mountains, Trinity Alps, and Yolla Bolly Mountains. The higher ranges, particularly the Trinity Alps and Siskiyous, were glaciated during the Ice Age but bear no glaciers today.

The geology of the Klamaths is exceedingly complex and has been studied relatively little. The mountains are made up mainly of metamorphic rocks derived from both sedimentary and volcanic sources. These are deeply folded, faulted, and intruded by granitic bodies. Underlying these rocks and outcropping over large areas are peridotite and serpentine, iron- and magnesium-rich igneous rocks thought to be derived from beneath the earth's crust.

California North Coast Range

Although California's North Coast Range lies outside what is normally considered to be the Pacific Northwest, it is included here because it is the principal home of the famous redwood forests, which share many features in common with other coastal forests in the Pacific Northwest. The range extends from Eureka south to San Francisco Bay. It is bordered on the west by the Pacific Ocean and on the east by the Klamath Mountains and the Sacramento Valley. The North Coast Range actually comprises a number of separate parallel ranges and their intervening valleys. Elevations range from sea level in places where the mountains plunge into the Pacific to more than 7,500 feet in the Mendocino Mountains bordering the Sacramento Valley. Summits are generally rounded, and the range was almost entirely free of ice during the Ice Age. Despite modest elevations, local relief is often impressive, especially where the mountains rise from the sea. The principal rocks making up these ranges are shales, sandstones, limestones, and cherts of marine origin. Outcrops of basalt and serpentine are also common.

Puget–Willamette Trough

Separating the two major coastal mountain chains of the Pacific Northwest is a long, narrow trough comprising Hecate Strait and the Strait of Georgia in British Columbia; Puget Sound and the valleys of the Chehalis and Cowlitz rivers in Washington; and the Willamette Valley in Oregon.

The Cowlitz and Willamette valleys are sunken blocks of the earth that are separated by faults from adjacent hills and mountains. The Cowlitz and Willamette rivers did not carve these broad troughs but rather, upon exiting the Cascade Range, were captured and diverted by them, the Cowlitz southward, and the Willamette northward, to the Columbia River. It is notable in this regard that the Columbia, which cuts straight through the Cascade Range, turns abruptly northward at its confluence with the Willamette in Portland, Oregon, and follows the line of the trough to the confluence of the Cowlitz River.

The Puget Lowlands and the Canadian coastal trough continue the northward trend established by the Willamette–Cowlitz depression and may mark the northern extension of the fault zone as well. The bedrock evidence that would confirm or deny this hypothesis, however, lies beneath thousands of feet of water or sediments or both.

The submerged portion of the trough extends southward to just beyond Olympia, Washington, and corresponds roughly to the part of it that was covered by continental glaciers during the Ice Age. Puget Sound and its associated waterways comprise a system of drowned glacial valleys. The surrounding plains are underlaid by as much as 3,000 feet of glacial and other sedimentary deposits and are interrupted by lines of hills consisting mainly of glacial till.

The Cascade–Coast Mountains Province

The Cascade Range and the Coast Mountains of British Columbia form a more or less continuous 1,700-mile mountain chain extending from northern California to Alaska. Owing to its great height, the Cascade–Coast Mountains chain forms the most important topographical barrier in the Pacific Northwest, dividing the mild, humid, densely forested coastal region from the drier, sunnier interior. The mountains intercept incoming Pacific storms and inhibit the eastward penetration of moderating marine air. They also partially protect the coastal lowlands from invasions of frigid continental air. The resulting differences in climate between the two sides of the mountains are responsible for their contrasting vegetation and patterns of land use.

The western flanks of the Coast Mountains and Cascade Range feature forests of Douglas-fir, western hemlock, western redcedar, Alaska-cedar, Pacific silver fir, and mountain hemlock. Along the upper timberline there are vast parklands featuring islands of trees surrounded by flower-filled meadows. Alpine tundra is limited in distribution because at elevations high enough to support it large areas are commonly buried beneath ice.

Conifer forests on the eastern side of the Cascade Range are generally Rocky Mountain types in which coastal species are important. Ponderosa pine, Douglas-fir, grand fir, western larch, Engelmann spruce, and subalpine fir are characteristic conifers both in the eastern Cascades and the northern Rockies. They are joined in appropriate habitats by the coastal conifers: western hemlock, western redcedar, and mountain hemlock. Timberline woodlands generally feature whitebark pine, though alpine larch is found in the North Cascades.

Similar forests occur on the eastern flanks of the Coast Mountains in southern British Columbia. Northward, however, conifers characteristic of the North American boreal forest, which stretches across Canada to the Atlantic, replace Northwest coastal and Rocky Mountain species. These northern interior forests lie outside the scope of this book.

Coast Mountains

The Coast Mountains of British Columbia are about 1,000 miles long and up to 200 miles wide. The range extends northward from near Vancouver, British Columbia, closely paralleling the shoreline and, in the north, forming the border with the Alaska Panhandle. In Alaska the Coast Mountains merge with the Fairweather and Saint Elias ranges, which are part of the same mountain system. The Coast Mountains rise abruptly from the saltwater of the Inside Passage, where the drowned valleys of former tidewater glaciers form fiords up to 60 miles long, two miles across, and 2,000 feet deep. The Alaskan portion of the range still contains a number of active tidewater glaciers, with the greatest concentration occurring in Glacier Bay National Park. Some of these glaciers are advancing, but the majority have been retreating steadily over the past couple of centuries. The range was deeply glaciated during the Ice Age, when it was one of the accumulation centers from which the continental ice sheet moved southward into what is now the northwestern United States. Extensive ice fields still occur in both the Coast Mountains proper and their Alaskan counterparts.

The highest peaks in the British Columbian Coast Mountains are over 13,000 feet, but a number of Alaskan and Yukon peaks, notably 18,008-foot Mount Saint Elias and 19,850-foot Mount Logan, are considerably higher. Nevertheless, several rivers draining the high plateaus to the east have succeeded in cutting completely through the Coast Mountains. The range consists primarily of granitic rocks of the Coast Mountain crystalline complex. Like all granitic rocks, these originated as molten rock (i.e., magma) that cooled in place deep within the earth. Later, as the mountains rose, the granite was exposed as overlying layers were stripped away by erosion. Smaller amounts of metamorphic rocks, principally gneiss, occur as caps on the higher peaks or as slices separating adjacent granite bodies.

North Cascades

The North Cascades extend southward from British Columbia to east of Seattle. They are bordered on the west by the Puget Lowlands and on the east by the Columbia Basin. The North Cascades are distinguished from the rest of the Cascade Range in age, rock types, mode of origin, and topography. Whereas the Southern Cascades are primarily volcanic in origin, the North Cascades, like the Coast Mountains, consist mainly of granitic and metamorphic rocks—except that the proportions are reversed. Whereas granite predominates in the Coast Mountains, metamorphic rocks such as schist and gneiss are more common in the North Cascades. Though separated by the Fraser River, the two ranges are geologically parts of the same mountain chain. During the Ice Age, the Cordilleran Ice Sheet, which originated partly in the Coast Mountains, all but buried the northern portion of the North Cascades. South of Glacier Peak, expanding alpine glaciers incised deep, sheer-walled valleys in the range en route to the lowlands.

Mount Baker and Glacier Peak, the two highest mountains in the North Cascades, are volcanoes of comparatively recent origin that formed atop the older granitic and metamorphic rocks. Elevations of the higher nonvolcanic peaks are modest, ranging between 6,500 and 9,500 feet, but their summits are sharply sculpted and their flanks are extremely steep, often rising as much as 6,000 feet in only three miles.

Southern Cascades

The Southern Cascade Range extends from central Washington to northern California. Its outstanding feature is the line of tall, symmetrical strato-volcanoes—the High Cascades—that occur at intervals along the crest. The two highest of these volcanoes are Mount Rainier and Mount Shasta, both of which top 14,000 feet. The two most active in this century have been Mount Saint Helens, which erupted in 1980, and Lassen Peak, which last erupted in 1917. Crater Lake, in southern Oregon, lies in what is actually a caldera, a depression created when a volcano, having emptied its magma chamber, collapses in upon itself. The enormous series of explosions that preceded the collapse occurred about 7,000 years ago and scattered pumice over most of the northwest. To the west of the High Cascade volcanoes, which mostly line up along the eastern crest of the range, are low, rounded ridges eroded from older Western Cascade volcanic rocks.

Elevations in the Southern Cascades have resulted less from uplift than from the piling up of volcanic materials. Because of the many low gaps in the range, the Southern Cascades have been cut through by three rivers: the Pit and Klamath rivers in California and the Columbia River along the border of Oregon and Washington. Of these the 1,200-mile Columbia is by far the greatest. Its present course apparently predates the formation of the mountains through which it passes. Over thousands of years, as lava flows and layers of pumice and ash gradually accumulated, the river was able to cut down through them fast enough to maintain its channel. The result of that persistence is the spectacular Columbia River Gorge.

Fraser Plateau Province

British Columbia's Fraser Plateau is a vast, rolling upland that lies between the Coast Mountains on the west and the Rocky Mountains on the east. The plateau is broadest in the north (about 200 miles across near Prince George) and narrows markedly toward the south. Only its southern part and the mountains adjacent to it fall within the area discussed in this book. Several rivers, including the Fraser itself, have carved deep, broad valleys through the plateau. In the south, where the plateau is highest, the valley rims appear as ranges of low mountains from river level. Farther north the topography is gentler. The rocks underlying the plateau are a mixture of volcanic and granitic types.

Valleys in the southern part of the Fraser Plateau are covered by bunchgrass or sagebrush steppe similar to that found in eastern Washington. Ponderosa pine and Douglas fir dominate foothill forests.

The Columbia Basin Province

The Columbia Basin Province includes the Columbia Basin proper, which covers most of eastern Washington; the Blue Mountains of eastern Oregon; and the high lava plains of eastern Oregon and southern Idaho. The province is bounded on the west by the Cascade Range, on the north and east by the Rocky Mountains, and on the south by the Great Basin.

Most of the Columbia Basin Province is covered by shrub steppe in which big sagebrush and other shrubs are scattered over a carpet of bunchgrasses such as bluebunch wheatgrass and Idaho fescue. Western juniper woodlands are widespread in south-central Oregon, with ponderosa pines forming open forests at somewhat higher elevations.

Forest vegetation in the Blue Mountains is similar to that along the east side of the Cascades, except that grand fir is more prominent and coastal elements are largely missing. The timberline region features forests of Engelmann spruce and subalpine fir and meadows dominated by Idaho fescue. Whitebark pine forms open woodlands on the highest rockiest slopes.

Columbia Basin

Though often called the Columbia Plateau by geologists, the Columbia Basin is actually a vast basin surrounded by mountains—the Cascades to the west, the Okanogan Highlands and Kettle Ranges to the north, the Rocky Mountains to the east, and the Blue Mountains to the south. The basin's area is about 180,000 square miles: It covers the southern two-thirds of eastern Washington, as well as a portion of north-central Oregon and a corner of northwestern Idaho. Elevations are mainly between 1,000 and 2,000 feet but drop to as little as 500 feet along the Columbia River.

The floor of the basin is covered by low hills and dissected by stream channels. Upon entering the basin from the north, the Columbia River flows westward along the base of the Okanogan Highlands, then south along the Cascades to the confluence with the Snake River. Just beyond, the combined rivers turn sharply west and enter the Columbia River Gorge, a spectacular basalt-walled canyon carved through the Cascade Range.

The entire basin is covered with thousands of feet of basalt, which erupted from vents along the Idaho border between 13 and 16 million years ago. In the eastern half of the basin the basalt flows lie nearly flat, but in the west the lava has been buckled into a series of low ridges, many of which run up against the eastern slope of the Cascades. In the extreme eastern basin, a line of small hills rising above the general level of the basin marks where outcrops of older Precambrian rocks escaped complete submersion by the surrounding floods of basalt. The best-known of these hills is Steptoe Butte, south of Spokane.

The Palouse Hills of southeastern Washington are old dunes made up of wind-blown silt, or loess, which accumulated to depths of about 200 feet. Although the hills formed after the basalt floods, the origin of the silt and the precise time of its deposition are unknown. It may have originated as exposed lake sediments, volcanic ash, and glacial outwash from the center of the basin and east slope of the Cascades. Alternatively, the silt may have originated in desert regions to the south. The soils that developed into the loess are among the most fertile in the world.

Among the most fascinating landforms in the Columbia Basin are the so-called channeled scablands, a complex network of dry channels and coulees cut into the Columbia basalt and overlying loess. Beginning near Spokane and running generally toward the southwest, the scabland channels were gouged out of the basalt flows by catastrophic floods, which repeatedly scoured the area some 15,000 years ago.

Blue Mountains

The Blue Mountains stretch across eastern Oregon from the Cascade Range near Bend to the mountains of central Idaho, separating the Columbia Basin to the north from the high lava plains to the south. They comprise a complex group of folded and faulted ranges that rise 2,000 to 5,000 feet above intervening lowlands and reach elevations of between 6,000 and 10,000 feet. The main ranges making up the Blue Mountains include the Ochoco, Elkhorn, Greenhorn, Strawberry, Seven Devils, and Wallowa mountains. The highest peaks are found in the Wallowa and Strawberry mountains. The Blue Mountains are a hodge-podge of old, highly deformed and scrambled sedimentary rocks that were intruded by granite and buried in places by Columbia basalt. In the eastern section of the Blue Mountains, Columbia flood basalts buried all but the highest ridges. The Snake River cut down through these flows and into the older sediments beneath to form Hells Canyon, the deepest major river valley in North America. The higher ranges in the Blue Mountains bore alpine glaciers during the Ice Age but are free of ice today. In the Wallowas, glaciers sculpted a spectacular alpine landscape from resistant granite, creating scenery reminiscent of the High Sierra.

High Lava Plains

The High Lava Plains comprise the Harney Lava Plain in southeastern Oregon and the Snake River Plain in southern Idaho. The Harney Lava Plain lies south of the Blue Mountains and runs parallel to them from the Cascades near

Bend to the Idaho border. From there, the Snake River Plain continues eastward to the Teton Range and other mountains along the Wyoming border. South of the High Lava Plains is the vast Great Basin province.

The Harney Lava Plain features level or gently inclined terrain punctuated, particularly in the west, by scattered volcanoes, cinder cones, and lava buttes. The largest of the volcanoes is Newberry Crater, which measures some 20 miles in diameter. The crater is actually a caldera not unlike that of Crater Lake, except that it contains two lakes rather than one. Scattered across the plain are several basins that lack drainage outlets. Some of the basins are dry; others contain wetlands and shallow lakes with seasonally fluctuating shorelines. The best known of these bodies of water is Malheur Lake, which each spring and fall hosts some of the largest concentrations of migrating waterfowl on the continent. The Owyhee Uplands lie east of Malheur Lake and extend into southwestern Idaho. They are essentially a high lava plateau into which the Owyhee River and its tributaries have carved deep, narrow canyons.

The Snake River Plain forms a broad arc through southern Idaho, separating the Northern Rocky Mountains on the north from the Great Basin and Middle Rockies on the south. The plain tilts gently westward from an elevation of about 6,000 feet near Yellowstone National Park, at its head, to about 2,200 feet near the Oregon border. The eastern half of the plain appears nearly flat, except for scattered cinder cones and lava domes. The Snake River winds its way along the length of the plain, but it did not carve this broad trench. In the western end of the plain the river has cut narrow, steep-walled gorges and terraces in the basalt flows that cover the floor of the plain. The Snake River Plain seems to occur along a rift zone, where the earth's crust is being pulled apart, possibly by stresses relating to the creation of the Basin and Range Province to the south.

Basin and Range Province

The Basin and Range Province covers most of the intermountain West lying between the Sierra Nevada and the

Rockies. The province includes the Sonora, Mohave, and Chihuahua deserts of the Southwest and the Great Basin desert to the north. The only section of the Basin and Range Province to extend into the Pacific Northwest is the Great Basin, which covers virtually all of Nevada and most of western Utah but also extends into south-central Oregon and southern Idaho. These portions of the Great Basin are accordingly the only parts of the Basin and Range Province to be discussed here.

The Basin and Range Province as a whole consists of a series of high mountain ranges that are uplifted along faults and separated by down-faulted basins. The result is dramatic washboard topography, which is evident both on maps and from the air. In southern Oregon, the principal fault-block ranges are Steens Mountain, the Abert Rim, the Pueblo Mountains, and the Trout Creek Mountains; in Idaho, the Portneuf Range, Bannock Range, Deep Creek Mountains, and Sublet Range. These ranges are essentially inclined plains, with abrupt eastern faces, which have risen along faults, and gradual western slopes. In their asymmetric profiles they resemble partly opened trap doors. East of the ranges are down-faulted basins, such as the Alvord Basin at the foot of Steens Mountain. These basins generally lack outside drainage and therefore often contain shallow saline lakes, or playas. Large areas of hard, white salt pan occur on dry lake beds. Most of the Great Basin in Oregon and Idaho is underlaid by basalt and other volcanic rocks that have erupted within the past 20 million years. Older rocks are exposed in a few of the mountain ranges.

Several species of sagebrush and perennial grasses together form the predominant vegetation of this region. Shadscale, a low desert shrub, dominates dry lake beds and other saline or alkaline areas. Steens Mountain and other fault-block ranges in the region mostly lack conifer forests, partly because these mountains are too remote from seed sources and partly because areas receiving sufficient precipitation are located at elevations too high, and therefore too cold, for most western conifers. Western juniper forms an open woodland on the lower slopes of Steens Mountain, while scattered groves of quaking aspen occur in moist soils upslope to timberline. Riparian woodlands are dominated by willow, alder, and cottonwood.

he Rocky Mountains Province

he Rocky Mountains Province in the Pacific Northwest is
presented almost entirely by the Northern Rocky Moun-
ins, though the Middle Rockies extend into the region
ong the Idaho-Wyoming border. The Northern Rocky
ountains include the Okanogan Highlands of northeastern
ashington; the Selkirk and Clearwater mountains and as-
ciated ranges of the Idaho Panhandle; the Salmon River,
wtooth, and other mountains of central and southern
aho; the Bitterroot Mountains along the Idaho-Montana
rder; and the Purcell, Selkirk, Cariboo, and Monashee
ountains of southeastern British Columbia.

The Okanogan Highlands consist of broad, rounded up-
nds, mostly below 5,000 feet elevation, but with a few
mmits reaching 8,000 feet. The upland areas are separated
 a series of north-south-trending river valleys, chief among
hich is that of the Columbia River, which divides the
kanogan Highlands into eastern and western halves. These
ghlands consist mainly of granitic rocks that have been
truded into older, folded, metamorphosed sedimentary
rmations. During the Ice Age, they were completely
ried beneath the Okanogan lobe of the Cordilleran Ice
eet. The Okanogan Valley forms a boundary between the
estern Okanogan Highlands and the North Cascades. The
lley of the Pend Oreille River separates the eastern high-
nds from the Selkirk Mountains of the Idaho Panhandle.

The Clearwater and Salmon River mountains, along with
her ranges of central Idaho, were all carved out of granitic
cks of the Idaho batholith. Although the river canyons
ssecting the rock are steep, the ridge summits are typically
ntle and of more or less the same elevation, so that from
e air the region looks like a dissected plateau. The highest
aks are just over 7,000 feet, and the ranges generally are
evated about 2,000 feet above the Columbia Basin to the
est. The most rugged and alpinelike of the mountains of
ntral Idaho are the scenic Sawtooths, just north of Boise,
here ice-fractured granite crags rise abruptly from the
arby lowlands. The Bitterroot Range—an uplifted fault
ock at the eastern edge of the Idaho batholith—runs along
e border separating western Montana and the Idaho Pan-

handle. The range consists mainly of highly folded an
faulted metamorphic rocks that have been intruded by ou
liers of granite. The Montana slope of the range is the highe
and craggiest, featuring sharp ridges separated by deep
glacially scoured valleys.

In British Columbia the Northern Rocky Mountain range
lying west of the Rocky Mountain Trench and east of th
Fraser Plateau are referred to collectively as the Columbi
Mountains. They comprise a series of lofty parallel range
separated by deep, north-south-trending valleys. Uplift ha
occurred along faults, and the highest peaks top 11,000 fee
All these ranges were deeply buried beneath the Cordillera
Ice Sheet during the last Ice Age and contain large ice field
and alpine glaciers today.

Ponderosa pine and Douglas-fir dominate the lowest for
ests in the mountains of Idaho. In southeastern Idaho, lim
ber pine may also be present. Mid-slope forests in centra
Idaho are dominated by Douglas-fir. In the Panhandle
grand fir, western redcedar, and western hemlock are als
prominent. Forests of western white pine, western larch
and lodgepole pine cover large areas that were devastate
by wildfire over the past few centuries. Engelmann spruc
and subalpine fir dominate subalpine forests, ranging up
slope to timberline where they are joined by alpine larc
and whitebark pine. Large parklands are common nea
timberline, but alpine vegetation is limited because mos
of the peaks in this section of the Rockies are not hig
enough to support it.

The varied landscapes of the Pacific Northwest represen
the response of vegetation to local permutations of regiona
geology and climate. The following three chapters discus
the geological processes that shaped the region, the climati
processes that make it distinctive, and the ways in whic
plants have responded to the physical habitats create
through the interplay of these processes.

CHAPTER TWO

The Record in the Rocks

THE PACIFIC NORTHWEST forms the leading edge of
North America, where the continent thrusts farthest into
the Pacific. It is here, at the boundary of land and sea, that
the most intense geologic activity on the continent is occur-
ing. The Alaska earthquake of 1964 and the eruption of
Mount Saint Helens in 1980 are but two of the more recent
dramatic events that punctuate the turbulent geologic history of the region. Both events provide keys to that history
and portend what yet is to come.

Earthquakes and volcanic activity occur most frequently
along the boundaries of the great moving plates that make
up the earth's crust. The plates bear relatively thin slabs of
heavy, black oceanic crust and much thicker chunks of continental crust. Oceanic crust consists of basaltic lava and
averages about 5.5 miles in thickness. Continental crust,
composed mostly of lightweight and light-colored granitic
rocks, has an average thickness of about 25 miles. Seven
major plates and several smaller "micro-plates" float on the
earth's mantle, which in turn surrounds the planet's iron
core. The mantle consists mainly of a dark, heavy rock known
as peridotite, which outcrops at various places in the Northwest, most notably in the Klamath Mountains. The plates
fit together like the patchwork polygons covering a soccer
ball, except that they are constantly moving—rifting apart,
scraping past each other, colliding, or diving one beneath
another. Why the plates move is not certain, but the most
frequent explanation is that they ride plumes of molten rock
within the mantle that circulate like water at a rolling boil.

Plates rift apart along mid-ocean ridges, such as the Mid-
Atlantic Ridge, which runs down the middle of the Atlantic

Ocean. Similar ridges snake across the floors of the world's other oceans. Molten basalt wells up along fissures that run along the crests of mid-ocean ridges and solidifies shortly after coming into contact with the cold ocean water. In this way new hunks of sea bed attach themselves to the trailing edges of the rifting plates and are borne away from the ridges.

As the plates move over the surface of the globe, they scrape past one another along transform faults such as the San Andreas Fault in California and the Great Glen Fault in Scotland. Since the shared boundary of the adjoining plates is seldom smooth, movement along such faults commonly occurs in jerks and starts, each of which is felt as an earthquake. The 1906 San Francisco quake, which measured 8.25 on the Richter scale, occurred when the land west of the San Andreas Fault all at once shifted 16 feet northward.

Movements and adjustments as one plate dives beneath another are manifested as deeply focused earthquakes of even greater magnitude and destructive power. The notorious Anchorage earthquake of 1964, which killed 130 people and caused $500 million in damage, occurred where the north-bound Pacific Plate is subducted beneath the North American Plate along the southern coast of Alaska. The Mexico City quake of 1985 also occurred along an active subduction zone, one marked as well by the great Mexican volcanoes Popocatapetl and Ixtaccihuatl.

The world's mountain ranges—volcanic and otherwise—occur along former or currently active zones of plate subduction and collision. Plate subduction generates the magmas that form volcanic chains such as the Cascade Range or the cores of granite ranges such as the Coast Mountains of British Columbia and the Sawtooth and Salmon mountains of central Idaho. Plate collisions cause rocks to crumple upward in great folds. The Himalaya, for example, is an artifact of the collision between the Indian and Asian plates. Great slabs of crust may also be pushed horizontally for many miles along glide planes known as thrust faults. The North Cascades and the mountains of Glacier National Park are dramatic examples of horizontally displaced terrain. Vertical adjustments result in the uplift of large sections of continental crust, elevating mountain ranges along faults that mark lines of stress.

A deep offshore trench forms where an oceanic plate dives beneath a continental plate. Over time, sediments are derived from the continent and carried by rivers to the sea, where they, along with slices of sea floor, are stuffed by the diving plate into the trench. In the process of subduction rocks are buried at great depth, brutally folded, squeezed like old cars in a junkyard compacter, and invaded by superheated magmas. In response, sedimentary, volcanic, and granitic rocks are transformed into entirely new metamorphic types such as gneiss, schist, greenstone, quartzite, and marble, all of which are especially well represented in the North Cascades and Klamath Mountains. The type of metamorphic rock produced depends on both the nature of the original rock and the degree of heat and pressure to which it is subjected. When temperatures are high enough to cause partial melting, individual mineral grains may fuse together. In this way sedimentary rocks such as sandstone transform into obdurate quartzite, and volcanic rocks such as basalt are hardened to form greenstone. Under greater stress, old minerals may actually break down and new ones form, all while the rock remains solid. Frequently the pressure is so great that rocks become plastic, spreading out into relatively thin sheets, like laundry run through a wringer. In the process, the minerals making up the rocks are flattened and realigned into swirly layers like those found in schist and gneiss.

As a subducting plate descends, it becomes progressively hotter until, finally, it is reabsorbed into the mantle. At a depth of about 60 miles, friction along the upper surface of a diving plate generates enough heat to melt the overlying continental rocks. The resulting molten rock—known as magma—is hotter, and therefore lighter in weight, than the rocks above it. In response the magma rises bouyantly, melting overlying rocks as it goes. As the magma rises it cools until it approaches the density and temperature of the surrounding rocks, at which point the rising ceases. In the process of cooling, the magma recrystallizes into bodies of granite called batholiths. Subsequent uplift and the removal of overlying rocks through erosion may eventually expose these deeply buried rocks. The huge batholiths revealed in the Coast Mountains of British Columbia, the mountains of central Idaho, and the Sierra Nevada originated in this way.

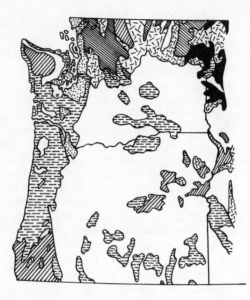

2a. Major rock units of Washington and Oregon (adapted from Highsmith and Kimerling, ed., *Atlas of the Pacific Northwest*)

Some of the rising magma, rather than recrystallizing deep within the earth, works its way to the surface to erupt in the form of lava either on the sea floor or the land. Chains of island volcanoes, such as the Aleutian Islands, commonly indicate the presence of offshore subduction trenches. The Olympic Mountains were carved from an enormous pile of basalt that erupted from submarine volcanoes. Volcanic chains, such as the Southern Cascade Range, may also develop onshore. Mount Saint Helens, Mount Rainier, Mount Shasta, and the rest of the Cascade volcanoes today mark a subduction zone where the offshore Juan de Fuca Plate dives beneath the continental margin.

As their common origin would suggest, granitic and volcanic rocks are closely related. Both are classified as igneous rocks, meaning rocks "born of fire." Containing the same minerals, they differ mainly in the size of their crystals. Granitic rocks have crystals large enough to be visible to the naked eye, while those of volcanic rocks are microscopic.

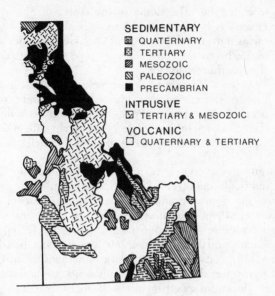

2b. Major rock units of Idaho (adapted from Highsmith and Kimerling, ed., *Atlas of the Pacific Northwest*)

The difference in size is mainly a result of the different rates of cooling. Magmas that are buried deep beneath the earth's surface cool slowly, providing ample time for the growth of large crystals. Magma erupted onto the earth's surface, however, cools rapidly upon exposure to air or, especially, water. As a result, there is little time for crystal growth.

The most common types of volcanic rocks exposed in the Pacific Northwest are basalt, andesite, and rhyolite:

- Basalt covers most of eastern Washington, eastern Oregon, and southern Idaho. Basalt consists almost entirely of dark minerals with low melting points. As a result it flows readily and is able to spread over large areas.
- Andesite is a mix of dark and light minerals, which together have a higher melting point than basalt. As a result, andesite has a pastier consistency and is often pushed upward out of a volcanic vent like toothpaste

from a tube. The dome in the crater of Mount Saint Helens is being built in precisely this way. Andesite forms most of the other great Cascade volcanoes as well and is by far the most common type of rock exposed in the Southern Cascades.

• Rhyolite and related volcanic rocks, though far less common in the region than either basalt or andesite, still occur widely. Lassen Peak, for example, is a dome of dacite (a rock intermediate between rhyolite and andesite) surrounded by a skirt of eroded debris.

Granite is a generic term that is commonly applied to any light-colored intrusive rock. These include true granite, quartz monzonite, granodiorite, and quartz diorite, which consist mostly of light minerals such as feldspar and quartz. Their volcanic counterparts are, respectively, rhyolite, rhyodacite, and dacite. Darker intrusive rocks such as diorite and gabbro consist mostly of dark minerals such as biotite and pyroxene; their volcanic equivalents are andesite and basalt. The entire spectrum of granitic rocks, from true granite to gabbro, is well represented in the Pacific Northwest.

Two hundred million years ago there was no Pacific Northwest as we now know it. The ancestral North American continent was smaller than it is today and together with all the other continents formed a single supercontinent named Pangaea. Pangaea began to break up into separate continents about 150 million years ago. North and South America began to drift westward, rifting apart from Europe and Africa and opening up the Atlantic Ocean. At that time the western margin of North America probably followed a line southward through what is now eastern British Columbia, northeastern Washington, central Idaho, central Oregon, and eastern California.

As the continent drifted west, its leading edge began to override the opposing oceanic plate, which was moving eastward from a mid-ocean ridge of its own. Subduction of this ancestral Pacific Plate was accompanied by widespread volcanic activity along the continental margin and by the formation of batholiths along a line stretching from British Columbia to Baja California.

Batholith formation along the Pacific Coast began about 150 million years ago in the Klamath Mountains and Sierra

Nevada and has continued more or less to this day. Granite began to invade the older sedimentary rocks of Idaho about 100 million years ago, but most of the plutons forming the Idaho batholith rose into place between 70 and 90 million years ago. The oldest batholiths in the North Cascades and Coast Mountains also date from this period. The youngest exposures of granite in the Cascades—the Mount Stuart batholith, for example—consolidated as recently as 12 to 15 million years ago. Younger ones still may lie unseen, buried deep beneath the surface rocks. What is more, ongoing volcanic activity in the Cascades suggests that batholith formation may still be underway.

The deformation, displacement, and uplift of rocks associated with the diving Pacific Plate created what was probably a single Andes-like mountain chain along the advancing western margin of North America. The mountains of central Idaho, the Blue Mountains, the Klamath Mountains, and the Sierra Nevada are the modern remnants of that ancient coastal range. The southern portion of the chain was displaced westward along a broad fault zone that today extends through the Snake River Plain and along the southern base of the Blue Mountains. The cause of this displacement seems to have been the growth and expansion of the Great Basin, which lies south of the fault zone and east of the Southern Cascades and Sierra. One consequence of this movement may have been the separation of the Klamath Mountains from the Sierra Nevada. A similar, though larger, gap occurs between the Klamath Mountains and the Blue Mountains. Both gaps are now occupied by volcanic terrain of the Southern Cascades.

Much of the Pacific Northwest did not form in place along the margin of North America but grew by the accretion of "suspect terrains"—odd pieces of continental crust that originated far to the west. Relics of the break up of Pangaea, these microcontinents rode the Pacific Plate eastward until, finally, they collided with the western edge of North America. Today these continental fragments make up most of Alaska, western British Columbia, Washington, and northwestern Oregon. The Okanogan microcontinent, which consists of the Okanogan Highlands of northeastern Washington and adjacent British Columbia, ran into northern Idaho about 100 million years ago. The huge North

Cascade microcontinent, which extends from Seattle to Alaska, arrived about 50 million years later.

Although this idea seems farfetched, it is quite plausible given our current knowledge of plate movement and explains why the rock suites occurring along the Pacific margin are so different from those of the old North American continent to the east. Moreover, such microcontinents still exist! New Zealand, New Guinea, Japan, and Madagascar are all examples of microcontinents that have yet to attach themselves to larger continents. The land west of the San Andreas Fault provides an example closer to home, one that will play an enormous role in the future geologic history of the Pacific Northwest. Known to geologists as the Salinian block, this land is drifting northward along the San Andreas Fault at the rate of about two inches per century. Eventually, millions of years in the future, the block will move out to sea and travel northward parallel to the coast, finally slamming into southern Alaska.

With the docking of the North Cascade microcontinent, subduction and trench formation shifted westward to near its present location. The Coast Range of Oregon and Washington consists of slices of basaltic sea floor and associated sedimentary rocks that were scraped off on the edge of the continent, rather than being carried below, and subsequently jacked upward to their present positions. These sea-bed rocks—known as pillow basalts for their bulbous, cushiony form—extend northward from the Willapa Hills to form a horseshoe-shaped flank of basalt enclosing the south, east, and north sides of the Olympic Mountains. Within the horseshoe are sedimentary rocks that were upended when the basalts were stuffed into the trench.

The pillow basalts that outcrop in the Olympics erupted from submarine vents between 55 and 35 million years ago. During this same period, onshore volcanoes strung out along the continental margin began spewing out huge volumes of lava and pyroclastics (airborne lava debris produced by volcanic explosions) along much of the west coast of North America. Extensive exposures of these rocks form the western foothills of the Southern Cascades from Mount Rainier southward. The name Western Cascades has been applied to this terrain, especially in Oregon, to distinguish it from the younger, higher major volcanoes to the east, the so called High Cascades. Volcanic rocks of an age comparable to those in the Western Cascades form the Clarno and John Day formations in eastern Oregon's Blue Mountains. Subsequent erosion of Western Cascade rocks has produced landforms bearing little resemblance to the great volcanoes that produced them. Among the most spectacular remnants of that period are Washington's Goat Rocks, south of Mount Rainier. The Goat Rocks are the remains of a volcano that was later sculpted by glaciers into a line of craggy peaks.

About 25 million years ago, for reasons as yet unclear, volcanic activity ceased among the old volcanoes of the Western Cascades. There followed a period of relative quiet that lasted about 10 million years. Then, sometime between 13 and 16 million years ago, highly fluid basalts erupted from a rift zone along the Idaho border, covering eastern Washington and Oregon to depths between 2,000 and 5,000 feet. Individual flows were as much as 100 feet thick. Lava pushed westward through what is now the Columbia River Gorge as far as the Willamette Valley and the Coast Range, which was rising from the sea at that time. During this same general period, basalt flows on a smaller scale were covering southeastern Oregon, northeastern California, and adjacent parts of Idaho and Nevada.

The pyrotechnic displays of both the Western Cascade and Columbia Basin volcanoes occurred in the heart of that long interval of geologic time known as the Tertiary Period. It began about 65 million years ago, when the great dinosaurs, along with innumerable other creatures, suddenly vanished from the earth, and ended about 3 million years ago, with the onset of the Pleistocene Epoch, or Ice Age. During most of the Tertiary Period, the earth's climate was far warmer and more stable than it is today. In the Pacific Northwest the climate was subtropical but grew cooler and drier as the eons passed.

The uplift that created the modern Coast Mountains and Cascade Range began late in the Tertiary Period, about 6 million years ago. Greatest uplift occurred in British Columbia and southeastern Alaska, with the amount declining steadily southward. Uplift amounted to about 8,000 feet in the North Cascades but only 3,000 feet in the Columbia River Gorge. Southward, even smaller displacements occurred. In fact, present elevations in the Southern Cascades have resulted far more from the piling up of volcanic lava flows and pyroclastics than from uplift.

By the end of the Pleistocene Epoch the mountain ranges of the Pacific Northwest had more or less reached their present height. At the same time, and for reasons unknown, the climate not only of the Pacific Northwest but of the entire northern hemisphere turned cooler, moister, and generally more unstable. Snowfall increased during the long, cold winters, while less and less of it melted during the cool, brief summers. As a result, large ice caps buried the mountains of the Pacific Northwest and spawned valley glaciers that pushed downslope into the lowlands. Ice accumulation was greatest in the Coast Mountains of British Columbia, where even today cold temperatures and a wet maritime climate combine to produce what are probably the greatest snowfalls on earth. At one time, that entire range, as well as the North Cascades southward to near Seattle, lay beneath a vast sheet of ice. Extensive ice caps also formed in the Northern Rockies. Farther south, alpine glaciers developed on the higher peaks and in places coalesced to form locally extensive ice fields.

Ice also covered vast areas of the lowlands during this period. Valley glaciers originating in the Coast Mountains coalesced in the lowlands to form the vast Cordilleran Ice Sheet, which pushed southward into northern Washington, Idaho, and Montana at least four, and perhaps several more, times. Most recently, about 15,000 years ago, the ice advanced as far south as Olympia in Washington, Pend Oreille Lake in northern Idaho, and the vicinity of Flathead Lake in Montana.

The Vashon Lobe of the Cordilleran Ice Sheet gouged out both Puget Sound and its outlet to the Pacific, the Strait of Juan de Fuca, from a gentle coastal plain. The ice reached a depth of 3,000 feet near Seattle and 8,000 feet farther north near the Canadian border. It banked up against the northern and eastern flanks of the Olympics as well as along the front of the Cascades as far south as Mount Rainier. Unsorted rock debris—glacial till—quarried from the sides and beds of its channels was carried southward by the ice and dumped in ridges throughout the Puget Lowland. These ridges, which generally run north and south to match the direction of glacial movement, form the low hills of Seattle and its outlying communities.

The push of the Cordilleran Ice Sheet southward into northern Montana and Idaho was responsible for the Spokane floods, the greatest deluges known to have occurred in the entire history of the planet. About 15,000 years ago a lobe of the Cordilleran Ice Sheet dammed the Clark Fork River near the site of present-day Pend Oreille Lake in the Idaho Panhandle. Behind the ice dam, waters backed up into western Montana to form a huge lake that geologists dubbed Lake Missoula. When rising water caused the ice dam to float and break up, the ensuing flood sent 500 cubic miles of water racing southwestward across the Columbia Basin. The power of the deluge was so great that giant channels—today's coulees—were cut into the basalt bedrock. The flood waters were temporarily ponded behind drainage bottlenecks such as the Wallula Gap near Pasco, Washington, and the Columbia River Gorge. They also backed up the Snake River to a depth of 600 feet near Lewiston, Washington, and filled much of the Willamette Valley south of Portland, Oregon. One such flood would have been a staggering spectacle, but geologists believe that the cycle of dam building and subsequent flooding may have occurred as many as forty times!

During the same general period, the Okanogan lobe of the Cordilleran Ice Sheet pushed southward over the Okanogan Highlands and out into the Columbia Basin. The ice diverted the Columbia River southward through what is now the famous Grand Coulee. Dry Falls marks the spot where this great river, fed by ice fields and floods, poured over a basalt cliff 400 feet tall and more than three miles across! When the Cordilleran Ice Sheet retreated northward, the Columbia abandoned the Grand Coulee for its old channel along the base of the Okanogan Highlands.

Beginning some 15,000 years ago, the climate in the Pacific Northwest began to grow warmer and drier, and by 10,000 years ago the Cordilleran Ice Sheet and associated alpine glaciers were in full retreat. The rapidity of that retreat can be gauged, if only approximately, by comparable events that have occurred over the past century in Glacier Bay National Park in the Alaska Panhandle. There, in the continent's optimum climate for ice formation, the great tidewater glaciers have retreated 60 miles in the past 200

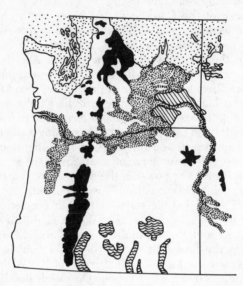

3a. Important glacial features of Washington and Oregon (adapted from Highsmith and Kimerling, ed., *Atlas of the Pacific Northwest*)

years. The retreat of the ice at the close of the Pleistocene Epoch may have been even faster.

Today, the most extensive glaciers in North America, outside Greenland, mantle the Coast Mountains of British Columbia and their Alaskan extensions, the Fairweather, St. Elias, Wrangell, and Chugach ranges. Large alpine glaciers also persist in the Canadian Rockies, Olympic Mountains, and North Cascades, and on the higher Cascade volcanoes south to Mount Jefferson. A few smaller glaciers are scattered southward in both the Northern Rockies and the Cascades.

Glaciation is responsible for most of the spectacular mountain scenery of the Pacific Northwest. Glaciers pluck rocks from the beds and sides of their channels and transport them downslope. In this way they carved the pyramidal peaks, knife-edged ridges, and steep-walled amphitheaters that distinguish alpine scenery the world over. The Coast Mountains, Cascades, Olympic Mountains, and Northern

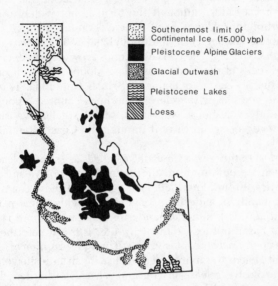

3b. Important glacial features of Idaho (adapted from Highsmith and Kimerling, ed., *Atlas of the Pacific Northwest*)

Rockies all provide extraordinary examples of glacial terrain. Glaciers also deepened and widened existing stream valleys and steepened the side walls, creating U-shaped troughs of uncommon beauty. Along the seaward flank of the Coast Mountain chain, the ice pushed all the way to tidewater, just as some glaciers do today in Alaska. When the tidewater glaciers eventually retreated, the valleys were flooded by rising seas, creating the fiords that today line the coast of British Columbia and the Alaska Panhandle. The southernmost fiord along the Pacific coast of North America is the Hood Canal, which extends southward from the Strait of Juan de Fuca along the east side of the Olympic Mountains.

Volcanic activity recommenced in the Southern Cascades several million years ago with the eruption of basalts from volcanoes located along more or less the same line as the present crest. The major Cascade volcanoes, from Mount Baker in the north to Lassen Peak in the south, all formed within the last million years. Together with associated younger volcanic rocks, they form what geologists call the High Cascades, although the term is not widely used in Washington. Mount Saint Helens, Mount Adams, Mount Rainier, Glacier Peak, and Mount Baker are all part of the High Cascades. The two latter cones grew atop older crystalline rocks of the North Cascades. Mount Garibaldi, in the southern Coast Mountains of British Columbia, is of the same age and is therefore sometimes counted among the Cascade volcanoes. Numerous, albeit smaller, volcanoes, however, occur northward through the Coast Mountains as well.

Most of the young Cascade volcanoes are stratovolcanoes, which are built up from alternating layers of lava and pyroclastics. From Mount Jefferson northward these cones consist mainly of andesite. Containing roughly equal parts of light and dark minerals, andesite is normally more viscous than basalt but less so than rhyolite. It is also intermediate in its potential for explosiveness. The 1980 eruption of Mount Saint Helens was more or less typical for an andesite volcano: an explosive release of volcanic ash as the hardened lava plug is ejected from the vent, followed by long, relatively quiet intervals of dome building, during which the thick, pasty lava is pushed upward by pressure from below. These dome-building episodes are interrupted periodically by explosive releases of ash, the two eruptive modes producing the alternation of pyroclastic and lava layers characteristic of stratovolcanoes.

From the Three Sisters southward, however, andesite gives way to rhyolite, which is extremely pasty and rich in light-colored silicate minerals. Rhyolite may also produce explosive eruptions that are truly catastrophic. If water becomes mixed with the lava, the magma chamber beneath a volcano's rhyolite plug may become an enormous pressure cooker whose power is clamped down only by the weight of the rocks overhead. If the weight is sufficient the rhyolite may slowly cool in place to form granite. If not, it may blow the mountain to pieces and devastate thousands of square miles surrounding the cone. About 7,000 years ago, this is precisely what happened to Mount Mazama, in the Cascades of southern Oregon. Before the eruptions commenced, Mount Mazama was a typical Cascade stratovolcano: about 12,000 feet tall, made up mostly of andesite, and possessing a more or less symmetrical profile. Deep beneath the mountain, however, granite/rhyolite magma impregnated with steam was slowly accumulating. In the ensuing explosions, more than 12 cubic miles of pumice were scattered over 350,000 square miles of western North America. When the magma chamber was emptied, the mountain fell in upon itself, creating the caldera that now holds Crater Lake.

Lassen Peak, the southernmost of the great Cascade volcanoes and the last to erupt prior to Mount Saint Helens, erupted explosively in 1914 and intermittently for three years thereafter. Since then it has lain dormant.

The eruption of Mount Saint Helens has fostered considerable speculation, both among the public and professional geologists, about the possibility of future eruptions by other Cascade volcanoes. The history of the High Cascades volcanoes has consisted of long periods of quiet punctuated by briefer intervals of considerable activity. Some of the volcanoes seem highly unlikely to erupt once again. Others, such as Mount Rainier, Mount Hood, or Mount Shasta, could well erupt sometime in the years ahead, though it is impossible to say whether such eruptions might occur within the lifespan of anyone likely to be reading this book.

Nor is volcanic activity in the Pacific Northwest restricted to the Cascades. A number of eruptions have occurred in this century along the southern coast of Alaska, and there is no reason to assume that volcanic activity has ceased entirely either along the Snake River Plain or in the Yellowstone region at the head of the plain.

Recent research suggests that the Snake River Plain may follow a rift in the earth's crust. The rift may well have formed as a consequence of the stretching of the crust that accompanied formation of the Great Basin. A notable feature of the rift is a magma hole or hot spot, where molten materials from the mantle are able to move upward to the surface. This hot spot seems to have migrated eastward along the general course of the Snake River Plain as the continent has moved west.

The Hawaiian Islands have migrated over a similar hot spot, which was centered in past times beneath Kauai, Oahu, and Maui, but which now fuels Kiluea volcano on the island of Hawaii. The present location of the Snake River Plain hot spot would seem to be somewhere in the vicinity of

Yellowstone National Park.

Just over 2 million years ago, a huge body of magma rose like a blister beneath the Yellowstone region. The growing pressure was released in a catastrophic eruption affecting more than a third of the present park. More than 2,500 cubic miles of rock debris were blown into the atmosphere. Subsequent build-ups of pressure resulted in a second monumental eruption about 1.2 million years ago and a third some 600,000 years ago. The active thermal areas for which Yellowstone National Park is renowned indicate that the fires beneath the surface have yet to cool. Previous Yellowstones may have occurred at intervals along the Snake River Plain, only to be buried beneath younger basalt flows. There is reason to believe that today's Yellowstone may yet produce future eruptions, and that future Yellowstones may develop northeast of the present one as the continent continues its westward push.

CHAPTER THREE

Wet Side, Dry Side

THE PACIFIC NORTHWEST has no single climate. Instead, it has several climates that are products largely of the interplay between latitude, the proximity of the Pacific Ocean, and the arrangement of the region's numerous mountain ranges. Latitude has a profound effect on air temperature and on the amount, type, and seasonal distribution of precipitation. In the Pacific Northwest, climates generally become warmer and drier from north to south, with snow declining in importance even though precipitation is increasingly confined to the fall, winter, and spring.

In much of the eastern United States, latitude is far and away the most important factor affecting climate. In the Pacific Northwest, however, climatic gradients induced by differences in latitude are profoundly altered by local topography. The region's mountain ranges channel the flow of air masses, some of which move inland from the Pacific, others coastward from the continental interior. The impact of a particular mountain range depends on its height, length, massiveness, orientation, and proximity to the ocean. Most of the region's mountain ranges run north and south directly across the path of the prevailing westerlies, which carry marine air, and the storms embedded in it, inland from the ocean. These ranges create a succession of north-south climatic belts in which the marine influence declines and the continental influence increases as one moves from the coast inland toward the Rocky Mountains.

Chief among the region's mountain barriers, of course, is the Cascade Range and its northern counterpart, the Coast Mountains chain of British Columbia and southeastern Alaska. West of the Cascades, maritime influences dominate the climate. Winters are wet and mild, summers are cool but dry. Rainfall exceeds 15 inches a year even at the driest locales. Relative humidity is often high, but thanks to cool temperatures normally falls within the human comfort range. Extensive, persistent cloudiness is characteristic through much of the year, though greatly reduced during the summer. Extreme temperatures are rare either during a single day or from season to season. Clouds retard daytime highs and act as a blanket, preventing the loss of accumulated heat at night.

East of the Cascades, the climate is more continental than maritime, though oceanic influences still play a significant role. Summers are hotter and drier; winters are colder and snowier. Rainfall exceeds 15 inches annually only at higher elevations. Daily and seasonal temperature fluctuations are greater than they are west of the mountains. Relative humidity is normally low.

These two different climates support distinct forms of vegetation. Conifer forests virtually blanket western Washington and Oregon from sea level to the upper timberline. Other types of vegetation occur only in special, atypical habitats or places where humans have cleared the forest for settlement or agriculture. In contrast, conifer forests are restricted in eastern Washington and Oregon mainly to the middle and upper slopes of mountain ranges. The drier lowlands, though popularly called "desert" by coastal residents, are covered mainly by semiarid grasslands, with or without sagebrush and other shrubs. True desert vegetation, however, occurs in southern Oregon.

In British Columbia and southeastern Alaska, the Coast Mountains and affiliated ranges rise abruptly from saltwater shores. As a result the coastal climate is confined to only a narrow strip of land sandwiched between the ocean and the mountain front.

Oceans have a moderating influence on the lands adjacent to them because great bodies of water gain and lose heat much less readily than great bodies of rock. Inland regions generally experience large daily fluctuations in air temperature as solar heating during the day is followed by rapid loss of heat on clear nights. Seasonal temperature shifts are even sharper, as both the land and the air above it warm and cool in response to changing levels of solar radiation.

The ocean, however, and the humid air above it, warm and cool far more slowly and never to as great a degree. As a result, coastal regions rarely experience sharp fluctuations in air temperature, either daily or seasonally, and tend to be warmer in winter and cooler in summer than inland areas.

A comparison of mean and extreme temperatures for Seattle and Spokane clearly shows the moderating influence of marine air and the role of the Cascade Range in blocking that air from entering the interior. Seattle is located on the shore of Puget Sound about 100 miles from the ocean. Although the Olympic Mountains lie due west, on the opposite side of Puget Sound, ample amounts of marine air (some would say too ample) flow around the mountains to fill the entire Puget Sound lowland. Seattle's winters are mild: The average temperature for January is about 40° F and the mean low temperature for the month is only 34° F. In the summer frequent morning clouds keep daytime temperatures low: The average temperature for July is just under 66° F, and the average high for the month is about 75° F.

Spokane is located about 275 miles east of Seattle, at the eastern edge of the state. To the west lies the vast Columbia Basin and beyond it the Cascade Range. Mountains to the north and east of Spokane protect it somewhat from incursions of continental air; at the same time, the marine influence is greatly diminished this far east of the ocean. As a result Spokane is much colder in winter and warmer in summer than Seattle. The average January temperature for Spokane is 25.3° F, and the average low for the month is a distinctly chilly 18° F. At the same time, these temperatures are significantly higher than those in Montana east of the Continental Divide. Spokane's average temperature for July equals Seattle's average maximum for the month, while its own average maximum is nine degrees higher. Between January and July, Spokane experiences an average temperature swing of some 50 degrees, compared to only 26 degrees of temperature variation in Seattle over the same period.

The marine influence extends farthest inland along the international border, and Spokane's relatively moderate climate, for a continental station, is largely a result of that incursion. This influence is greatest in winter, when a succession of wet storms marches eastward along a corridor more or less straddling the border. This inland push of marine air has allowed coastal conifers such as western hemlock and western redcedar to thrive on the windward slopes of the Northern Rockies east to the Continental Divide. In summer, as the storm track moves northward, the marine influence declines, and the region is invaded by continental air from the east. In passing over the Continental Divide, as well as each successive range to the west, this air becomes increasingly dry. As a result, the climate of this corner of the Northwest is wet, cloudy, and relatively mild in winter, with extraordinary amounts of snow falling at higher elevations, while summers are warm and extremely dry.

The marine influence is negligible in southeastern Oregon, which is part of the Great Basin, and virtually nonexistent in southeastern Idaho, which experiences—at different locations to be sure—among the hottest summers and coldest winters in the region.

From central California north, fog commonly blankets the Pacific Coast during the summer months. It forms through condensation as relatively warm, moist ocean air from the northeastern Pacific Ocean passes over cold waters welling up along the northwestern Pacific Coast. San Francisco is famous for fog—indeed, has made a virtue of it—but every coastal town gets its share. Along most of the coast, mountains confine the fog—and the coastal forests—to a relatively narrow shoreline strip. In western Washington, however, major breaks in the mountain barrier—the valleys of the Columbia and Chehalis rivers and the Strait of Juan de Fuca—permit maritime air masses to penetrate deep into the interior, dragging overcast skies along with them. The resulting cool, frequently cloudy summer weather, combined with ample winter rains, has allowed conifers to spread across the lowlands to the Cascade front, more than 100 miles from the sea.

The Pacific Ocean is also the source of virtually all major storms to enter the region. Most Pacific storms originate as cyclonic low-pressure cells in the Gulf of Alaska, whence they are swept southeastward by the jet stream into the west coast of North America. Some storms, however, originate farther south, over warmer waters. These storms occur less frequently but are usually wetter, bringing abundant rain to the western lowlands and heavy, wet snow to the Cascades. Winds move around the low-pressure centers in a counterclockwise direction, so that while the storm track may strike the coast at various angles, surface winds from an approaching front always originate from the south.

The frequency of storms depends on the position of the jet stream. During the winter, the jet stream sags southward so that a succession of storms crosses southern British Columbia, Washington, Oregon, and northern California. Through spring and into summer the storm track is displaced far to the north by a developing high-pressure cell over the northern Pacific. Winds circulate clockwise around the cell, generally striking the West Coast from the northwest. These prevailing northwesterly winds generally mean clear, dry weather, except along the immediate coast, where summer fog is frequent.

As a result of seasonal shifts of the storm track, most precipitation received by Washington and Oregon arrives during the winter months, while summers are mostly dry. Seattle, for example, receives an average of 35 inches of rain a year, of which only about 3 inches—or 9 percent—fall from June through August. The trend to summer dryness increases steadily from north to south. For example, Portland receives only 6 percent of its annual rainfall during the summer months, while at Port Orford, on the southern Oregon coast, summer precipitation amounts to a mere 4.5 percent of the yearly total. In most of California west of the High Sierra virtually no rain falls during the summer.

The climate along the immediate coast in southwestern Oregon and northwestern California is a slightly warmer, slightly drier version of the coastal climate farther north. In response, there is a gradual shift in the kinds and relative proportion of conifers and other plants making up the coastal forest. Even so, the similarities in both climate and forest between northwestern California and northwestern Washington are greater than the differences. Summers are cool and fogbound; winters are mild and extraordinarily wet and overcast. Inland from the coast, summers are hotter and drier, but at higher elevations precipitation remains ample.

The steady decline in summer precipitation from north to south through the Pacific Northwest has a pronounced effect on vegetation. In southwestern Oregon, for example, coastal conifers characteristic of most of western Washington and northwestern Oregon are confined to a narrow shoreline belt. Inland, California conifers increasingly replace coastal species in mid-slope forests, while drought-resistant broad-leaf evergreen trees and shrubs dominate the lower slopes and valleys. East of the Cascades, the steppes of the Columbia Basin give way in southern Oregon to desert communities characteristic of the Great Basin.

The region along the U.S.–Canadian border is far enough north that it remains somewhat under the influence of the storm track even in midsummer, when the jet stream is located over Alaska and northern Canada. As a result the northwestern corner of Washington and the southwestern corner of British Columbia tend to be somewhat cloudier and wetter during the summer than areas to the south. Northward through coastal British Columbia, summer rainfall steadily increases until, in the Alaska Panhandle, precipitation occurs in great quantity throughout the year.

When cyclonic storms strike the coast of Washington and Oregon, they first pass over the line of coastal mountains lying west of the Cascades. These ranges include the Klamath Mountains, Oregon Coast Range, and Olympic Mountains. As moist air masses rise up and over these ranges, cooling causes prodigious amounts of moisture to fall on their western and southern slopes. Coastal totals range from about 70 inches a year in southern Oregon to more than 130 inches on the Olympic Peninsula. The lower western slopes of the Olympic Mountains regularly receive more than 150—and sometimes more than 200—inches of rain a year. Snowfall at higher elevations in the Olympics normally ranges between 350 and 500 inches a year. Snow is also the characteristic form of winter precipitation at higher elevations in the Klamath Mountains.

As storms pass over the coastal ranges, precipitation lets up as the descending air masses grow warmer and therefore able to retain greater amounts of moisture. The warming also increases evaporation, so that clouds tend to dissipate as water droplets are reabsorbed into the air. As a result, lowlands in the lee of these ranges are a lot drier and sunnier than the region as a whole.

For example, the northeastern corner of the Olympic Peninsula, which lies in the lee of the Olympic Mountains, is the only place in western Washington to receive less than 19 inches of rain a year. The "rainshadow" cast by the

Olympics extends northeastward to include southern Vancouver Island and the San Juan Islands. Known locally as the Banana Belt, this area supports a number of plants—including the region's only cactus!—that are more characteristic of eastern Washington or southern Oregon than of western Washington. Southward, along the eastern side of the Olympics, the rainshadow effect is less pronounced, but even there the forests are notably drier, as evidenced by the presence of pines and Pacific rhododendron.

The Olympic Mountains are high enough to create near-desert conditions in their lee were they not so easily out-flanked. On the north, marine air pours through the broad Strait of Juan de Fuca into the Puget Sound lowlands, creating ocean-shore conditions some 100 miles inland from the outer coast. On the south side of the Olympics is the even broader valley of the Chehalis River, through which marine air spreads into southwestern Washington and the southern Puget Sound region. Marine air pushes farther inland in western Washington than anywhere else along the Pacific Coast. As a result, the coastal forest belt here reaches its greatest width—roughly 175 miles from the outer coast to the upper limit of the forest on the western slopes of the Cascade Range.

The Willamette Valley, which lies in the rainshadow of the Oregon Coast Range, is much hotter and drier than the Puget Sound region. The Coast Range is neither as high nor as massive as the Olympics, so its effect on passing storms is less profound. Nevertheless, precipitation at stations in the Willamette Valley is about half what it is along the coast. In addition, summers are much hotter and drier than they are in western Washington. As a result, large areas on the floor of the valley are grassland and oak woodland rather than forest. The Umpqua and Rogue valleys are even drier, partly because of their more southerly location, partly because they lie northeast of the Siskiyou Mountains, which are higher and more massive than the Coast Range.

In the Willamette Valley, the rainshadow effect of the Coast Range is mitigated in part by the Columbia River valley, which provides an open corridor along which marine air can pass eastward into the interior. The marine influence is greatest near Portland, at the north end of the valley, and diminishes southward. The average maximum temperature for July thus increases from 78.4° F in Portland at the north end of the valley to 82.2° F in Eugene at the south end. East of Portland, the Columbia River Gorge provides a major passage for milder marine air to flow through the Cascade Range to eastern Washington and northeastern Oregon. This same corridor exposes Portland to occasional severe ice storms in winter, as cold continental air rushes downriver toward the coast.

For most of its length, the Cascade Range is separated from the coast by an intervening mountain range. In western Washington, however, the isolation of the Olympics, and the broad lowland areas on all sides of those mountains, permit marine air direct access to the western slopes of the Cascades. As a result, this part of the range, which also happens to be the highest, receives nearly as much precipitation as the western Olympics do. Snowfall commonly exceeds 400 inches at higher elevations; Paradise, on Mount Rainier, has received more than 1,000 inches during at least three different seasons.

Extraordinarily high rainfall totals for the elevation are recorded along the western base and foothills of the Cascades, where clouds pile up, like people jammed at the door of a movie theater, before slowly moving up and over the range. This effect is even greater where river valleys exit the mountain front. There, the clouds are confined not only vertically but horizontally, creating local parcels of supersaturated air that drop large amounts of rain as they wait their turn to head east. This same phenomenon occurs on the western slopes of the Olympics and helps to account for the extraordinary rainfall totals recorded in the Hoh, Quinault, and Queets river valleys, where the finest rain forests are located.

Because of their proximity to the Pacific Ocean, the Cascades and Olympics are both warmer and snowier than the Rockies to the east. The warmest winter temperatures throughout the region are normally associated with incoming storms. As a result, snowfall in the mountains often occurs at temperatures at or not much below freezing. The heavy, wet snow produced under such conditions has earned the dubious if appropriate sobriquet "Cascade cement." It is also common at middle elevations in the mountains for heavy rains to melt already fallen snow, resulting in extraordinarily igh volumes of runoff and consequent flooding in lowland alleys. The combination of deep snow and relative warmth, owever, is also responsible for the vast flowery parklands hat mantle the slopes of the Cascades and Olympics.

As a consequence of cool summers and abundant precipitation, the mountains of western Washington contain the greatest concentration of glaciers in the conterminous United States. The North Cascades alone count for more han half the glaciers found south of Canada, with some 750 bodies of ice covering more than 104 square miles. Mount Rainier, in Washington's Southern Cascades, contains 26 named glaciers covering 34 square miles. The Olympics also bear rivers of ice. Mount Olympus alone supports 15 square miles of glaciers, two of which, the Hoh and the Blue, extend more than three miles from their sources high on its flanks. The coastal mountains of British Columbia and Alaska, which rise directly from the sea to elevations ranging from 13,000 to more than 19,000 feet, are even more heavily glaciated than the mountains of western Washington. In southeastern and south-central Alaska, where cool temperatures combine with year-round precipitation, great tongues of ice extend dozens of miles from their sources in mountain ice fields down broad U-shaped valleys to tidewater.

By the time storms push over the Cascade crest, they are much cooler and drier than they were at the beginning of their ascent. Normally air sinks as it cools, but since high winds are pushing this air upslope, it has no option but to continue rising. Once over the crest, however, the super-cooled air begins to rush downslope. In the process, it rapidly heats up, both from compression and as a result of the heat released by continued, though dwindling, precipitation. As the air grows warmer and drier, its capacity for absorbing and holding moisture increases accordingly, so that it acts like a huge sponge, soaking up moisture from soil and vegetation. In winter and early spring, these warm, dry winds—called Chinooks—often race down the lee slopes of the Cascades and other ranges to the east, bringing unseasonably warm weather and melting large amounts of snow.

As storms move east from the Cascade crest, their energy dissipates. Clouds become thinner and more ragged; openings appear in the overcast. Powerful winter storms are only

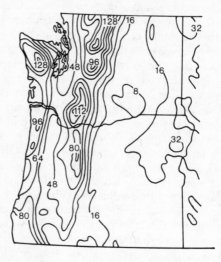

4a. Annual precipitation of Washington and Oregon (adapted from
Highsmith and Kimerling, ed., *Atlas of the Pacific Northwest*)

momentarily disorganized, however, and quickly regroup
during their passage eastward toward the Rockies. Weaker
systems, such as those associated with Chinook winds, may
dissipate entirely, creating clear sunny skies on the eastern
slopes of the Cascades even as drizzle and overcast continue
to prevail in the west.

All of eastern Washington, eastern Oregon, and Idaho lie
in the vast rainshadow cast by the Cascades. Annual precipitation at lower elevations is generally 10 to 15 inches a year,
with even lesser amounts recorded in south-central Washington
and southeastern Oregon. Snowfall amounts range from an
inch or so to as much as 40 to 50 inches and, depending on
locale, account for anywhere from a trace to as much as 40
percent of the total annual precipitation. A somewhat larger
percentage of total precipitation falls there during the summer than does west of the Cascades, primarily as a result
of increased thunderstorms east of the range.

Thunderstorms form when intense afternoon heating

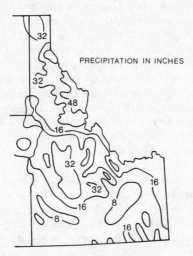

PRECIPITATION IN INCHES

4b. Annual precipitation of Idaho (adapted from Highsmith and Kimerling, ed., *Atlas of the Pacific Northwest*)

creates large masses of turbulent, rising air. Rapidly cooling in its ascent, the rising air condenses to form great, puffy cumulus clouds, which coalesce into a single huge, black, ominous mass—the cumulonimbus cloud or "thunderhead." As the thunderhead grows, the upper portion of the cloud acquires a positive charge and the lower portion a negative charge. This disequilibrium results in massive discharges of electricity—sheet lightning—from the negative to the positive portion of the cloud. Fork lightning is a discharge that travels from the lower portion of the cloud to the positively charged earth.

Throughout the western United States, and especially along the Pacific Coast, thunderstorms mostly occur over mountain ranges, where updrafts are strongest. West of the Cascades, however, afternoon heating is seldom intense enough to generate them. As a result, the Olympics and the western slopes of the Cascade Range experience far fewer thunderstorms than either the Sierra Nevada to the south or the Rockies to the east, where they may occur nearly every afternoon. Thunderstorms are more common east of the Cascades but play an important role only in the mountains of northern Idaho, northwestern Montana, northeastern Washington, and southeastern British Columbia. In this region, ample daytime heating combines with relatively humid marine-air masses to create a broad lightning zone stretching east to the Continental Divide. The frequent summer lightning storms that plague this region cause numerous forest fires but release too little precipitation to put them out. As a result, frequent fires seem to be a natural characteristic of forest environments in the Northern Rockies.

During a thunderstorm, large amounts of rain and hail may fall over a relatively short period. In the Northwest, however, relative humidity in the summer is rarely high enough to fuel the torrential downpours associated with thunderstorms in the east. As a result, thunderstorms do little to relieve moisture stress experienced during the summer by plants.

For the great majority of time the procession of weather in the Pacific Northwest is from west to east. During the winter, the entire region lies in the flow of eastward-moving storms. During the summer, the warming of the interior creates a low pressure area that draws marine air inland from the coast. Sometimes the resulting movement of air is so strong that mountain passes and the eastern flank of the Cascades may experience westerly winds in excess of 30 miles an hour. On occasion, however, a reverse movement occurs, as air from the continental interior flows westward over the Rockies and the Cascades toward the coast, bringing the hottest and coldest weather experienced by the region. In summer, easterly winds descending the western slope of the Cascades may cause temperatures in the Puget Sound area to hover in the eighties or nineties for several days—or even weeks! Even higher temperatures are recorded along the coast during such periods as a result of the air gaining additional heat as it passes over the Olympics. Most of the major fires to hit western Washington and northwestern Oregon have occurred during such periods. Southward, in the Willamette Valley, thermometers often top 100°F on these occasions. Winter invasions of continental air bring cloudless skies and subfreezing temperatures, which may persist for a week or more. The greatest snowfall west of the Cascades usually occurs at the end of such a period, when the storm track sags into the region, causing moist ocean air to push inland over the residual, freezing continental air.

Mountain ranges not only affect the climates of the lowlands adjacent to them but, by virtue of their great height, create their own climates, which tend to feature cooler, cloudier weather, greater amounts of both total precipitation and of snow as a percentage of that total, and higher, more frequent winds. Air temperatures generally drop at an average rate of about 3.5° F per each 1,000-foot gain in elevation. The actual rate varies according to a number of factors, including the temperature of the rising air masses, the amount of moisture they contain, the temperature and humidity of the air they are displacing, and the season. Since cold air is able to hold less water vapor than warm air, the cooling that attends the passage of air over a mountain range usually results in increased cloudiness and precipitation. Since temperatures aloft are commonly below freezing in winter, a large percentage of the precipitation received arrives in the form of snow. Mountains are windier partly because they thrust their tops into more vigorous and persistent upper-level air currents, partly because diurnal temperature changes create daily mountain and valley breezes, and partly because air accelerates as it is squeezed in its passage over a high mountain range.

When high upper-level winds pass over a mountain range, they form a giant wave. The existence of these winds is often betrayed by the presence of a lenticular (i.e., lens-shaped) cloud perched like a cap on a mountain top or levitating just above it. Such clouds are common sights atop Mount Rainier, Mount Hood, and the other great Cascade volcanoes. Although the winds that produce lenticular clouds (also called mountain-wave clouds) travel at high speeds, the clouds themselves are stationary. They form when the air rises above the condensation level, where air temperatures reach the dew point. The flat bottoms of lenticular clouds mark that level; their rounded upper surfaces inscribe the arc of the wave. Since high winds aloft often presage a coming storm, lenticular clouds are normally heralds of bad weather.

Climatic gradients induced by increasing elevation produce marked changes in vegetation, which are most commonly expressed in sequences of elevational zones or belts.* While adjacent zones commonly blur along their shared boundary, they are normally distinct enough to suggest marked differences in climate and related factors. Such changes are most conspicuous east of the Cascade crest, where moisture regimes are profoundly affected by elevation. Forests on the eastern slope of the Cascades, as well as ranges farther east, form lower timberlines where the commencement of grasses and shrubs marks the elevation below which moisture levels are too low to support trees. The upper timberline, however, is a response to increasing cold, occurring where too little energy is available during the growing season to support upright trees. Optimal conditions of moisture and temperature occur on the middle mountain slopes, which accordingly support the richest forests.

Climate is the controlling factor governing the distribution of vegetation. Yet rarely does it act in isolation. Topographic, edaphic, and biotic factors act alone or in concert to alter or supplement climate in ways that produce dramatic changes in vegetation. The interplay of these factors and the patterns of vegetation they have produced in the Pacific Northwest are the subjects of the following chapter.

* The vegetation zones of the Pacific Northwest are summarized in Chapter 4, Patterns on the Land.

CHAPTER FOUR

Patterns on the Land

O MOST PEOPLE the Pacific Northwest means conifer forests. This is entirely fitting, for the region offers the finest conditions for the growth of conifers to be found in the entire world and therefore contains the most magnificent and varied conifer forests on the planet. Conifer forests, however, are not the only type of vegetation in the region. The eastern two-thirds of Washington and Oregon, as well as southern Idaho, are mostly covered by grasslands and shrub steppes. There, in the rainshadow of the Cascade Range, forests are restricted to higher elevations, where cooler temperatures and increased precipitation reduce moisture stress during the dry summer months. Grasslands are also the characteristic vegetation of Oregon's interior valleys and of scattered places in western Washington where local climates or soils are unsuited for conifers.

Oak woodlands often occur with grasslands in drier areas west of the Cascades, from Vancouver Island through Oregon. In western Washington their distribution is patchy but from Tacoma southward they become increasingly widespread, particularly in western Oregon's interior valleys. Oak woodlands also extend eastward through the Columbia River Gorge to the lower eastern slopes of the Cascades. In south-central Oregon a distinctive western-juniper woodland extends from the lower Cascade foothills out onto the High Lava Plains. Deciduous woodlands or forest are conspicuous along the margins of lakes and streams on both sides of the mountains. In addition, large areas of deciduous forest have grown up west of the Cascades on clearcut lands. Within the forest are innumerable meadows, particularly near timberline, where they open up into large open parklands.

Timberline, of course, marks the upper limit of trees in the higher mountains of the region. Above that line the vegetation comprises various alpine communities dominated by prostrate, mostly perennial, herbs and shrubs.

The great diversity of vegetation in the Pacific Northwest results mainly from alterations in regional climatic patterns caused by the presence of numerous high mountain ranges. Environmental conditions in any given locale, however, often vary significantly from regional norms, creating patchwork, or mosaic, of habitats, each supporting a distinctive assemblage of plants. In some instances the resulting change in vegetation can be dramatic, as when grassland suddenly gives way to a corridor of deciduous trees along a stream. In most cases, however, the changes are subtle, sometimes involving merely a shift in the relative abundance of species. Many people notice the shift without knowing the reason; others simply don't see it, missing the trees for the forest, as it were.

The four main factors determining plant habitats are climate, topography, soil, and interactions among plants and animals, including humans. These factors do not operate independently, and it is usually difficult to speak of one without referring to one or more of the others. Even so, on a particular site a single factor is often the controlling one, with the others subsidiary to it. For example, moisture controls the lower timberline, the place where forest gives way to steppe. The moisture available to plants, however, depends on social characteristics, local topography, and interactions among competing plants, in addition to several important climatic factors. In other places, soil, topography, or even the activities of animals may be the controlling factor. Regardless, climate, topography, soil, and biotic influences invariably act in concert to determine plant habitats.

The single most important factor is climate, which includes air temperature, humidity, precipitation, and wind. Each of these elements plays an important role in determining a region's flora (the plant species it contains) and vegetation (the formations in which they occur). In addition, climate exerts an indirect influence on vegetation through its role in soil formation. For example, gardeners understand that climate limits the types of ornamental plants they can grow; climate exerts comparable constraints on naturally occurring plants. Western hemlock, for instance, cannot survive in the rolling hills of southeastern Washington's Palouse region, and big sagebrush is doomed along the Oregon coast. It is notable too that forests are largely restricted to areas of ample precipitation and relatively cool air temperatures, while steppes are limited to semiarid rain-shadow lands east of the Cascades.

In mountainous regions such as the Pacific Northwest, regional climate is modified by topography to create local variations—microclimates—that often may be detected by corresponding changes in vegetation. For example, in the northern hemisphere, slopes that face south receive more hours of more intense sunshine throughout the year than do those facing north. As a result, a southern slope is commonly warmer than a northern one. Snow melts first and sticks last on southern slopes, which therefore enjoy appreciably longer growing seasons. Since Pacific storms generally approach from the south or southwest, southern aspects may also receive greater amounts of wind and rain. Even so, moisture stress is usually less on northern slopes, where cooler conditions lower evaporation rates. Plants growing on south-facing slopes commonly experience greater moisture stress because higher air temperatures there increase evaporation from both plant surfaces and the soil. Differences in vegetation resulting from slope aspect are greatest in regions of drought and smallest in areas where moisture is abundant. In western Washington, for example, northern and southern exposures normally both support forest. Moreover, that forest will more than likely contain the same kinds of trees. What may be different is the relative proportion of each species and the types and abundance of plants growing in the understory. Western hemlock and sword fern, for instance, may be more common on a northern slope, while Douglas-fir and ocean spray have the edge on a southern exposure. All four species, however, are likely to be found in varying numbers on both slopes. In southern Oregon, however, where summer drought is often critical, not only are the kinds of trees likely to vary according to aspect, but the types of vegetation as well. Where soil drought is extreme, conifer forest may be limited to cool northern exposures, while oak woodland, chaparral, grassland, or some combination thereof covers the southern flanks.

The effects of topography on climate, and therefore vegetation, are not limited to slope aspect. Significant variation in vegetation also occur in areas that are either concave on the one hand or convex on the other. Concave surface include valley bottoms, cirques, shallow bowls, and other depressions; convex terrain refers to ridgecrests, hilltops and similar raised areas. The changes in vegetation exhibited by such terrain occur in response to the tendency of warm air to rise and cold air to sink. Cold air often flows downslope at night, filling low-lying areas and local depressions. Therefore, such places—often called frost pockets—tend to be colder than surrounding areas of comparable elevation and exposure. Conversely, ridgetops tend to be warmer than nearby slopes or basins because of warm upslope breezes nighttime cold-air drainage, and overall greater exposure to the sun. As a result of such local temperature inversions vegetation characteristic of higher, colder habitats commonly ranges farthest downslope in basins and valleys, while vegetation of lower, warmer habitats extends farthest upslope on ridges. In the Northern Rockies, for example, subalpine conifers extend downslope into the warmer, drier Inland Fir Zone only along valley bottoms and in other depressions. Conversely, Douglas-fir ranges upslope into the subalpine forest mainly along ridgetops. As one would expect, variations in vegetation resulting from surface contours are most evident in high, rugged mountains, where great local relief can produce abrupt changes over short distances.

Topography also affects vegetation through determining local wind patterns. Areas with good air circulation, for example, are less likely to experience killing frosts. At the other extreme, high winds may prevent certain plants—trees in particular—from growing in certain areas. The impact of wind on vegetation is greatest at and above timber line, where abrasion, desiccation, and cooling caused by high winds are critical factors governing the distribution of plants. In this hostile environment the shelter provided by even the smallest topographic rises or obstructions, such as a rock, may allow plants to persist that otherwise would have little chance of survival.

Even at lower elevations, however, wind plays an important role in shaping plant habitats. Trees, for example, vary in their resistance to wind according to the depth or breadth of their root systems. Trees with low resistance to windthrow (i.e., felling by high wind) are therefore excluded from some habitats. By toppling trees, winds also create openings in the forest and initiate the process by which the nutrients tied up in standing timber are recycled to the soil.

As the rooting medium for plants, the role of soil in determining plant habitats is both obvious and difficult to overstate. Yet the relationship between climate, soil, and vegetation is more complex, and therefore interesting, than many people realize. Soil isn't just dirt. Rather, it is a blend of organic and inorganic materials, of clay, sand, and gravel on the one hand and organic materials—mostly composted plant debris—on the other. The type of soil present in a given locale therefore depends on the nature of the parent rock material, the climate, and the type of vegetation it supports.

The parent rock determines the mineral content of the soil and has a direct bearing on the rate at which weathering, and therefore soil formation, can occur. Fine-grained volcanic or sedimentary rocks, for example, tend to weather more rapidly than coarse-grained granites. As a result they often feature deeper soils and thicker vegetation. Some of the finest forest soils in the Pacific Northwest have developed on deep layers of wind-deposited ash and pumice derived from innumerable volcanic eruptions. Since a few common minerals—quartz, feldspar, and mica, for example—recur in the great majority of rocks, differences in soil chemistry are often too small to produce major changes in vegetation. But there are exceptions. In the Klamath Mountains, for example, the vegetation on soils developed from peridotite is noticeably sparser and significantly different in its constituent species than that on nearby soils formed on other adjacent types of rock.

Climate affects soil formation directly through the weathering of rock materials to form clay particles and the activities of the decomposer organisms—chiefly fungi and bacteria, but also various invertebrates. Weathering and decomposition proceed most rapidly in warm, humid climates, most slowly in cool, dry ones. Climate also affects soil indirectly through the crucial role it plays in determining the types of plants and vegetation that occur from place to place.

Within the constraints imposed by particular climates and types of parent rock, plants create the soils in which they grow. Plants and their soil develop together, each leaving their mark upon the other. Plants are the source of humus, the dark, rich, fresh-smelling material that gardeners call compost. Soil bacteria and fungi break down plant debris into finer, softer particles. In the process they release nutrients bound up in those materials and convert them into forms available to plants. They also improve soil texture, which has a direct bearing on its moisture characteristics. Humus gives soil its blocky texture like that of pie-crust dough before the water is added. This texture allows organic soils to retain moisture better than sand and gravel yet drain faster than clay. Soils that drain too rapidly experience periods of drought, while those that drain poorly are deficient in oxygen because the spaces between the particles are filled with water. Both extreme conditions are severely limiting to most plants.

As stated, by supplying the source materials for the humus in which they grow, plants have a large role in shaping their own soils. Conifers provide an excellent example. The soils that develop beneath conifer forests are generally acidic and deficient in essential nutrients. Both conditions are direct consequences of the chemical and physical qualities of conifer needles. Because of their tough skins, which are essential for leaves that must last throughout the year, conifer needles decompose slowly. The process is further retarded by low soil temperatures, which reduce the activity of soil bacteria but which are nevertheless characteristic of the latitudes and altitudes at which most conifer forests occur. Thanks to the delay, nutrients that otherwise would be released to the soil remain bound up in thick mats of partially decomposed needles that collect beneath the trees. At the same time, water draining through this needle mat forms a mild humic acid that leaches out what nutrients may be present and carries them downward through the soil to depths below the reach of many plants. The resulting soils, known as podsols, are generally characteristic of conifer forests, though the degree of podsolization differs from region to region and even from one place to the next in a single forest. Podsolization is very weak in Pacific-slope forests, where the mild, wet climate promotes microbial activity.

The ability to thrive in podsols is an essential attribute for plants that take root beneath conifers. The heath family seems to have specialized in this trait and is therefore well represented in the understories of conifer forests throughout the northern hemisphere. In our own region, the family is represented by such abundant forest plants as salal, huckleberries, and rhododendron.

The role of soil fungi and bacteria in the lives of higher plants would be enormous even if they did nothing else but break down organic litter into water-soluble forms. But they do much more. For example, both conifers and ericads, as well as other plants, are able to survive in dry, acidic, impoverished soils largely through the assistance of soil fungi. Each soil fungus consists of filamentous strands called hyphae, which together form the fungal body, or mycelium. The hyphae enter into intimate unions called mycorrhizae with the roots of numerous plants. Some fungi merely sheathe the roots; others penetrate them. In either case, the fungi obtain carbon dioxide and carbohydrates from their hosts while supplying moisture and soil nutrients in return. Mycorrhizae increase the range and effectiveness of the root systems and provide the fungi with essential substances that they cannot obtain otherwise.

Some plants are able to improve soils by incorporating atmospheric nitrogen gas into organic ammonium, in which form the nitrogen is available to the roots of other plants. Legumes, such as locoweeds and lupines, are able to fix nitrogen through the assistance of *Rhizobium* bacteria, which form root nodules on the host plants. Similar associations are formed between *Actinomyces* bacteria and various woody plants including species of alder, ceanothus, serviceberry, waxmyrtle, antelope bitterbrush, and buffaloberry. Many of these plants are pioneers on bare ground, where nitrogen is in short supply. By increasing soil nitrogen, they improve the ground for later stages of vegetation. In addition to bacteria, certain blue-green algae form nitrogen-fixing unions with a variety of plants.

Although soil obviously plays a major role in determining plant habitats, many details of the relationship remain obscure. Changes in soil type from one place to another may or may not show up as corresponding changes in vegetation. Most plants, it seems, are less picky about the particular type of soil in which they grow than that it provide sufficient moisture, nutrients, and oxygen.

Climate, topography, and soil define the physical environment in which plants grow. Plant habitats, however, are not simple reflections of that environment. Plants must share their habitats both with one another and with a variety of animals (meaning *all* animal life, not only mammals). The resulting interactions modify the physical environment in important ways. For example, plants compete with one another for space, light, moisture, and other resources supplied by the environment. Plants also form mutually beneficial relationships, including some that are absolutely essential to their success in particular locales. The importance of mycorrhizae and nitrogen-fixing bacteria has already been noted.

Since resources are finite, competition occurs among all the plants sharing a habitat. At the same time, no single species of plant is so perfectly adapted to its habitat as to exclude all competitors. Consequently, plants growing together must also accommodate themselves to the presence of others. The resulting assemblages are appropriately called plant communities.

Plants and animals also interact in a variety of ways. Through providing particular types of food and cover, plants largely determine animal habitats. In return, animals pollinate flowers, transport seeds to new locales, improve soils, assist in the decomposition of plant materials, and through selecting certain plants over others for food strongly influence their relative abundance and distribution. Through such interactions, plants and animals together form biotic communities—associations of organisms that have evolved together in response to particular habitats. Biotic communities together with their habitats constitute ecosystems, which are elaborate networks of mutual dependence whose chief function is the circulation and recycling of the energy derived from sunlight.

Green plants trap the energy of sunlight and use it to synthesize simple sugars from carbon dioxide and water. The process, known as photosynthesis, is the engine that drives all life on earth. The energy produced passes first to plant-eating animals and from them to flesh-eating animals. Ultimately the energy passes to soil fungi and bacteria, which obtain it by breaking down the tissues of plants and animals. In the process they release nutrients into the soil in forms that plant roots can utilize. At each stage of transfer, however, most of the energy is lost in the form of waste heat. As a result, less and less energy is available to the next level of consumers. This is why there are always fewer carnivores than herbivores and fewer herbivores than the plants on which they depend. This degradation of energy is also why natural communities require continuous infusions of new energy through photosynthesis.

Although animals and plants form intimate associations, the animal component is usually elusive and accounts for but a fraction of a community's total biomass (mass of living tissue). Moreover, while plants virtually determine animal habitats, animals are far less important than climate, soil, and topography in determining plant habitats. For this reason, and because animals tend to roam among several habitats while plants clearly cannot, it is customary to identify habitat types by the plant communities they support.

A plant community and its habitat are inseparable. Where one occurs the other—in the absence of severe disturbance—will be found as well. Plant ecologists don't always agree where the boundaries of a particular habitat or community should be drawn. Some prefer to designate larger units that emphasize similarities over wide areas. Others place greater importance on local differences in vegetation and define their communities accordingly. However individual communities are defined, there is no debate that they do in fact exist.

Plant communities are the collective product of individual plants responding to shared habitats. Each species of plant tolerates varying degrees of sunlight, moisture, soils, nutrients, and other elements that make up its physical environment. For each species these tolerances fall within certain more or less broad ranges that all together define its ecologic amplitude. The broad ecologic amplitude of Douglas-fir allows it to range through numerous habitats over a wide geographic area. The narrow ecologic amplitude of red mountain-heather, however, restricts it to a narrow range of habitats—namely, moist places near timberline. A plant species normally exhibits different degrees of tolerance for the multitude of conditions that make up its habitat. It can survive, however, only in habitats that at least minimally satisfy *all* its requirements. As a result, a plant species' ecologic range is governed by the element for which it has the least tolerance. For example, lady fern, a common resident of coastal conifer forests, can grow in either full sun or full shade so long as soil moisture is abundant throughout the growing season. In other words, because lady fern tolerates a greater range of light than moisture, the latter is the more critical factor governing its distribution. Of course, the ecologic amplitudes of plants sharing a particular patch of ground are never identical; instead, their association represents habitats where their tolerance ranges overlap. Thus lodgepole pine may be found growing with both western larch and Sitka spruce, although the latter two trees do not occur together in nature. Finally, competition commonly limits a species' range well below its physiologic limits.

Community boundaries can be abrupt or gradual. Abrupt boundaries usually reflect either sudden changes in the soil or parent rock or the edges of disturbances such as fire or logging. The abrupt change from sagebrush to grasses in eastern Washington and eastern Oregon often marks where deep, well-developed soils suddenly give way to shallower, rockier types. More gradual changes of vegetation occur along normal climatic gradients in response to variations in elevation, topography, latitude, and other factors. Timberline, for example, marks a gradual transition from forest to alpine tundra in the face of increasing cold. Where the transition between communities is gradual, transitional zones called ecotones separate adjacent communities. Ecotones normally feature plants from both communities. They are of particular significance to wildlife owing to the so-called "edge effect"—the tendency for greater numbers and varieties of animals to occur along community margins, where habitat diversity is greatest.

Not all species of plants growing on a single piece of real estate, of course, are equally suited to their location. Typically, a single species will occur in several habitats, in which the particular conditions essential for its growth and reproduction range from marginal to optimum. As one would expect, a species increases in abundance as conditions approach the optimum. Each habitat favors one or a few species over all the rest. As a result the favored species tend to increase in number or grow larger than their companions. In this way they gradually dominate their habitats.

Grasses dominate grasslands by virtue of their number; trees dominate forests mainly as a consequence of their height. In each case the dominant class of plants commands the largest share of available resources and by virtue of its size or numbers reshapes the habitat for its companions. When the dominant plants of a community are removed by fire or other disturbance, the community is so drastically changed in appearance, composition, and ecological characteristics that it essentially becomes a totally new community. The most widely encountered example of such drastic change in the Pacific Northwest is the conversion from forest to brush that results from clearcutting.

Plants are quick to move into new habitats as they become available. Lichens and mosses commonly invade bare rock surfaces, while higher plants become established in crevices where wind-blown soil has accumulated. Once established, these pioneer plants alter the habitat in ways that make it available to other species. Lichens, for example, break down the rock surface, creating a thin skin of rudimentary soil that mosses and other plants may colonize. Plants growing in crevices contribute to the buildup of soil and, if large enough, may provide shelter to other plants that tolerate less exposure to the elements. Young conifers, for example, often invade crevices in advance of other plants and by shading the areas beneath them open them up to plants that could not endure the high temperatures and intense solar radiation that characterized the initial habitat.

Similar sequences characterize the colonization of wet ground. In lakes and ponds, sediments deposited by streams are initially invaded by aquatic plants such as quillworts and pondweeds. Their accumulating remains produce a steady shallowing of the marginal waters and provide a rooting medium for emergent plants such as sedges, which tolerate partial submersion. Sedges in turn contribute their remains to the accumulating organic mass and thereby continue the gradual filling in of the pond. As the shores extend toward the center of the pond, a progressive drying of the soil allows other plants, such as willows, to invade the area.

A similar process occurs in the aftermath of a serious disturbance such as a fire. In the years following a forest fire, the burned area normally supports successive communities of herbs, shrubs, and finally trees. Opportunistic, fast-growing, sun-loving species are usually the first trees to dominate a disturbed area. In the Pacific Northwest these include red alder, lodgepole pine, quaking aspen, western larch, western white pine, noble fir, ponderosa pine, and even Douglas-fir. Once the canopy closes, shade inhibits the germination and seedling growth of these pioneer trees, but not of shade-tolerant species such as western hemlock and Pacific silver fir. As a result, the latter eventually gain dominance of the stand as the former die out one by one.

The process whereby plant communities gradually replace one another is called succession. Primary succession refers to the initial sequence of communities that develop on bare ground, such as a rock outcrop or the bottom sediments of a pond. Secondary succession refers to the sequence that occurs following a disturbance. Each community in the sequence is called a sere (coined from the word series), and plants that make up a sere are referred to as seral or secondary species.

In theory—and often in fact—succession eventually leads to association of plants that are so well suited to their habitats as to remain more or less stable for indefinite periods. These stable associations are called climax communities. For instance, western hemlock dominates climax forests on most lowland habitats in western Washington. Similarly, bluebunch wheatgrass and big sagebrush dominate large areas of climax vegetation in eastern Washington and eastern Oregon. Changes do occur in climax communities, but they tend to be local and more or less random. They do not result in removal of the dominant climax species or build on one another to cause significant, long-term changes in the structure or composition of the community.

Massive disturbances occur frequently enough that the course of succession is often interrupted before climax vegetation can become established. Such disturbances include fires, landslides, volcanic eruptions, high winds, insect infestations, disease epidemics, overgrazing, logging, and the clearing of land for other commercial purposes. Natural disasters have always occurred often enough in the Pacific Northwest to assure that seral vegetation is well represented. Typically, the vegetation of a given area includes stands in various stages of succession. Since the coming of white settlers to the region, however, human disturbances have profoundly altered natural vegetation patterns, with the result that climax, or near-climax, vegetation has been eliminated from many areas. For example, the native grasslands of the Palouse have been converted mostly to winter wheat and lentils, while overgrazing has produced weedy communities dominated by alien plants throughout much of the eastern steppes. Similarly, climax-forest stands are scarce in the lowlands of western Washington and western Oregon. Lands that remain forested mostly support seral communities that have developed following logging earlier in the century. Some of these older "second-growth" stands are now being cut once again. Human activities in general tend to arrest the process of succession, keeping vegetation in a perpetually seral state known as a disclimax. The largest remaining stands of climax vegetation—whether forest or steppe—are to be found in various parks and wilderness areas.

Vegetation Zones

Climax vegetation often represents the potential rather than the actual vegetation to be found in a given area. Attempting to classify the vegetation of the region according to existing types, however, has a couple of major drawbacks. First, the pattern of vegetation resulting from human disturbances obscures basic environmental features operating over large areas. Second, since the timing and location of human disturbances are governed by human wishes rather than natural conditions, the resulting hodge-podge of vegetation bears only an incidental relationship to natural habitat patterns.

The following system of vegetation zones* is therefore based largely on potential, or climax, vegetation. Each zone designates a region of more or less uniform climate in which distinctive types of climax vegetation form on deep, well-developed soils. Various seral communities, however, occur in each zone and in places may even be more common than

* The zonal system presented here is a simplified version of the one employed by Jerry F. Franklin and C. T. Dyrness in their classic survey *Natural Vegetation of Oregon and Washington*.

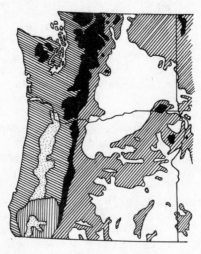

5a. Vegetation zones of Washington and Oregon (adapted from Highsmith and Kimerling, ed., *Atlas of the Pacific Northwest*, and from Franklin and Dyrness, *Natural Vegetation of Oregon and Washington*)

climax vegetation. Individual plant species commonly occur in more than one zone.

In mountain ranges the zones are segregated by elevation. Their boundaries, however, are usually broad ecotones in which species from neighboring zones occur together. Although upper and lower elevation limits are given for each zone, these are approximate and, depending on soil, topography, and other factors, may vary locally by as much as several hundred feet. As a rule, zone boundaries increase in elevation from north to south. They also tend to rise from west to east in response to the increasingly continental flavor of the climate. Typically, zone boundaries are undulating, curving upward on warm exposures and ridgetops, sagging on cool slopes and valley bottoms.

In the following accounts the zones are grouped to correspond with discussions in later chapters, which are noted following the name of each zone. The locations of the zones are shown in Figure 5.

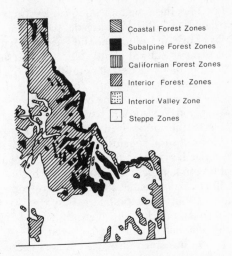

5b. Vegetation zones of Idaho (adapted from Highsmith and Kimerling, ed., *Atlas of the Pacific Northwest*, and from Franklin and Dyrness, *Natural Vegetation of Oregon and Washington*)

Northwest Coastal Forest Zones (Chapter 6)

The Sitka Spruce Zone is confined to a narrow coastal strip from northwestern California to south-central Alaska, ranging farther inland among major river valleys. The zone generally occurs below 500 feet elevation, up to 2,500 feet in southeastern Alaska. Lush forests dominated by Sitka spruce characterize the zone. Western hemlock, Douglas-fir, and western redcedar are important associates. Shore pine is common along the immediate coast and the margins of rivers and lakes. Bigleaf maple and red alder are locally common.

The Western Hemlock Zone occurs inland from the Sitka Spruce Zone from southwestern Oregon to southeastern Alaska. It is the principal forest zone of Oregon's Coast Range, the lowlands of western Washington, the Olympic

Mountains, and the lower to middle elevations along the western flanks of both the Cascade Range and the Coast Mountains of British Columbia. The Western Hemlock Zone also occurs sporadically at middle elevations on the east side of the Washington Cascades, generally above the Inland Fir Zone and below the Subalpine Zone. Along the Oregon, Washington boundary, the zone occurs at elevations ranging from 500 to 3,300 feet. Although western hemlock dominates climax forests, the zone is best known for old-growth stands of Douglas-fir, a seral species on all but the driest habitats. Western redcedar is a common associate, especially in western Washington and British Columbia. At higher elevations Pacific silver fir dominates stands that are transitional between lowland and subalpine forests. Extensive logging in the Western Hemlock Zone has produced large areas of deciduous woodland dominated by red alder and bigleaf maple. In southwestern Oregon, conifers characteristic of the Sierra Nevada enter the zone.

Southwestern Oregon and Californian Zones (Chapter 7)

The Coast Redwood Zone extends along the coast from extreme southwestern Oregon to south of San Francisco. It normally forms a strip 5 to 30 miles wide, but extends inland along major river valleys. The upper limit of the zone generally occurs at about 2,500 feet. Forests dominated by coast redwood characterize the zone. Pure redwood groves develop on river flats subject to periodic flooding. Douglas-fir is a major associate, and other coastal conifers may be present, particularly toward the northern end of the zone. Tanoak, a broadleaf evergreen, is a frequent understory tree in mixed stands. Inland, the zone butts up against the Mixed Evergreen Zone.

The Mixed Evergreen Zone is the principal lower montane zone of northwestern California and southwestern Oregon, where it occurs in the North Coast Range and the Klamath Mountains (including Oregon's Siskiyous) at elevations generally between 2,500 and 4,600 feet. Douglas-fir dominates climax forests in which tanoak, Pacific madrone, and canyon live oak are important associates. A large number of other tree species, drawn from both Northwestern and Californian sources, may also be present, though rarely in a single stand. Large areas of serpentine and peridotite support distinct plant communities in which Jeffrey pine and Port-Orford-cedar are prominent.

The Sierran Mixed Conifer Zone occurs on the western slope of the Oregon Cascades northward to, roughly, the North Fork Umpqua River drainage, where it blends gradually with the Western Hemlock Zone. The Sierran Mixed Conifer Zone generally occurs between 2,500 and 5,200 feet elevation on the west slopes of the Cascades, somewhat higher on the east. At lower elevations on the west slope it borders Oregon's Interior Valley Zone; at its upper limit it merges with subalpine forests dominated by Shasta red fir. The forests of the Sierran Mixed Conifer Zone are similar to and northern extensions of the mixed conifer forests that cover the western slope of California's Sierra Nevada. White fir appears to be the dominant climax species, but except at higher elevations most stands also contain significant numbers of Douglas-fir, incense-cedar, sugar pine, and ponderosa pine. California black oak and Oregon white oak are also fairly common. In the Klamath Mountains, the mixed conifer forest is largely replaced by the mixed evergreen forest, save for a narrow belt of white fir at higher elevations.

Interior Valley Zone (Chapter 7)

Oregon's Interior Valley Zone includes the Willamette Valley in the north and the valleys of the Umpqua and Rogue rivers in the south. All lie in the rainshadow of the Coast Range and are subsequently much drier than the lowlands of western Washington. The natural vegetation of the valley floors comprises a mosaic of oak woodlands and grasslands. Conifer forests are largely restricted to nearby foothills; deciduous woodlands occur along streams and in other reliably moist areas. Chaparral occupies hot, dry, south-facing hillsides in the Umpqua and Rogue valleys.

Inland Forest Zones (Chapter 8)

The Western Juniper Zone covers a large area in central Oregon and from there occurs sporadically eastward into southern Idaho. Normally occurring at elevations between 2,500 and 4,600 feet, it is the lowest, driest zone east of the Cascades that is dominated by trees, forming a transition between shrub-steppe below and ponderosa pine forest above. The only common tree is western juniper, which forms an open woodland throughout the zone. Ponderosa pines occasionally occur along the upper fringe of the zone. Sagebrush is the juniper's most common woody companion, though several other shrubs also occur in the woodland.

The Ponderosa Pine Zone is the lowest forest zone along the east side of the Cascade Range and eastward to the Northern Rockies, where it occurs as low as 2,000 feet in northeastern Washington and 6,600 feet in the pumice region of south-central Oregon. The zone borders the Steppe Zone at lower elevations and merges with the Inland Fir Zone upslope. Ponderosa pine is the overwhelming dominant species, often forming pure or nearly pure forests. Several other trees occur and are even locally prominent in the Ponderosa Pine Zone, but none are of general occurrence.

The Inland Fir Zone is the next one upslope from the Ponderosa Pine Zone, occurring at elevations between about 1,000 and 4,000 feet in northeastern Washington and 5,400 to 6,000 feet in southern Oregon. Forests may be dominated by Douglas-fir, grand fir, or white fir, depending on location. Ponderosa pine, lodgepole pine, and western larch are frequent associates in seral stands. The Inland Fir Zone extends along the entire eastern side of the Cascade Range into British Columbia and eastward to the Northern Rockies. It is the single most extensive forest zone in the vast mountain region of central Idaho, as well as in the Blue Mountains complex of northeastern Oregon. In northern Idaho and adjacent areas the zone blends upslope with the higher, drier Inland Maritime Zone. Elsewhere it lies just below the Subalpine Fir/Engelmann Spruce Zone.

The Inland Maritime Zone occurs in northern Idaho, northeastern Washington, southeastern British Columbia, and northwestern Montana. It is best developed on the seaward slopes of north-south-trending mountain ranges, such as the

Selkirks and the Purcells. Occurring at elevations between 1,800 and 5,500 feet, the zone lies above either the Ponderosa Pine Zone or Inland Fir Zone and below the Subalpine Fir/Engelmann Spruce Zone. The dominant trees are western hemlock and western redcedar. Western white pine dominates seral stands, which cover vast areas once devastated by fire. Western larch, Douglas-fir, and lodgepole pine also occur in this zone.

Subalpine and Alpine Zones
(Chapters 9 and 11)

The Pacific Silver Fir Zone occurs on the west slope of the Coast Mountains and Cascade Range south to near Crater Lake. Elevations for the zone range from 3,300 to 4,900 feet in Oregon and from 2,000 to 4,300 feet in northern Washington. The Pacific Silver Fir Zone is transitional between the lower Western Hemlock Zone and the higher Mountain Hemlock Zone and includes trees and understory plants from each. Pacific silver fir is the dominant climax species, though western hemlock is usually present. Alaska-cedar is an important associate, and Douglas-fir, western redcedar, and mountain hemlock are all fairly common. In southern Washington and Oregon, noble fir is a long-lived member of seral stands.

The Shasta Red Fir Zone occurs in southwestern Oregon and northwestern California at elevations between 5,200 and 6,600 feet in the Cascades and 5,900 and 7,200 feet in the Siskiyous. The zone forms a narrow belt sandwiched between lower mixed conifer forests and higher mountain hemlock forests. In the Cascades the zone features nearly pure stands of Shasta red fir. Lodgepole pine is the most common seral species. White fir and sugar pine occur in the lower part of the zone, mountain hemlock in the upper. In the Siskiyous and other ranges making up the Klamath Mountains, Shasta red fir cohabits with as many as two dozen different conifer species to form what are probably the most diverse conifer forests on the planet.

The Mountain Hemlock Zone is the highest forest zone on the west slope of the Coast Mountains and Cascades, ranging as far north as south-central Alaska (where mountain hemlocks grow at sea level) and as far south as the southern Sierra Nevada. Mountain hemlock forests also occur in the Olympic Mountains and Klamath Mountains. The most extensive mountain hemlock forests occur in the Cascades of central and southern Oregon. The lower and upper limits of the zone are typically 4,100 and 6,000 feet in northwestern Washington and 5,600 and 6,600 feet in southwestern Washington. Mountain hemlock, with or without Pacific silver fir, dominate climax forests. Alaska-cedar, lodgepole pine, and whitebark pine are common associates. Douglas-fir, subalpine fir, and western white pine may also be present. The zone includes a lower closed-forest section and an upper parkland section consisting of tree islands scattered over a sea of subalpine meadows. The meadow communities are dominated by sedges, broadleaf herbs, and members of the heath family. Timberline marks the upper limit of the zone.

The Subalpine Fir/Engelmann Spruce Zone is the highest forest zone in the Northern Rockies, where it generally occurs at elevations between 4,500 and 7,500 feet. The zone also occurs along the east side of the Cascades, though Engelmann spruce is less common there. In its place are mountain hemlock and other conifers from the Mountain Hemlock Zone of the western slope. The lower part of the zone consists of closed forests of fir and spruce in which Douglas-fir is often common. Alpine larch and whitebark pine form open woodlands on rocky slopes in the upper part of the zone. Lodgepole pine often dominates cirque basins and other frost pockets. Timberline marks the upper limit of the zone.

The Alpine Zone is the region above timberline. The zone contains a variety of communities dominated by herbs and low shrubs. It also includes the scattered dwarfed trees (Krummholz) that occur along the upper timberline.

Steppe Zones (Chapter 13)

The Bunchgrass Steppe Zone designates the grasslands that still mantle areas of north-central Oregon and the Palouse region of southeastern Washington. The dominant plants are bunchgrasses—bluebunch wheatgrass, Idaho fescue, and Sandberg's bluegrass. The native grasslands of the Palouse have now been converted almost entirely to agriculture.

The Shrub Steppe Zone covers much of eastern Oregon, southern Idaho, and Washington's Columbia Basin. The shrub steppe is a two-layered formation in which the lower layer is dominated by bunchgrasses and the upper by well-spaced shrubs. The principal bunchgrasses are the same ones that dominate the bunchgrass steppe communities. Big sagebrush is the most common and widespread shrub. Other important shrubs include rabbitbrush, antelope bitter-brush, and common snowberry. Downy cheatgrass, an alien species, has replaced native bunchgrasses throughout most of the region. The shrub steppe is a northern extension of cold-desert communities common to the Great Basin. Distinctive vegetation occurs within the zone on damp, rocky, and saline soils. The so-called meadow-steppe of northeastern Washington is a type of shrub-steppe in which herbaceous plants are particularly conspicuous.

CHAPTER FIVE

The Kingdom of Conifers

THE MOST DIVERSE conifer forests in the world mantle the mountains and coastal lowlands of the Pacific Northwest. All together, more than thirty species of conifers inhabit the region, more than in any other area of comparable size in North America. These species are drawn from three regional floras that combine and mingle in the Pacific Northwest:

- A distinctive group of Northwest coastal conifers dominates the lowlands and foothills of the Pacific slope, from northwestern California to south-central Alaska. They also grow on the wet seaward slopes of the Northern Rockies eastward to the Continental Divide.
- Forests characteristic of California's Sierra Nevada and Coast Range are the prevailing types in southwestern Oregon, where they blend with coastal elements in the Siskiyou Mountains and on the west side of the Cascades and with Rocky Mountain elements on the east side of the Cascades.
- Rocky Mountain conifers occur not only in the Northern Rockies but also on the east side of the Cascade Range and in the mountains of central and northeastern Oregon.
- Finally, subalpine conifers drawn from all three regions form distinctive upper timberlines on the higher mountain ranges of the region.

Conifers are among the oldest seed plants on earth. Their earliest fossils date back some 350 million years to the middle of the Paleozoic Era, before the advent of flowering plants, when spore-bearing, tree-sized ferns, club mosses, and horsetails formed swampy forests. The conifers—probably hardy ancestors of today's pines—were the first plants to leave the swamps and venture onto high ground. We can imagine them sprouting from crevices in barren rock because we can see their descendants doing the same thing today in the mountains of the Northwest.

Spores, which consist only of a microscopic cell surrounded by a stout wall for protection from rapid dehydration, can be blown far and wide but have to land on damp ground in order to germinate. Because of their rudimentary structure, days or weeks must pass before an embryo is formed and even before a plant is visible to the naked eye. In contrast, seeds come equipped with an already formed embryo and a mass of starchy cells to fuel rapid growth. This built-in food supply gave seed-bearing conifers a clear advantage over spore-bearing trees in colonizing harsh environments.

Conifers and their close relatives, the cycads and gingkos, are collectively known as gymnosperms, meaning plants with naked seeds. True flowering plants bear their seeds in ovaries found at the bases of the flowers. Conifer seeds are born naked, as it were, on the scales of woody cones. Actually, conifers produce two kinds of cones: The large, woody female cones are the seed bearers, the ones most people call "pine cones" regardless of whether they come from pines, firs, spruces, or whatever; the smaller male cones produce pollen, which is carried by wind, rather than insects, to the exposed ovules on the upper sides of the female-cone scales.

Most conifers belong to two great families: the pine family and the cypress family. In the Pacific Northwest the pine family is represented by firs, larches, spruces, pines, Douglas-fir, and hemlocks; the cypress family by Baker cypress, incense-cedar, Alaska-cedar, Port-Orford-cedar, junipers, and western redcedar. Two smaller families are also represented: the baldcypress family by coast redwood and the yew family by western yew.

The leaves of conifers are simple and durable. Members of the pine, baldcypress, and yew families possess needlelike leaves, which have a central vein for conducting water and a waxy coat that insulates them from heat and cold and increases their resistance to drought. The central vein concentrates water in the leaf while the coating prevents freezing and helps to retard moisture loss through evaporation. The needles are impregnated with resin, which acts as an

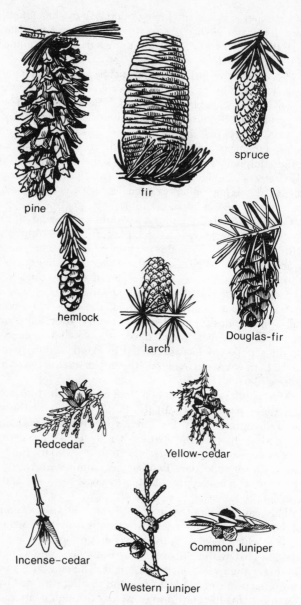

pine

fir

spruce

hemlock

larch

Douglas-fir

Redcedar

Yellow-cedar

Incense-cedar

Western juniper

Common Juniper

6. An assortment of conifer leaves and cones

NATURALIST'S GUIDE TO THE PACIFIC NORTHWEST

ntifreeze but also makes them resistant to decay. Conifer needles are built to last, to remain on the trees through winter blasts and summer drought. Lacking the elaborately structured leaves of flowering trees, with their superstructure of veins supporting a broad photosynthetic surface, conifer needles are less efficient in warm, moist climates but are longer lasting and superior under conditions of stress.

Members of the cypress family have leaves that resemble scales rather than needles. If a conifer needle were severely abbreviated and more or less flattened, the result would be very much like the leaves of western redcedar, Alaska-cedar, incense-cedar, Port-Orford-cedar, and Rocky Mountain juniper. This shape allows the needles to cluster tightly around the stems, creating flat sprays of foliage.

All conifers but the larches are evergreen. Although their leaves fall more or less continuously, as the thick needle carpets in conifer forests attest, individual needles last up to several years. The principal advantage of evergreenness lies in not having to produce a new crop of leaves each year. This is an advantage in extreme environments, where the growing season may be sharply curtailed or where essential resources may be in short supply. Evergreenness allows conifers to respond immediately to favorable changes in the environment and to avoid yearly expenditures of energy on entirely new sets of leaves.

The conifer forests of the Pacific Northwest are descendants of a richer, more widespread, mixed conifer-hardwood forest that 50 million years ago spanned the continent from ocean to ocean. Fossil evidence shows that a mixed conifer forest at that time occurred along the northernmost margin of the continent, including the arctic islands and Greenland. Ancestral firs, pines, and baldcypresses were present in this forest, along with birches, hazelnuts, poplars, and willows. Except for the baldcypresses, which are today limited to the warm, humid southeastern United States and tropical America, all these species are members of the several conifer forests currently found in the Pacific Northwest.

South of this subarctic forest was a rich temperate forest that included the forerunners of trees that are now found in both the continent's eastern and western forests. Among the western species represented in those forests were conifers such as firs, arborvitae, incense-cedars, spruces, pines, hemlocks, and Douglas-firs. The eastern species included deciduous species such as maples, buckeyes, chestnuts, hazelnuts, beeches, ashes, walnuts, and elms. Baldcypresses, redwoods, giant sequoias, and dawn redwoods were also present, as were gingkos, which are today known only from cultivation. Gingko State Park in eastern Washington contains the only petrified gingkos in the world and offers dramatic insights into the nature and composition of this ancient temperate forest.

The Pacific Northwest was still being assembled from fragments of continents during this period (see Chapter 2), but what parts of it were in place occupied a broad transitional belt, or ecotone, between the temperate forest to the north and subtropical vegetation to the south. Much of the latter consisted of scrub, savanna, and steppe, vegetation like that found today in East Africa and other tropical areas. The first horses and other hooved mammals appeared during this period, suggesting that grasslands were extensive.

The Tertiary Period came to an end about 3 million years ago with the onset of the Pleistocene Epoch, or Ice Age. The cooling that led to the Ice Age began about 30 million years ago. In response, vegetation zones shifted southward to near their present positions. At the same time, the uplift of the Rockies began to cast a rainshadow over lands to the east. The drier conditions that ensued over what is now the Great Plains region allowed grasslands to extend northward up the center of the continent, dividing the forest into eastern and western halves. Over the next 20 to 30 million years, the eastern and western populations of many species evolved along different lines in response to different environmental conditions. As a result, single species that once occurred across the continent are today represented by distinct eastern and western descendants. Examples include the Pacific dogwood, bigleaf maple, and western redcedar in the western forest and their counterparts flowering dogwood, sugar maple, and northern whitecedar in the east. The eastern and western forests remained connected only in the far north, but even there the rise of the lofty coast ranges of northwestern Canada and southeastern Alaska virtually severed contact between Northwest coastal and eastern conifers. The modern descendant of this northern transcontinental forest is the North American boreal forest, or taiga, which is heavily dominated by eastern species that have close relatives among the western mountain and coastal conifers.

The rise of the Sierra Nevada and Cascade Range cast a rainshadow over the entire region stretching east to the Rockies. As a result, desert conditions prevailed then as now, allowing plants of southwestern and Mexican origin to push northward as far as southern British Columbia. Another result was to limit western conifers to the mountain ranges or immediate coast, where air temperature, humidity, and precipitation were more congenial. This is more or less the situation that exists today.

During the Pleistocene Epoch, or Ice Age, which began about 3 million years ago and ended about 10,000 years ago, the climate was significantly cooler and at least as wet as today's. As a result ice caps formed in the western mountain ranges and spawned valley glaciers that moved outward into the lowlands. In western Canada the valley glaciers buried their intervening ridges and coalesced in the lowlands to form the vast Cordilleran Ice Sheet, which pushed as far south as what are now Olympia, Washington, and Missoula, Montana. As a result, the forest was also displaced southward and pushed downslope out of the mountains onto nearby plains.

The ice began to retreat slowly about 15,000 years ago. The pace quickened with the dramatic warming that began about 10,500 years ago. Over the next 3,500 years the forest advancd northward at the rate of roughly 18 miles a century, colonizing the rubble and scoured bedrock left in the wake of the retreating glaciers.

We have an excellent picture of how forest reclaimed the lands abandoned by the ice because for the past century and more we have been able to observe the process at work in many places throughout the Northwest. On recently abandoned glacial till in Glacier Bay National Park in southeastern Alaska, seral and climax plants are both included among the first invaders. Herbs dominate the first sere, particularly mats of mountain avens and masses of taller plants such as red willowherb and lupine. Dense thickets of Sitka alder succeed the herbaceous vegetation. These shrubs are able to fix nitrogen and therefore increase soil fertility. Eventually, fast-growing black cottonwood shades out the alder and is replaced in turn by Sitka spruce. Finally, western hemlock, the climax species, grows up in the shade of the spruces. The course of succession at the end of the Pleistocene Era must have been nearly identical to this throughout the Puget Sound region and northward along the coast to Alaska. Inland, several different species may have been involved at various stages, but the overall process would have been virtually the same.

Today, conifers dominate western forests because they are better adapted than hardwoods to combinations of warm winters and dry summers. Deciduous hardwoods, which rule the eastern forest, are admirably suited to long cold winter but require warm, moist conditions during the growing season. In the west, however, summers are either too cool at higher elevations or too dry in the lowlands. As a result, at lower elevations deciduous trees are limited in the wild mainly to lakeshores, streamsides, and wetlands, where moisture and warmth combine during the growing season. At higher elevations, where moisture may be sufficient to support deciduous growth, cool, brief growing seasons favor conifers.

Conditions suitable for deciduous hardwoods would seem to exist along the mild, humid Northwest coast, yet there too conifers reign supreme. In fact, the Northwest coastal forest is unique among the world's temperate forests for the overwhelming dominance of conifers over hardwoods. In other temperate regions, such as western Europe, eastern Asia, and eastern North America, hardwoods, or a mix of hardwoods and conifers, normally dominate mature forests. Often, conifers are relegated to rigorous borderline habitats or are temporary forest residents that are eventually evicted by hardwoods. This is certainly the case in eastern North America. In the Northwest coastal forest, however, conifers dominate hardwoods, in terms of timber volume, by a ratio of 1000:1! There hardwoods are largely confined to marginal sites and the early stages of succession, and conifers dominate mature forests in typical regional habitats.

Mild temperatures and abundant moisture from fall through spring permit significant ongoing photosynthesis during what in most other temperate-forest regions would be considered the dormant season. Evergreen conifers are able to take advantage of this situation but deciduous hardwoods are not. For example, conifers can assimilate carbohydrates over a broad temperature span, including temperatures below freezing. In addition, their conical crowns are admirably suited for intercepting maximum light when the winter sun lies low in the southern sky.

In the Pacific Northwest conifers also maintain their advantage over deciduous hardwoods during the summer, when moisture deficits are commonplace throughout the region, including the coastal section. In response to this moisture stress, the small pores (stomates) on the leaves, through which gas exchange occurs, are forced to close. The result is a sharp drop in the uptake of carbon dioxide, without which photosynthesis is impossible. Deciduous hardwoods, which have no choice but to carry on photosynthesis during the summer months, are therefore restricted to habitats where the supply of moisture is reliable.

Conifers, however, possess several structural and physiological features that make them admirably suited to endure summer drought. First, conifers have a larger proportion of sapwood and therefore can store more water than hardwoods can. They are also able to recharge cells with water more readily during occasional summer showers. Second, conifer needles, which are insulated with a wax, are able to conserve moisture more effectively than the leaves of deciduous hardwoods. Mature conifers are also able to avoid moisture stress during the summer by reducing metabolic processes for as long as may be necessary. Since their leaves remain intact, they are able to resume activities just as soon as enough moisture again becomes available. This strategy wouldn't work for deciduous hardwoods because they wouldn't have enough time each summer to complete growth, set fruit, and put on new buds for the following year.

Most types of vegetation consist of two or more distinct layers. The uppermost layer comprises the largest class of plants able to survive on the resources available in a particular habitat. Below this layer are successively smaller classes of plants, consisting of species that have evolved various strategies for surviving on the leftovers. Trees, by virtue of their great height, permit the elaboration of multiple layers, a tendency that achieves its extreme expression in the tropical rain forest, where all the necessities of life are in abundant supply. Temperate conifer forests also support several layers of vegetation, although the relative paucity of resources often results in fewer or less fully developed layers than exist in tropical forests. The closest approximation to tropical richness occurs in old-growth coastal forests, where mild temperatures, year-round growing seasons, and abundant moisture generally permit the elaboration of several distinct layers.

The top forest layer is the canopy, which comprises the crowns of the principal trees. The layers beneath the canopy collectively make up the forest understory. These may include layers dominated by smaller trees, shrubs, herbaceous plants, and mosses or lichens. Old-growth coastal forests commonly contain all these layers. At the other extreme, dense second-growth forests may contain no understory layers to speak of. Or if they do, the layers are often sparse and poor in species. As competition among the young trees thins out such stands, increasing numbers of plants are able to establish themselves in the understory. Some old-growth forests also have little or no understory vegetation, but as pointed out below, this often has more to do with deficiencies of moisture and nutrients than of light alone.

Leaves absorb a large percentage of the light that strikes them. As a result, understory plants rely on the light that passes through the gaps between the leaves of the canopy. Moreover, each layer of vegetation acts as an additional filter, reducing the light available to the one beneath it. In response to conditions of low light in the understory, many forest conifers abandon their lower branches, concentrating their photosynthetic energies on the upper ones, which intercept most of the incoming solar radiation (insolation). This self-pruning accounts for the long, clear trunks so characteristic of western conifers.

Some plants require shade; others merely tolerate it. Prince's pine is an example of the former; salal, of the latter. Whichever, a plant growing in the forest understory must above all be able to carry out photosynthesis at light levels well below normal. The ability—or inability— to survive in shade, however, is not necessarily a response to light alone. Heat and moisture are both closely tied to light levels. Thus, some plants require shade because they cannot stand the overheating or increased evaporation rates associated with full sunlight. In addition, several other factors critical to plant growth are associated with low light levels within a forest. For example, wind speeds are significantly lower within a forest than in the open. When winds carry humid air away, the higher vapor capacity of the incoming air increases evaporation both from plant surfaces and the soil. Nutrient deficiencies are also associated with low light. For example, decomposition proceeds more slowly in shade than in sunlight, not because light is a factor but because lower temperatures inhibit the activities of soil fungi and bacteria.

The tendency of conifers to dominate soil resources not only makes nutrient deficiencies worse but creates drought in the upper soil horizons. It is not uncommon to see well-developed understory vegetation on sites where light may be low but moisture is plentiful. Often, the paucity of understory plants in certain old-growth stands, where light levels are clearly high enough to permit their presence, is a result of depleted soil moisture (either alone or in combination with other factors) during the growing season.

The adaptations exhibited by plants growing beneath conifers must therefore address a complex of environmental factors. Nevertheless, shade plants as a group possess a number of anatomical and physiological features that are mainly responses to low light. As one would expect, these adaptations are usually most evident in the leaves, which are the primary photosynthetic organs. The leaves of shade plants are normally large and thin, allowing maximum surface with minimum weight. They also tend to be held at right angles to the sun, either in basal rosettes or in sprays of foliage held aloft. The leaves are generally dark green because they have high levels of the green pigment chlorophyll, the chemical that enables plants to trap light. The absence of fine hairs, which act as sun screens and heat radiators for plants growing in the open, also contribute to the deep, often lustrous color of shade plants.

Tolerance, the measure of a tree's ability to withstand low overhead light and intense root competition, is the driving force behind forest succession. The relative tolerance of the various tree species that are able to occupy a given habitat largely determines which of them will occur in the climax forest and which will be limited primarily to earlier seral stages (see following table). A tolerant species can reproduce

NORTHWEST TREES: Ages, Dimensions, and Relative Tolerances

Species	Age (years)	Diameter* (inches)	Height* (feet)	Tolerance
Alaska–cedar	1,000+	40–60	100–130	tolerant
Alder, Red	100	22–30	100–130	intolerant
Cottonwood, Black	200+	30–35	80–115	intolerant
Douglas–fir	750+	60–90	230–260	intolerant
Fir, Grand	300+	30–50	130–200	tolerant
Fir, Noble	400+	35–60	150–230	intolerant
Fir, Pacific Silver	400+	35–45	150–180	very tolerant
Fir, Shasta Red	300+	40–50	130–165	intermediate
Fir, Subalpine	250+	20–25	80–115	tolerant
Fir, White	300+	40–60	130–180	tolerant
Hemlock, Mountain	400+	30–40	80–115	tolerant
Hemlock, Western	400+	35–50	165–215	very tolerant
Incense–cedar	500+	35–50	150	intermediate
Larch, Western	700+	55	165	intolerant
Maple, Bigleaf	300+	20	50	tolerant
Oak, Oregon White	500	25–35	50–80	intolerant
Pine, Lodgepole	250+	20	80–115	intolerant
Pine, Ponderosa	600+	30–50	100–165	intolerant
Pine, Sugar	400+	40–50	150–180	intermediate
Pine, Western White	400+	45	200	intermediate
Port–Orford–cedar	500+	50–70	200	tolerant
Redcedar, Western	1,000+	60–120	200+	tolerant
Redwood, Coast	1,000+	60–70	250–320	tolerant
Spruce, Engelmann's	500+	40+	150–165	tolerant
Spruce, Sitka	800+	70–90	230–250	tolerant
Tanoak	180	10–60	50–160	tolerant

* Typical dimensions on better forest sites.

Adapted from a table appearing in *Natural Vegetation of Oregon and Washington*, by Jerry F. Franklin and C. T. Dyrness, USDA Forest Service, General Tech, Portland, Oregon, 1973.

and survive beneath a canopy of taller trees and upon release can accelerate growth to take advantage of diminished competition and increased sunlight. An intolerant species, however, requires full sunlight, and perhaps the lack of competition that such a state implies, for reproduction and growth.

Tolerant species are able to carry on photosynthesis at lower light levels than intolerant ones. And as light increases, tolerant species achieve maximum rates of photosynthesis at lower light levels than intolerant species. Since intolerant species are generally able to increase their rates of photosynthesis beyond the maximums attained by tolerant species, the former normally outgrow the latter in open areas. As shade increases, the difference in growth rates declines until at some point the tolerant species begins to outgrow the intolerant one.

Observation and comparison of species growing together allow a subjective ordering of them according to apparent tolerance. Normally, species are grouped into broad categories of tolerance without much attempt to make finer distinctions among them. Western hemlock, Pacific silver fir, and mountain hemlock are among the most tolerant conifers in the Pacific Northwest; ponderosa pine, western larch, and lodgepole pine, among the least.

Major disturbances that remove the dominant trees tend to favor intolerant species and are largely responsible for their continued presence in the landscape. On the other hand, minor interruptions in the canopy may favor the tolerant species by releasing suppressed understory trees, which rapidly shoot upward to fill the gaps. Chief among these disturbances (at least prior to the arrival in this century of clearcut logging) is fire. Wildfire has long been part of the natural environment in which the forests of the Pacific Northwest have evolved.

The role of fire has been greatest in the Northern Rockies, where dry summers and frequent lightning storms create ideal fire conditions. Frequent holocausts have consumed hundreds of thousands of acres of forest in the region. As a result, large areas are dominated by western white pine, western larch, and lodgepole pine, seral conifers that rapidly invade recently burned sites. Before the onset of fire-suppression policies early in this century, the resulting fires often raged unchecked until the first storms of autumn put them out.

Fire has also played a major role in northern California and southern Oregon, where mild, wet winters cause understory fuel to proliferate, while hot, dry summers create tinderbox conditions in which the merest spark can cause the materials to ignite. Lightning is uncommon in the region, however, so wildfires have generally been less frequent, if not necessarily less extensive, than in the Northern Rockies. The importance of fire to the region's vegetation, however, is suggested by the large number of plants showing specific adaptations to fire. These adaptations include serotinous (i.e., late-developing) cones, dormant seeds, and sprouting from stumps or root crowns. Serotinous cones remain closed and on the trees until fire melts the resin sealing their scales.

Knobcone pines, for instance, have serotinous cones that may cling like withered ornaments to their branches for years. Many shrubs and herbs in the region produce seeds that remain dormant in the soil, often for decades, until scarified by fire. Serotiny and seed dormancy not only allow plants to survive fires but assure that their resurgence occurs under conditions where competition is minimal. Coast redwood and greenleaf manzanita are among the many plants that sprout vigorously from stumps or root crowns following a fire. Sprouting gives such plants a head start in the post-fire environment and allows the new generation to exploit root networks that are already in place.

Fire has played a lesser role in the coastal forests of the Pacific Northwest, where lightning is rare, summers are cool, and drought is seldom severe. When fires do occur, however, they are often disastrous. Luxuriant understories that provide abundant fuel, combined with the thin, highly flammable bark of many of the resident trees, set the stage for crown fires that may devastate hundreds of thousands of acres. Such fires normally occur every 300 to 400 years on a given site. Since the region's two major fire-dependent conifers—Sitka spruce and Douglas-fir—both live for 1,000 years or more, their continued presence in the forests is assured.

Throughout the Northwest, fire has arrested forest succession at various stages short of climax (subclimaxes). We are so conditioned to equate changes over time with the nineteenth-century notion of beneficial social progress that we sometimes forget that nature doesn't always move in that direction. As a matter of fact, true climax vegetation commonly shows far less diversity and energy than seral

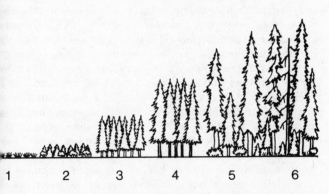

1   2   3   4   5   6

The six major stages of forest succession: (1) grass forb, (2) shrub-seedling, (3) pole-sapling, (4) young, (5) mature, and (6) old growth (adapted from Brown, ed., *Management of Wildlife and Fish Habitats in Forests of Western Oregon and Washington*)

ypes. Personification is the cardinal sin of natural science, but the analogy here to human society is irresistible. Seral forests offer varied opportunities and therefore attract a large number of entrepreneurs, opportunists, and hustlers, all with an eye for the main chance. Competition is intense, the potential rewards are great, and the rise and fall of successive groups of plants can be relatively rapid. Climax forests, however, are dominated by the establishment, which hogs most of the resources and effectively eliminates most potential competitors. Often, production actually declines in climax forests, as increasing amounts of raw materials are trapped in nonproductive tissues or thick carpets of litter. Fire and other disturbances may actually serve to reinvigorate forest stands, increasing the diversity of both species and vegetation types. The resulting mosaic of vegetation in turn provides more different kinds of habitats for wildlife, which in response may increase in both numbers and species.

Fires therefore are not merely agents of destruction. Relatively cool ground fires actually improve the soil by releasing nutrients bound up in forest litter. Moreover, the fire pioneers in each area always include one or more species that improve the soil through the fixation of nitrogen. In the Pacific Northwest, several species of alder and ceanothus are particularly noteworthy in this regard. Fires also destroy diseased or insect-infested trees, thereby paving the way for healthier young stands. This has happened in the Northern Rockies, for example, where younger generations of western white pine show greater resistance to white pine blister rust than their ancestors.

For most of this century the official policy of forest management agencies at all levels of government has been to suppress fires. This policy has had several unfortunate consequences. First, the enormous amounts of fuel that accumulated in the absence of more frequent burning made truly devastating fires more likely. Second, fire suppression favored the regeneration of shade-tolerant conifers over seral species, which include such important timber trees as Douglas-fir, ponderosa pine, and western white pine. Third, the forest steadily advanced into clearings that were created and maintained by fire, including communities such as meadows, brush, and huckleberry fields, that are highly valued as wildlife habitat, recreation resources, and sources of food.

Prior to the coming of white settlers, Indian people throughout the west regularly burned areas of forest to improve wildlife habitats and maintain foraging areas. The large open huckleberry fields scattered throughout the Cascades were largely maintained in this way. Fire suppression in this century has allowed forests to steadily invade these areas so that today management agencies are searching for an effective way to maintain them as openings.

While true climax forests, owing to the frequency of fire and the considerable longevity of many seral conifers, have probably always been rather uncommon, old-growth forest containing a mix of seral and conifer species once occurred over a vast area and even today cover hundreds of thousands of acres. Old-growth stands, whatever their make-up, share several features that distinguish them from younger managed and unmanaged stands. The following discussion of those features is drawn largely from field studies carried out by ecologists and foresters associated with the Forest Sciences Laboratory in Corvallis, Oregon. Although the findings were mainly gathered in old-growth Douglas-fir forests in the Oregon Cascades, they apply nearly as well to old-growth conifer forests in general.

Old-growth forests in the Pacific Northwest commonly take at least 175 years to develop, though most remaining stands are between 350 and 750 years old. Stands over 1,000 years old occur in moist canyon bottoms and river flats, where fire is virtually excluded. Even so, most old-growth forests are not climaxes, thanks to the longevity of the major seral species in the region. As a result, these stands typically contain several species of trees representing several age classes—the "graduates" of past disturbances. The largest trees may reach enormous size, particularly in the coastal forests. They are normally spaced at fair intervals, but the density of their crowns creates areas of deep shade. High winds and the undermining of roots by water or soil creep, however, cause trees already weakened by fire, disease, or insects to fall, creating small openings in the canopy. The

8. Stages in the decomposition of standing snags

resulting patchwork of light and shade typically results in patchy understory vegetation, save where abundant moisture counteracts the effects of low light. In addition to abundant fallen timber, old-growth forests also feature numerous standing snags in various stages of decomposition. These are critical habitats for wildlife but also contribute to the aesthetic quality of old-growth forests.

Old fallen logs act as nutrient reservoirs, accumulating phosphorus and smaller amounts of calcium and magnesium. They are also sites of nitrogen fixation, whereby bacteria active in the wood are able to convert atmospheric nitrogen to forms useful to plants. These nutrients are released over two or three centuries, as the log slowly succumbs to the incessant attacks of fungi, bacteria, and insects. Through this gradual release, fallen timber not only contributes to the recycling of nutrients back to the forest community but also serves to stabilize it as well.

Old logs also arrest the flow of water out of the forest, thereby retarding erosion and the loss of nutrients. Forest streams usually consist of alternating pools and riffles (or rapids). The pools commonly form behind logs that have fallen into the stream or behind dams formed as debris has become wedged between log, rock, and water. Sediments carried downstream are deposited in the quiet water of the pools, increasing stream clarity and preventing mineral and soil resources from washing away. Moreover, small forest streams depend on downed timber and other woody debris supplied by the forest for carbon and other nutrients essential to biological activity. Researchers in the Oregon Cascades found that large fallen trees accounted for 85 percent of the organic material in forest streams. These logs and branches served to retain conifer needles long enough in one place to allow microbes to begin breaking them down. Otherwise, these important nutrient resources would have been washed downstream out of the system. Research has shown too that the restoration of stable stream habitats in the wake of landslides, floods, and other serious disturbances proceeds more rapidly where woody debris is present than where it has been removed.

Downed timber also provides food and shelter for wildlife. Numerous birds and small mammals clamber over the logs in search of insects or conifer seeds. Woodpeckers bore into the soft wood in quest of the larvae of termites, carpenter ants, and wood-boring beetles. Bears, coyotes, raccoons, and other large mammals use hollow logs as dens or temporary shelters.

Fallen timber also plays an important role in establishing forest traffic patterns, providing easy pathways for some animals but blocking the way for others. Logs that lie across slopes seem to function as wildlife corridors more often than those pointing up- and downslope. Fallen trees lying across slopes also help retard erosion by capturing soil that otherwise would be carried downhill into streams. Soil that piles up on the upslope sides of fallen logs provides an excellent seed bed for forest plants, including conifers.

The forests of the Pacific Northwest have been disturbed extensively and repeatedly during the last century. In western Washington and Oregon unrelenting clearcut logging has left a patchwork of clearings and second-growth woods stretching from the Cascade foothills to the coast. Broadleaf deciduous trees such as red alder and bigleaf maple have replaced conifers over large areas. Conversion to conifers is very slow in many urban and suburban stands, presumably owing to a lack of reliable nearby seed sources.

Having cut most prime lowland stands, timber operations have moved upslope. Logging on steep mountainsides at high elevations has become increasingly common on both private and national-forest lands. Steep slopes, of course, are more vulnerable to erosion, and the transfer of topsoil downslope to streams threatens both terrestrial and aquatic environments. In addition, upper montane and subalpine forests have developed under extreme conditions of cold, wind, and snow. As a result the colonization of clearcut areas is likely to be painfully slow and unlikely to be completed until the men who cut the trees have long been dead. In such a prolonged time frame, lip service paid to "sustained yield" rings hollow. This is not forestry; it is timber mining.

The forests of British Columbia were long spared by the economic and logistical difficulties posed by the remoteness and ruggedness of most of the forest lands in the province. Today, however, with the aid of modern logging methods and transportation and the active encouragement of provincial forestry officials, the cutting of old-growth forests is proceeding at an alarming pace throughout the province.

Opponents of the province's timber policies are hampered by the absence of a strong tradition of conservation and the lack of effective legal recourse under Canadian law.

Current logging practice in the Pacific Northwest consists of cutting every tree of commercial size and burning the slash—that is every noncommercial piece of wood, including downed timber. In this way, diverse old-growth forests are converted to even-aged tree farms, where trees grow like turnips and are harvested nearly as often. These managed, second-growth stands are less diverse than old-growth forests and therefore less stable. Diversity increases ecological stability because disruption of any single element in the system is unlikely to destroy the whole. Slash fires may help to return nutrients to the soil by freeing compounds bound up in the woody debris, but they contribute to loss of diversity and resulting instability and may volatilize substantial amounts of nitrogen. In breaking the link between forests that were and forests that will be, the combination of clear-cutting, slash burning, and reduction of the "harvest" rotation period is likely to have disastrous consequences for the productivity, scientific value, and beauty of tomorrow's forests.

CHAPTER SIX

Rain Forests

THROUGHOUT MOST of the western United States, the only places that are at once cool and wet enough to support conifer forests are mountain ranges. The vegetation of intervening valleys is usually some combination of grassland, woodland, and brush and features plants that can tolerate long periods of hot, dry weather. But along the Northwest Pacific Coast, from northwestern California to southeastern Alaska, moisture is plentiful even at sea level and dense conifer forests mantle all but the driest parts of the lowlands, from mountainside to ocean shore.

The magnificent Douglas-fir forests of Oregon, the lush, verdant rain forests of Washington and British Columbia, and the spruce-hemlock forests of Alaska are all manifestations of what has been variously called the Northwest coastal forest, north-coast temperate conifer forest, Pacific coastal forest, and the like.* The Northwest coastal forest—as it shall be known here—occurs along the Pacific slope from northwestern California to south-central Alaska. Throughout this range, the forest grows at or near sea level, lining saltwater shores, even venturing onto wave-battered headlands and seastacks. But the Northwest coastal forest is not restricted to the shoreline. It also extends eastward to mantle the western flanks of the Coast Mountains and Cascade Range, ranging upslope to elevations as high as 2,000 feet in southeastern Alaska, 2,500 feet in British Columbia, 3,000

* Although the coast redwood forest of northwestern California shares many species and characteristics in common with coastal forests farther north, it is also part of a unique complex of distinctly Californian communities that are discussed together in the following chapter.

feet in western Washington, and 4,500 feet in northwestern Oregon.

Before the coming of white settlers, coastal conifer forests formed a nearly unbroken blanket over the western Washington lowlands. Today, despite past and continuing clearance of large areas for settlement and agriculture, 80 percent of the region is still classified as forest, although most of the old-growth stands that grew here a century ago have been logged. Conifers also cover most of western Oregon, except in the valleys of the Willamette, Umpqua, and Rogue rivers, which lie in the rainshadow of the Oregon Coast Range. Although conifers range down out of the foothills along streams and grow in other moist places, natural vegetation in these valleys consists largely of oak woodlands and grasslands.

Forests of western hemlock and western redcedar also occur on the seaward slopes of mountain ranges in southeastern British Columbia, eastern Washington, northern Idaho, and northwestern Montana. The inland forests are surprisingly similar to those growing along the coast, and their anomalous occurrence well east of the Cascade Range apparently stems from the frequent position of the jet stream over this region. The resulting strong, persistent, upper-level winds, combined with an only moderately high mountain barrier to the west, permit moist, relatively mild marine air to penetrate deeply into the interior, dragging as it were the coastal forest along with it.

Spanning more than 20 degrees of latitude, the Northwest coastal forest exhibits considerable variation over that distance. From Oregon northward through British Columbia, the vast majority of stands are dominated by one or a combination of four conifers: western hemlock, Douglas-fir, Sitka spruce, and western redcedar. Douglas-fir is missing from coastal forests in Alaska, and western redcedar ranges only as far north as Sitka. In northwestern California, coast redwood is the most important conifer, followed by Douglas-fir. Sitka spruce, western hemlock, and western redcedar are sporadic in distribution and only locally common.

While no single conifer occurs throughout the entire Northwest coastal forest, there is a good deal of overlap among plant and animal species, and the several forest types merge imperceptibly one into another. Widespread plants include shrubs such as salal and low Oregon-grape, ferns such as common sword fern and deer fern, and wildflowers such as evergreen violet and youth-on-age. Widespread and characteristic animals include mountain-beaver, black-tailed deer, winter wren, varied thrush, and roughskin newt.

The Northwest coastal forest enjoys the mildest and most humid climate in the Pacific Northwest. The moderating influence of marine air produces cool summers and mild winters in which extremes of temperature are rare. Though hard freezes and periods of hot weather do occur from time to time, they are generally modest in degree and of short duration. Rainfall, however, is decidedly immoderate. Most locales along the coast receive between 80 and 120 inches a year, most of it falling from October through April. Seattle and Portland both receive only about 40 inches of rain annually, but some areas along the coast receive 200 inches or more in some years. Precipitation also increases in the coastal mountains as a result of adiabatic cooling, as well as the constriction and piling up of air masses in their passage over the ranges. At lower elevations, snowfall is insignificant except in northern British Columbia and Alaska, where a foot or more normally remains on the ground through the winter. Summers commonly have extended periods of fog or high clouds, particularly along the coast. Intervals of warm weather, when temperatures exceed 80° F, occur most summers but are usually infrequent and brief. Truly hot weather is a novelty.

Summer fog provides coastal conifers and other plants with much-needed moisture during the driest season of the year. For that reason, the distribution of lowland conifer forests in the Pacific Northwest closely corresponds to the coastal fog belt. Fog helps young conifers and other forest plants in a couple of ways. First, it provides a significant shot of moisture in the form of fog drip. Fog droplets adhere to the needles of conifers, where they coalesce to form larger drops that slide off slender tips and fall through the forest like soft rain. Measurements taken in a mid-elevation old-growth Douglas-fir forest in the Western Cascades near Portland indicated that fog drip added 30 percent to the precipitation over that received in adjacent open areas. Measurements from some coastal forest areas have yielded comparable results.

The second way in which fog helps forest plants is by reducing the rate at which they lose moisture to the atmosphere. Overcast skies lower air temperatures, which in turn lowers the rate of evaporation from leaf surfaces. Fog also increases relative humidity, which further reduces evaporation.

Fog and overcast skies are the rule in coastal British Columbia and southeastern Alaska, but there drought is rarely a problem. Forests of Sitka spruce and western hemlock are restricted to the immediate coast not by too little moisture but by too little warmth. The abruptly rising wall of the Coast Mountains, with their mantle of glaciers, forms a frigid barrier to the inland push of coastal conifers.

The Pacific Northwest is famous for the great size and longevity of its principal trees. Indeed, all ten of the conifer genera that occur in the region are represented by their largest and, often, their longest-lived species. Larger or older conifers are found elsewhere, but as a group those of the Northwest are unsurpassed for overall age and size (see table, page 80). Among the 11 most important conifers occurring in the Northwest coastal forest, six commonly exceed 500 years of age, and three normally live longer than 300 years. Coast redwood is exceeded in size only by the giant sequoia of California's Sierra Nevada. Coastal Douglas-fir, Sitka spruce, and western redcedar are somewhat less massive than coast redwood but nevertheless must be counted among the world's largest trees. Before the wholesale logging of old-growth coastal stands that began during the last century and has continued to this day, individual trees exceeding 200 feet in height, ten feet in diameter, and 500 years of age were not uncommon. Today, such giants are rare but still may be found in national parks, wilderness areas, and other forest preserves. Apparently, conifers that are genetically predisposed to great size and long life stand an excellent chance of realizing that potential in the Northwest coastal forest, where moisture stress is normally minimal and the growing season is 12 months long.

In old-growth coastal forests the trunks of the dominant conifers rise like columns, often free of branches for 60 feet or more. While their crowns touch to form a more or less continuous canopy, the trees themselves may be rather widely spaced, each presiding over its own sphere of influence. In places, however, several large conifers may be clumped in circles or arrayed in straight lines, their tidy geometric patterns echoing their origins as either sprouts or seedlings growing atop old stumps or fallen trees. The canopy is often so elevated above the forest floor as to form a vaulted space not unlike that of a cathedral, where the soft, diffuse light creates a sense of serenity rather than gloom. This impression, which is felt by nearly all who visit these forests, is reinforced by their profound stillness, in which sounds are muffled and even birds seem to whisper.

Coastal forests on mesic sites with deep, rich soils commonly feature lush, multitiered understories in which small trees, shrubs, wildflowers, ferns, and mosses are all well represented. In the best-developed stands every available growing space is utilized, including fallen logs and old stumps, which usually sport a variety of ferns, shrubs, mosses, herbs, mushrooms, and even young conifers. Thick, bright green cushions of moss commonly pad rocks and trees or carpet large areas of the forest floor, making the woods look as if they had been upholstered in emerald plush.

Sunnier, more open versions of the Northwest coastal forest develop on drier sites. The dryness, however, is relative, for plants growing on these sites still experience less moisture stress than their counterparts on typical forest sites in the Rocky Mountains or Sierra Nevada. Such stands are more common in Oregon than in Washington or British Columbia.

Visitors to the Northwest coastal forest cannot help but notice that most young conifers seem to have sprouted atop fallen timber and old stumps. In fact, conifer reproduction in lush, humid coastal forests may be confined mostly or entirely to such "nurse logs" or "mother stumps," as they are called, because dense moss and other vegetation on the forest floor inhibit the germination of conifer seeds and, where that happens to succeed, the subsequent growth of young trees. The decaying wood of fallen timber provides a rich, reliably moist rooting medium, one, moreover, that is elevated well above the strenuous competition for space, light, water, and nutrients that is the hallmark of life on the forest floor. Moreover, because fallen logs create openings in the canopy, young conifers growing on them generally receive more sunlight than they would on other sites.

Western hemlock routinely begins life on fallen logs and

9. Western redcedar (*Thuja plicata*) played a central role in the life of Northwest coastal Indian tribes, who relied on the tree for fiber, food, medicine, and wood.

old stumps, though it does not require them. Sitka spruce and western redcedar do so with less regularity. Douglas-fir only occasionally grows on nurse logs because its seeds normally require bare mineral soil for germination. So do those of coast redwood. But redwood often originates from nurse logs of a different sort. Instead of relying on wind-blown seeds that happen to alight on suitable logs or stumps, these conifers readily sprout from the still-living tissues of recently cut, burned, or fallen timber.

By acting as nurse logs, fallen timber helps to determine spatial relationships within the forest. As nurse-log seedlings grow into saplings, their company thins, leaving a number of fair-sized young trees lined up along the log. One or more roots from each tree usually embrace the fallen giant as they reach down to the forest soil. Eventually, when the log has completely decomposed, a line, or colonnade, of young trees that are perched on flaring, stiltlike roots, mark where it once lay. Where regeneration begins on a stump rather than a log, the mature trees often form a semicircle, with their trunks more or less fused at the base.

A wide variety of understory plants also take advantage of nurse logs and mother stumps. One of the most common is red huckleberry, a relative of commercial blueberries and cranberries. Its sweet red berries attract not only humans and bears but also forest birds, which digest the pulp but deposit the seeds along with their feces—often on other stumps and logs. This huckleberry grows abundantly in the damper forests of the region but is almost never seen except on one of these woody perches. Birds perform the same service for coast red elderberry.

The strategy of the huckleberry has also been adopted inadvertently by certain ornamental trees imported from Europe. In the Puget Sound region, for example, English holly and European mountain-ash, both of which bear small red berries, are commonly found growing on nurse logs and mother stumps in city and suburban parks.

Sitka spruce is the reigning conifer of the coastal fog belt from southern Oregon to south-central Alaska. In fact, wave-battered headlands and seastacks crowned with wind-pruned Sitka spruce are emblematic of the Northwest coast. In northwestern California, Sitka-spruce forests often replace redwoods on exposed headlands and seaside slopes, buffering the latter tree from high winds and excessive salt spray. Though normally restricted to the coastal fog belt, Sitka spruce also ranges inland along major rivers for 60 miles or more. In western Washington, spruces occur in forested wetlands around Puget Sound and in humid valleys on the west slope of the Cascades. A near-rain forest featuring Sitka spruce, western hemlock, and western redcedar occurs along the Carbon River in the extreme northwest corner of Mount Rainier National Park, more than 100 miles from the Pacific Ocean.

Throughout its range, Sitka spruce's nearly constant companion is western hemlock. The spruce-hemlock forest normally occurs below 500 feet elevation but may extend upward to 2,000 feet where mountains are immediately adjacent to the coast. Stands consisting solely of Sitka spruce are common on coastal bluffs and headlands, where high winds may exclude hemlocks. Sitka spruce also is among the first conifers to invade bare, open, recently exposed ground such as glacial till, landslides, abandoned stream terraces, old floodplains, and uplifted beaches or dunes.

The raw mineral soils, exposure to the sun, and greater drought of such habitats is generally sufficient to exclude western hemlock at least for a time.

Sitka spruce has stiff, sharp, flattened needles that radiate in bottle-brush fashion from all sides of the twigs. The bark is also distinctive: purplish-brown and divided into large, loose, scaly plates. The light-brown, cylindrical cones are two to three-and-a-half inches long and have papery scales. Sitka spruce grows rapidly, and when openings in the forest occur it is quick to fill them. Young spruces may reach heights of 150 feet and more in a century, while old ones are known to add from several inches to a foot or more in girth every 30 to 35 years. Spruces eight feet thick and 200 feet tall are common. In humid coastal valleys sheltered from the wind, Sitka spruces may exceed 12 feet in diameter and 300 feet in height.

Unlike western hemlock, Sitka spruce often requires sunny openings and bare soil for reproduction. It can use nurse logs, however, and does so exclusively in the Olympic rain forest. Over the spruce's several-century lifespan, however, wind, landslide, flood, and even fire create enough openings to assure its continued presence in the forest. In fact, old-growth forests along the coast are more often dominated by spruce than hemlock. The hemlock's greater vulnerability to windthrow and lower tolerance for salt spray are severe handicaps in seaside habitats.

Throughout most of the world's conifer forests, western hemlock would rank among the largest trees. After all, mature hemlocks commonly exceed three feet in diameter and 150 feet in height. In the Northwest coastal forest, however, the hemlock is the smallest major conifer. Douglas-fir, western redcedar, and Sitka spruce all greatly exceed it in height, girth, and longevity. (see table, page 80). Yet western hemlock's prolific seeding habit and ability to reproduce in deep shade assures its continuing presence among these giants. Though often not the most abundant conifer in old-growth stands, it is almost always present, if sometimes only in the form of young understory trees. Often, in fact, western hemlocks are the only young conifers found in coastal forest stands. A few young redcedars are sometimes present but rarely in great numbers. Young Douglas-firs or Sitka spruces, both of which require full sun and bare mineral

10. Western hemlock (*Tsuga hetrophylla*)

soil to reproduce, are normally conspicuous by their absence.

Western hemlock seeds are not so picky. They will germinate in mineral soil, forest duff, even on old logs and stumps—wherever moisture is available. Moreover, the seeds are produced in profusion. A one-acre hemlock forest in Oregon, for example, yielded an average of eight million seeds a year! Attached to each seed is a membrane that serves as a wing, and even the slightest breeze is enough to carry the seeds great distances.

Because western hemlock is able to reproduce in the shade of its larger, longer-lived associates, given enough time it would eventually replace them. And since the other trees are in varying degrees less tolerant of shade, they would not be able to reproduce in great enough numbers to replace the hemlocks. As a result, western hemlocks would continue to dominate the forest indefinitely, until some major disturbance—fire, landslide, volcanic eruption, windthrow, logging, or flood—created an opening large enough to permit significant reproduction of other conifers. Hemlocks also have large leaf areas and cast very dense shade. In fact, most of the heavy shade in old-growth stands is cast by hemlocks rather than the Douglas-firs.

In short, western hemlock is the dominant climax species in all but the driest Northwest coastal forest stands. Yet climax forests are rare. It appears that natural and human disturbances open up the forest often enough to assure the continuing presence of its long-lived companions. As a result, old-growth stands may be dominated by other conifers. In most stands, however, hemlock is more numerous and grows more densely than its companions.

Western redcedar is a frequent member of spruce-hemlock forests from Sitka, Alaska, south, particularly on wet flats and river bottoms. A number of other conifers are present on such sites in much smaller numbers. Douglas-fir occurs mainly on drier sites from northern California to near Bella Coola, British Columbia. Coast redwood and Port-Orford-cedar may be present in extreme southwestern Oregon and northwestern California. Pacific silver fir, which normally grows at higher elevations in the mountains, occurs sparingly in spruce-hemlock forests in Washington and increasingly so in British Columbia. Alaska-cedar and mountain hemlock are two more subalpine conifers that occur in coastal spruce-hemlock forests in Alaska. In fact, on the west side of the Cook Peninsula, south of Anchorage, the hemlock species in spruce-hemlock forests is the mountain hemlock, not the western.

The Sitka spruce-western hemlock forest is most widespread in and characteristic of southeastern Alaska and adjacent portions of coastal British Columbia, but it achieves perhaps its finest expression in the famous rain forests of Olympic National Park in Washington. The rain forest is a special type of spruce-hemlock forest that has developed in the valley bottoms along the Quinault, Queets, Hoh, and Bogachiel rivers, all on the west side of the Olympic Mountains. The distinguishing characteristics of these forests are (1) the presence of huge, ancient Sitka spruces, (2) an abundance of bigleaf maple and vine maple in the understory, (3) dense layers of moss and other epiphytes ("air plants") growing on the limbs of trees, and (4) open understories created by the selective browsing of Roosevelt elk.

Away from the immediate coast, Douglas-fir and western hemlock, in various combinations and proportions, dominate the great majority of coastal forest stands in Washington, Oregon, and British Columbia. Although western hemlock is the climax conifer in most of these forests, Douglas-fir is usually the dominant of the two. Pure or nearly pure stands of either conifer are rare, however, and the vast majority contain both fir and hemlock in varying proportions. Their nearly universal companion, growing in all but the very driest places, is western redcedar.

As a rule, Douglas-firs tend to increase and western hemlocks to decrease as available moisture declines. On the driest forest sites in the Cascades of western Oregon, mature western hemlocks are often not even present, while Douglas-firs not only dominate but are considered to be climax as well. As soil moisture increases, so does the coverage and constancy of western hemlock, but this increase normally is not accompanied by a corresponding decrease in Douglas-fir. Indeed, increases in the number of western hemlocks even on the most favorable sites usually just brings their numbers about even with those of Douglas-fir. Evidently, the longer life and greater size of Douglas-fir assures that it will dominate western hemlock just about wherever the two occur together. Nevertheless, Douglas-fir is able to reproduce successfully only in the driest, most open stands; elsewhere it depends on periodic disturbances to open up the forest. Western redcedar is present in all but the driest stands and may be codominant with either hemlock or fir in the wettest ones. Old-growth fir-hemlock stands on mesic sites are usually true mixed forests in which Douglas-fir, western hemlock, and western redcedar, plus a smattering of other conifers, are all well represented.

Depending on location and habitat, Douglas-fir-western hemlock forests may also include grand fir, Pacific silver fir, western white pine, shore pine, coast redwood, or Sitka spruce. In the Oregon Cascades, typical Sierran conifers such as white fir, sugar pine, incense-cedar, or even ponderosa pine may also be present.

Away from the immediate coast, where cool, foggy weather favors Sitka spruce, Douglas-fir is the dominant conifer in old-growth forests from southern Oregon through northern British Columbia. In northern California, Douglas-fir occurs both with or without coast redwood and dominates a mixed evergreen forest that replaces the redwood forest in drier inland habitats.

Although Douglas-fir ranges more widely than any other Western conifer, it reaches great size only in the Northwest coastal forest, where specimens eight feet in diameter and more than 200 feet tall are not uncommon. Douglas-firs more than 300 feet tall have also been found in the region. The oldest trees may be more than 750 years of age.

Botanists recognize two geographic races of Douglas-fir: the coastal Douglas-fir and Rocky Mountain Douglas-fir. The Rocky Mountain form is a smaller tree than its coastal cousin, rarely taller than 130 feet, but is able to withstand colder, drier conditions. The foliage and cones of the Rocky Mountain Douglas-fir are also slightly different from those of the coastal form.

Mature Douglas-firs commonly have long, clear trunks and broad, rounded, often wind-damaged crowns. Young trees are pyramidal, with branches that sweep upward. The cones are quite unique—about two inches long with slender, flat, three-pointed bracts protruding from between the woody scales. They hang in profusion from the outer tips of branches and often thickly litter the ground beneath. The bark is thick, corky, and in mature trees deeply furrowed. When cut it shows wavy bands of lighter and darker brown. The needles are flat, flexible, about one inch long, and blunt or rounded at the tip. They grow on short, twisted stalks from all sides of a twig, giving the foliage a dense, luxuriant look.

Except where redwoods are numerous, or in damp coastal valleys where Sitka spruce reign, Douglas-firs dominate most old-growth forests in sheer size as well as numbers. Yet such forests are not considered climax formations. The abundant reproduction of western hemlock combined with the virtual absence of seedling or sapling Douglas-firs suggests that in the absence of significant disturbance the former conifer would eventually replace the latter in most stands. Douglas-firs at all stages of growth are less tolerant of shade than most of their coastal companions, and their seeds are able to germinate only in bare mineral soil. As a result, Douglas-fir reproduction in old-growth Douglas-fir forests is virtually nil, leaving the field to western hemlock.

11. Douglas-fir (*Pseudotsuga menziesii*)

The conditions of light and soil that favor Douglas-fir reproduction generally follow large-scale disasters such as forest
fires, landslides, volcanic eruptions, and clearcut logging.
When such disruptions do occur, Douglas-fir is quick to
reinvade disturbed areas, and the seedlings grow so rapidly
that the conifers completely dominate such sites within just
a few years. It is rare to see just one or two Douglas-fir
seedlings; where one is found a hundred more are likely to
be nearby.

Douglas-fir's thick, corky bark provides a measure of protection against fire, which periodically rages through inland
forests but is rare along the humid Northwest coast. When
fires do occur—usually during periods of prolonged summer
drought—they can be devastating, owing to the abundance
of dry fuel provided by the lush understory vegetation characteristic of coastal forests.

Extensive old-growth forests of Douglas-fir fueled settlement of the Pacific Northwest. The conifer was recognized

early on to be a nearly ideal lumber tree because its wood is of medium weight and hardness yet has good strength. The large size and rapid growth of Douglas-fir also made it economical to log. Even today, this splendid conifer provides more lumber than any other tree in North America.

Western redcedar is the most abundant of all the conifers associating with Douglas-fir and western hemlock in Northwest coastal forests. It is most common in areas that receive well over 30 inches of rain a year but reaches greatest size in coastal valleys where precipitation may be two to four times as great. In the drier mountains east of the Cascade crest, western redcedar is common only along streams or in damp bottomlands. Redcedar swamps, where the trees grow in shallow standing water much or all of the year, are common in the coastal lowlands and in major river valleys within the mountains to the east. In such habitats redcedars frequently grow with black cottonwood, bigleaf maple, and, on the Olympic Peninsula, western white pine and shore pine. Western hemlock is a nearly constant companion in most situations, though it does not fare well in either the wettest or the driest habitats tolerated by western redcedar.

Among coastal conifers only coast redwood exceeds redcedar in girth. Redcedars 200 feet tall and six feet in diameter are routine, and trees with trunks 16 to 20 feet across were once fairly common. A few specimens of this stature still exist in Olympic National Park and on other unlogged lands. Large redcedars reach 800 to 1,000 years of age, and some in eastern Washington may be 2,000 years old.

Western redcedar is more tolerant of shade than any of its lowland companions save western hemlock. And like hemlock it is a prodigious seeder. Moreover, the seeds are so tiny that even small forest rodents ignore them. Even so, there are always far more young hemlocks than redcedars in the forest understory. While a large percentage of redcedar seeds germinate, few seedlings survive for long. Fungi, birds, insects, strong sunlight, dry soil, and smothering by fallen leaves or dense vegetation all kill their share of the tiny tree sprouts. Redcedars are so long-lived, however, that only a few seedlings need survive each year to assure the tree's continuing place in the forest.

Western redcedar was the single most useful tree to the various Native American peoples of the Pacific Northwest.

They made beautiful ocean-going dugout canoes from large trees and sculpted totem poles from smaller ones. They also used the wood for housing planks and siding, cradles, boxes, and household implements. The fibrous bark was separated into individual strands that were woven into fabric. Larger pieces of bark were plaited to make mats and platters, and roots were woven into baskets. Various tonics and other medicinals were prepared from all parts of the tree.

Redcedar wood is highly prized for shakes, siding, and other outdoor uses, partly for its beauty and partly because it is more resistant to decay than most other woods. Chemicals called thujaplicins that are present within the heartwood are known to inhibit the growth of numerous species of fungi and bacteria and to repel certain insects. Nevertheless, certain fungi seem able to neutralize thujaplicins and thus are able to withstand increasingly high concentrations of the chemicals. This may explain why heart rot is common in mature redcedars despite the presence of thujaplicins.

Redcedar bark is thin and stringy, ranging from light cinnamon brown on young trees to warm gray on mature specimens. The trunks of older trees flare at the base and taper dramatically within the first 16 feet of the ground. They are also typically fluted, with pronounced bark seams. Branches on younger trees point up, but as the trees mature, the branches relax, only to sweep upward at the very tips. The leaves are scalelike and grow in opposing pairs that are tightly pressed along their stems. The resulting sprays of foliage are distinctive. The seed-bearing (female) cones are about a half-inch long and grow upright at the tips of upper branches. They consist of five to six pairs of scales arranged to resemble fleur-de-lis.

Deciduous trees form a distinctly minor element within the Northwest coastal forest. Nevertheless, they are conspicuous along streams, in clearings, and as members of the woody understory. Red alder is the most common of the deciduous trees in the coastal forest region mainly because it is usually the first tree of any sort to invade recently logged or burned areas, where it grows rapidly and may form dense groves that persist for decades. This familiar tree also grows abundantly in wet bottomlands where old-growth redcedars have been removed. Lakeshores and low, flooded streambanks often support tangled deciduous thickets in which red alder, black cottonwood, and Oregon ash dominate the canopy, while smaller deciduous trees such as Pacific crabapple, cascara, bitter cherry, various willows, and Pacific dogwood form an understory layer. A well-developed layer of deciduous shrubs normally includes red osier, hardhack, swamp birch, and willows. The ample sunlight along highway corridors, combined with runoff from pavement, provides an artificial habitat favored by red alders and other deciduous trees, as well as other plants that fare poorly within shade of conifer forests.

Bigleaf maple ranks only after red alder as the most abundant deciduous tree in the Northwest coastal forest, where it is able to reproduce in small openings. Its chance of regeneration greatly improves in recently disturbed areas, where it often grows along with alder in the mixed deciduous-conifer woods that frequently follow fires or clear-cutting. Bigleaf maple is a conspicuous and characteristic

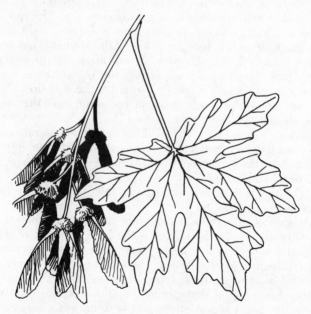

12. Bigleaf maple (*Acer macrophyllum*)

member of the Olympic rain forest, where it tends to occupy damp flats, leaving the somewhat higher, drier ground to spruces and hemlocks. Rain-forest maples are thickly draped with mosses and clubmosses. The nooks and crannies in their bark are the favored habitats of the epiphytic licorice fern, which commonly festoons trunks and branches.

A number of small shade-tolerant trees commonly form a distinct understory-tree layer beneath the dominant conifers. Among the more common of these understory trees are western yew, Pacific dogwood, vine maple, or cascara.

Western yew is a conifer without cones. Instead, its seeds are borne singly in small, red, berrylike cups that attract birds. Along with all other parts of the tree, the cups—called arils—are reputedly toxic to humans. They are eaten by birds, however, which pass the seeds and thereby help to spread the tree. Yews are often large, sprawling shrubs but also occur as trees up to 60 feet tall in well-watered canyons and moist bottomlands. Yew not only tolerates shade but requires it, turning brown if exposed to prolonged sunlight.

Pacific dogwood is among the most beloved trees in the Northwest and has been widely planted in parks and gardens, along with its close eastern relative, flowering dogwood. The showy white "flowers," which appear in spring (and sometimes in a smaller, late-summer bloom), are actually leaves that have been modified to resemble petals. The actual flowers are quite small and are set in the center of the ring of pseudo-petals. Pacific dogwood is among the most shade-tolerant of trees, requiring as little as one-third the sunlight as plants growing in the open.

Vine maple is a frequent and nearly constant member of the understory, where it supplies a delicate counterpoint to the boldness of the conifers. Though tolerant of dense shade, it also grows well in the open. Following fire or clearcutting, maples that were present in the forest commonly sprout new shoots and quickly become one of the dominant post-disturbance shrubs. Vine maple displays two rather different forms, however, depending on whether it is growing in full sun or deep shade. In the open it forms a large, compact, more or less rounded shrub. In the forest it usually forms a small wiry tree with contorted branches that support horizontal sprays of bright yellow-green foliage. Like the popular Japanese maples with which it is closely allied, vine maple puts on a spectacular autumn show. Plants growing in the open or at the forest margin turn shades of fiery red and orange, while those growing in the shade usually become only pale yellow. The difference is due to the presence in the open-area plants of reddish pigments whose function is to protect leaves from excessive ultraviolet radiation. Vine maples growing in the forest have no need to concentrate those pigments.

Closely allied with the understory tree layer, though sometimes separate from it, is the tall-shrub layer, which can vary from a smattering of plants to a nearly continuous layer. The types and relative abundance of shrubs also varies greatly from stand to stand, depending on local climate, available light and moisture, soil characteristics, and other environmental factors.

In the coastal lowlands of western Washington, red huckle-berry is a nearly ubiquitous understory shrub, sprouting freely from old stumps and logs, which it often shares with coast red elderberry, wood fern, sworn fern, salal, and a host of herbaceous plants. Vine maple and California hazel-nut are frequent companions. Osoberry (also known as Indian plum) does not tolerate dense shade but grows commonly in the dappled sunlight found in small openings and along the forest's edge. It is usually the first shrub to put on leaves and flowers in the spring.

Drier forest habitats are often the province of Pacific rhododendron, salal, and Oregon-grape, though these same plants also grow on moister sites. The hyphen in the name Oregon-grape indicates that this low shrub is not really a grape, despite its clusters of juicy, dark purple berries, which appear in midsummer. Oregon-grape prefers drier sites than sword fern and moister sites than salal but has a broader range of tolerance than either and commonly occurs with both. The plant's leathery leaves provide a measure of insulation from subfreezing winter temperatures and help to retard moisture loss during warm, dry summer weather. Tall Oregon-grape is similar but taller and prefers open sunny rock outcrops to forest shade.

Pacific rhododendron is a large shrub with clusters of showy pink flowers that rival in beauty those of cultivated varieties. In forests where rhododendron is common, the spring flower show is breathtakingly beautiful. The plant is an evergreen whose thick, waxy leaves provide a measure of protection against cold as well as drought.

Dry, exposed ridgetops in the Oregon Cascades, where the dominant trees are Douglas-firs, commonly support dense undergrowths of rhododendron and golden chinquapin, while the driest forest sites typically feature thick growths of salal or ocean spray.

Salal, rhododendron, and evergreen huckleberry also thrive on steep coastal slopes and sand dunes, where rapid drainage and exposure to drying winds and salt spray eliminate most competitors. All three shrubs are ericads, that is, members of the heath family. As a family the ericads seem to have specialized in adversity. Mountain-heathers withstand the high winds and frigid temperatures of timberline; manzanitas are superbly adapted to California's prolonged summer droughts; Pacific rhododendron is often an indicator of forest soils that are deficient in nitrogen; and Labrador-tea and swamp laurel thrive in the highly acidic

13. Pacific rhododendron (*Rhododendron occidentale*)

peat soils of forest swamps and bogs. Since relatively few plants are well adapted to such environments, the ericads often have little competition.

Rank, impenetrable understory vegetation is characteristic of well-watered sites, such as spring-fed slopes, canyon bottoms, and poorly drained flats. The most common shrubs in such habitats are salmonberry, devil's club, and coast red elderberry. They are usually accompanied by lady fern and skunk-cabbage.

Salmonberry often forms dense, nearly pure thickets in such habitats. This nearly thornless relative of the blackberry has lavender-pink blossoms and berries that range in color from pale salmon to bright red. Alas, their flavor is bland and watery.

Devil's club has heavily spined, kinky stems and huge palmate leaves with thorns on the underside of the veins. Even so, it is a favorite food of herbivores such as deer and elk, which eat it despite the thorns. Traversing damp areas overgrown with devil's club can be a misery. Before trails and roads were established, early explorers and pioneers in the Pacific Northwest generally followed the riverbottoms, where growths of devil's club were both dense and extensive. As a result, the history of the region is richly spiced with curses and imprecations called down upon this strange relative of the Asian ginseng.

Skunk-cabbage is one of the first herbaceous plants to bloom in the spring. Its small flowers, like those of the garden calla lily, grow in a dense spike (spadix) surrounded by a showy yellow sheath (spathe). The fetid, skunklike odor of the flowers attracts flies, which serve as the principal pollinators.

Rich herbaceous cover distinguishes the finest, most productive habitats within the Northwest coastal forest. Where soils are rich and deep and moisture is abundant, lush herbaceous understories dominated by sword fern and redwood sorrel are characteristic. Other common herbs include Smith's fairybell, bunchberry, false lily of the valley, inside-out flower, foamflower, bedstraw, vanilla leaf, evergreen violet, western bleeding heart, and starry Solomon's plume.

Most forest herbs have small white or yellow flowers that are easily visible within the shade. These pale blossoms are designed to attract such pollinators as flies, beetles, or nocturnal moths. Since bees, butterflies, and hummingbirds are not abundant within the forest, the various brightly colored and irregularly shaped flowers that appeal to those pollinators are also less numerous. One exception is the salmon-berry, whose pink blossom attracts rufous hummingbirds.

The impression of almost tropical lushness that people remember from visits to the Olympic rain forest, river-flat redwood groves, and other moist habitats within the Northwest coastal forest comes mainly from the abundance of ferns in the herbaceous understory. Common sword ferns form nearly pure, dense stands on cool, moist, shady slopes. Lady fern's large plumelike fronds lend a primordial aspect to streamsides and wet bottoms, as if giant dragonflies might wing through the trees or some huge lumbering amphibian emerge from the goo. Bracken fern invades disturbed soils and does much to soften the harsh aspect of clearcuts or recent burns. Deer ferns form flat rosettes on damp slopes, while wood ferns sprout from decaying logs and old stumps. And perhaps the most beautiful of all, the delicate northern maidenhair, is the centerpiece of hanging rock gardens dampened by seepage or the spray from waterfalls.

Ferns reproduce from spores rather than seeds and actually comprise two distinct generations, each represented by a different plant. The plants we normally call ferns actually represent the spore-bearing, or sporophyte, generation. The spores are borne on the undersides of fertile leaflets and upon release are carried far and wide by the merest forest breezes. A spore lucky enough to land on a suitable substrate absorbs water and develops into a tiny green plant called a prothallus, which is the sexual generation. Eggs and sperm produced by the prothallus unite to form the plants we know as ferns.

Deer fern has evolved specialized fronds, very likely in response to low light and wind conditions within the forest. The sterile fronds are relatively broad and form flat rosettes that face upward like satellite dishes in order to better intercept whatever light is available beneath the forest canopy. In contrast, the fertile fronds are slim and have wiry stems, which hold them well above the basal rosette. In this position, the ripe spores can take advantage of the forest's slight air currents, which are nonetheless greater a foot above the ground than at ground level.

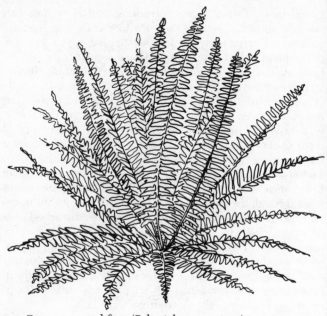

14. Common sword fern (*Polystichum munitum*)

Common sword fern is by far the most abundant and wide-spread fern in the Northwest coastal forest, occurring in a variety of shady habitats from Alaska to as far south as northern Baja California and east to Idaho and western Montana. As evergreens, it and wood fern provide welcome touches of summer green to the winter forest.

The distribution of sword fern and lady fern within the forest provides an excellent example of what ecologists call "the law of the minimum." First expressed in 1840 by the agronomist Justus von Liebig, the law says, in effect, that the growth or distribution of a plant or animal species is governed by that factor in its environment for which it has the narrowest range of tolerance. Lady fern, for example, can grow in a variety of light conditions, from nearly full sun to deep shade, so long as moisture is plentiful throughout the growing season. In contrast, sword fern tolerates drier habitats so long as they are shaded. Lady fern does not join sword fern on well-drained slopes, and sword fern rarely grows with lady fern in sunny, wet bottomlands. The two ferns are frequent companions, however, in damp, shaded places such as spring-fed slopes and soggy bottoms within the forest.

The damp coastal forests of the Pacific Northwest are well suited to the growth of mosses, none of which have a mechanism for circulating water and therefore must absorb it directly from the environment. But that's a two-way street: The thin leaf surfaces that permit easy absorption of moisture also provide no barrier to its loss. Consequently, mosses must either grow in habitats where moisture stress never occurs or must possess a high tolerance for partial or complete cellular dehydration. As a matter of fact, mosses do possess such a tolerance. Many species shrivel during times of drought but quickly revive when moisture is once more available. Even so, environments where moisture stress is seldom a problem generally host more species of moss than others. The more humid parts of the Northwest coastal forest provide just such a reliably moist environment and therefore host a rich moss flora.

Mosses are particularly varied and abundant in coastal spruce-fir forests, reaching a climax perhaps in the Olympic rain forest, where they carpet large areas of ground and pad logs, stumps, rocks, and the trunks and limbs of living trees. A single fallen tree often hosts a half-dozen or more different moss species within a relatively small area. As many as 40 or 50 species may be encountered in a single stand of woods.

Moss growth is generally opportunistic, occurring whenever conditions are favorable. In the lowlands of the Pacific Northwest, where temperatures are mild and snow cover is infrequent and of short duration, growth occurs largely in winter. Mosses, like ferns, comprise two separate generations: a gametophyte generation that produces eggs and sperm, and a sporophyte generation that produces spores. Unlike ferns, however, the familiar plant, the one we call "moss," is the sexual rather than the spore-bearing generation. In spring mosses produce eggs and sperm, which combine to produce spore-bearing capsules—the sporophyte generation—that are held aloft atop slender, wiry stems. When the spores mature, the capsules pop open, releasing spores into the air, where the wind may waft them great distances from the parent plants. Spores that fall on moist surfaces form spreading mats (protonema) that give rise to the leafy plants we know as moss.

Smaller, compact mosses whose leaves are in direct contact with the ground, decayed wood, or other growing surface derive at least some of their nutrients from those sources, but most of the larger, more elaborate types are epiphytes, or "air plants." Epiphytes are plants that grow on various surfaces, including living plants, but do not depend upon them for nutrients. Since mosses lack vascular systems for circulating nutrient solutions derived from the soil, most are epiphytes.

One example among the most common mosses of the coastal forest is mountain fern moss, which is named for its branching, fernlike growth. Often forming rather large, pure stands, mountain fern moss grows on both the ground and decaying logs, as well as on rocks where adequate soil exists or other moss colonies have become established. A study of this moss concluded that it derived most of its nutrients from a combination of atmospheric dust in rainwater and minerals leached from forest trees by water dripping off foliage and limbs. The greatest supply of minerals was available directly beneath trees, but the moss grew most vigorously just outside the projected crown border, where conditions of both nutrients and light were most favorable.

Among the showier epiphytic mosses inhabiting coastal rain forests is Isothecium, which festoons the limbs of trees and shrubs. Comprising filamentlike strands up to four inches long, this moss resembles the famous Spanish moss—a flowering plant—that drapes live oaks in the southeastern United States and tropical America. Away from the coast, Isothecium more often grows on rocks, tree trunks, and dead wood, where it assumes a coarse, much branched habit quite unlike its aerial form.

Following fire, clearcutting, or other catastrophe, formerly forested areas are quickly revegetated by a variety of herbs, shrubs, and young trees. Many of the plants are holdovers from the former forests; others are opportunists that rarely grow anywhere other than disturbed areas. Post-disturbance succession within coastal lowland forests generally commences with the rapid growth of weedy herbs such as bracken fern, fireweed, and pearly everlasting. This herbaceous stage is shortly followed by the rapid dominance of shrubs. Along the coast, dense brush stands dominated by salmonberry, thimbleberry, salal, coast red elderberry, huckleberry, and vine maple may persist many years before finally being topped by invading red alders or conifers. Away from the coast, the shrub stage frequently includes Pacific rhododendron, low Oregon-grape, Pacific blackberry, mountain balm, and various willows, as well as the shrubs mentioned above. Conifers may not appear until the shrub stage is well established or, where nearby forests permit rapid natural reseeding, they may be present from the beginning. Sitka spruce, Douglas-fir, and western redcedar all readily colonize disturbed sites. Western hemlock, which quickly succumbs to overheating, is usually confined to cooler, moister microhabitats within such openings.

In the Washington Cascades the coastal forest undergoes a subtle change at an elevation of about 3,000 feet. Western hemlock, western redcedar, and Douglas-fir are still present but in fewer numbers, and at this altitude they no longer dominate the forests. Instead, Pacific silver fir, which is nearly as tolerant of shade and better adapted to cold and snow than western hemlock, presides. Silver fir is present at all stages of growth, from seedlings to giant trees three to four feet thick and 150 to 200 feet tall. At these altitudes it outcompetes even western hemlock, whose seedlings are prone to snow damage. Silver fir is therefore considered to be the climax tree in these upper montane forests. Silver-fir forests also occur northward into British Columbia and southward into northern Oregon, as well as in the Olympics.

Pacific silver fir is named for the silvery color of its bark. Its needles, like those of other firs, tend to grow in two ranks, spreading on lower branches and curved upward on the upper ones. The upper branches also bear the purple, barrel-shaped cones, which stand upright and disintegrate in place. About every three years, Pacific silver fir produces abundant crops of relatively large winged seeds, but the number that germinates is low and the seeds do not remain viable for long. What's more, the seeds are among the favored foods of Douglas' squirrel, which strips away the cone scales to get at the treasures contained inside.

In British Columbia, Pacific silver fir ranges downslope to sea level. Throughout its range it also occurs with subalpine conifers in the islands of trees that are commonly scattered about timberline parklands. Its downward limit appears to be governed by decreasing amounts of rainfall during the growing season. Its upward range is limited by the intolerance of its seedlings to summer frosts, which are frequent at subalpine heights, combined with the inability of the tree to reproduce through layering, the rooting of stems that touch the ground, and the sprouting of new upright shoots that follows.

Many researchers recognize a distinctive silver fir zone, which forms a transition between the lower western hemlock zone and the higher mountain hemlock zone. At the upper level of the Pacific silver fir zone, coastal conifers dwindle in number, while subalpine species, notably Alaska-cedar and mountain hemlock, become increasingly common.

In the Cascades from Stevens Pass, Washington, south to Crater Lake, Oregon, noble fir dominates seral forests in the Pacific silver fir zone. Noble fir also occurs in the Siskiyou Mountains, where it ranges southward barely into northern California. At the southern limits of its range, noble fir hybridizes with the closely related Shasta red fir. These two trees alone among the firs of the Pacific Northwest have bracts that extend well beyond the tips of the cone scales, and in the noble fir the papery bracts nearly obscure the scales.

Largest and longest-lived of the world's true firs, noble firs often exceed 200 feet in height and 600 years in age. The largest specimen, which grows in southwestern Washington, is 278 feet tall, with a trunk nine feet thick at breast height. Mature trees commonly have clear, straight trunks that taper but slightly and are free of branches to heights of 100 feet or more. The bark is grayish brown and furrowed into long narrow ridges. The needles are stiff and curve upward along the twigs to form a dense brushlike effect. Ranging in color from silvery to blue-green, they are unique among local firs in having *two* white bands on both their upper and lower surfaces.

Noble fir is highly intolerant of shade and depends largely on fires and other disasters to create openings in which its seedlings are able to survive. Once established, however, noble fir's great size and longevity enable it to maintain itself in dense mixed forests for centuries. It prefers cool, ather moist sites but thrives in rocky areas where deep ources of moisture are available. Ample summer precipitaion is essential for seedling survival. The most common eedlings found in forests dominated by noble fir, however, re those of the highly shade tolerant Pacific silver fir.

The transitional nature of Pacific silver-fir forests is also evident in the understory, which includes a mix of species common to both lowland and subalpine forests. Lowland hrubs include salal, Oregon-grape, and—in Oregon—Pacific rhododendron, which generally occupy warmer, drier sites within the forest. Alaska huckleberry and big huckleberry, subalpine shrubs, commonly dominate moister, cooler habitats, often growing with Cascade azalea, another subalpine species, or menziesia, a huckleberry look-alike hat ranges from sea level to subalpine heights. Poorly drained places commonly support dense growths of devil's club, huckleberries, and vine maple. Vine maple is also common in sunny openings, where its flaming autumn colors provide an outstanding display.

Pacific silver-fir forests commonly feature rich herb layers hat, again, feature both lowland and montane or subalpine species. Low shrublets, such as twinflower, strawberry bramble, dwarf bramble, and bunchberry are particularly characteristic of these forests. Twinflower, a tiny shrublet with creeping woody stems, may form a dense ground cover. At intervals along the stems sprout leafy upright stalks that terminate in two delicate, nodding pink flowers. Strawberry bramble resembles a strawberry plant in its leaves, flowers, and creeping stems. The berries, however, are rather hard and unpalatable. Bunchberry is actually a tiny dogwood, and its white "flowers" and leaves resemble miniature versions of those found on dogwood trees. In shady, moist places bunchberry grows in compact masses only a couple of inches tall. Queen's cup, or beadlily, does not form massed displays, but it is nonetheless very common in these forests. A member of the lily family, this lovely forest herb normally bears but one white blossom. When the flower dies, an unusual turquoise berry appears in its place. In dry, shady habitats, herbaceous members of the heath family are common. These include prince's pine and Pyrolas.

Natural forest openings related to local topography are relatively numerous in the Pacific silver fir zone, where relief often changes abruptly from flat cirque or valley floors to nearby steep slopes. Openings on gentle terrain where poor drainage discourages the growth of conifers usually support various wet meadow communities. Dense thickets dominated by salmonberry and bracken fern commonly occupy somewhat drier habitats bordering wet meadows, along stream corridors, and on well-watered rocky slopes. Sitka alder, which is popularly known as slide alder, forms nearly impenetrable thickets on steep slopes subject to snow creep or avalanching. The shrubs are ten to 16 feet tall and feature stems that are strongly bowed, generally in a downhill direction. In the Washington Cascades avalanche tracks filled with slide alder are conspicuous as light green corridors snaking downward through the darker forest. On slopes especially prone to avalanching, alder corridors and intervening forest may form a series of vertical stripes on the mountainside. In the Oregon Cascades, where steep slopes are less common, communities of Sitka alder commonly occur on sites that are not prone to avalanching, but where snows lie deep and seepage water is abundant.

The vast clearcuts that so often shock visitors to Oregon, Washington, and British Columbia are attempts to harvest conifers like wheat. The trees, along with all other vegetation, are, in effect, mowed down. The resulting debris, called slash, is burned, mainly to reduce the fire hazard but also to return nutrients bound up in the dead vegetation to the soil. The devastated land may then be restocked with young Douglas-firs or left to natural reseeding. In the latter case, red alder, a deciduous hardwood, may quickly invade the area and postpone the reestablishment of conifers for several decades.

Whatever the method of restocking, the second-growth forests that grow up in the wake of clearcutting lack the diversity of species and habitats that characterize old-growth stands. Conifers other than Douglas-fir are scarce or missing in densely stocked second-growth stands, where the shade may be so complete as to virtually eliminate vegetation from the understory. The idea is to log these stands within 70 or 80 years, long before the trees have reached maturity or the forest has diversified—in other words, to make trees a crop.

In the process a highly complex and diverse ecological

system is replaced with a simpler, less stable one. In the process a multitude of values, or benefits, are summarily traded in for a single benefit—lumber. Wildlife habitats, including valuable sport fisheries, are lost or degraded, with accompanying declines in, or even extinction of, species that depend on old-growth forests. Valuable topsoil, minerals, and nutrients are lost as a result of increased runoff and the removal of naturally occurring fallen timber. Recreational opportunities, including camping, hunting, angling, hiking, and birding, are reduced. Scenic values are severely compromised. As regrettable as the above losses are, the most serious consequence of wholesale clearcut logging of old-growth timber is the loss of genetic and ecologic diversity and the stability they provide. Genetic diversity and a mix of species provide old-growth forests with excellent protection against insects and disease, as evidenced by the very longevity of the forests. After all, the greater the number of elements in a system, the less likely it is that the loss or malfunction of any single element will disrupt the whole. By reducing complex forest systems to single-species crops, large-scale tree farming increases the instability and vulnerability of the nation's forest resource for short-term economic gain.

CHAPTER SEVEN

A Touch of California

MOVING SOUTHWARD down the Pacific Coast of North America, rainfall declines and is increasingly restricted to the winter months. At the same time, summers become increasingly long and hot. These climatic gradients are paralleled by corresponding shifts in vegetation from Northwestern to typically Californian types. Northwestern elements extend farthest south along the immediate coast while Californian elements range farthest north in Oregon's interior valleys. In a way, then, the coast redwood forest is a southern extension of the Northwest coastal forest just as the Oregon white oak woodlands of Oregon's Willamette Valley are northern versions of similar oak woodlands that blanket most of northern and central California. The redwoods of Big Sur live in their own little "Seattle"; the oaks of Eugene hark south to Monterey.

Driving south from Seattle down Interstate 5, one first becomes aware of the California influence near Tacoma, where large tracts of Oregon white oak grow next to the freeway. Oaks grow north of this area but sparsely and in isolated stands. Southward, however, oak woodlands become increasingly common until, in the Willamette, Umpqua, and Rogue River valleys, they are a prominent part of a vegetation mosaic that also includes grassland and conifer forest. The Umpqua and Rogue River valleys and their surrounding hills also feature sizable tracts of chaparral.

Prior to white settlement, the Willamette Valley was largely prairie, with savannas of widely scattered oaks and intersected by riparian woodlands that grew along streams and rivers. Since conifer forest appears to be the climax vegetation throughout most of the valley, it is likely that the open landscape of grassland and savanna was originally maintained by Indian fires. Since white settlement, the suppression of fires, except for agricultural burning, has allowed development of extensive oak woodlands. At the same time, the conversion of grasslands to crops has maintained the open character of the valley landscape.

Oregon white oak dominates oak woodlands in the Willamette Valley. Stands range in structure from open savanna in which big old oaks are widely scattered over a grassland understory to closed forests in which conifers are important associates. Douglas-fir reproduces abundantly beneath open oak canopies and has become an important component of some stands. Bigleaf maple and grand fir are important associates on moister sites. Pacific madrone is often present on drier ones.

Oregon white oak (also known as Garry oak) ranges from southwestern British Columbia southward to the foothills of central California. This large, spreading tree is also common at the eastern end of the Columbia River Gorge, where

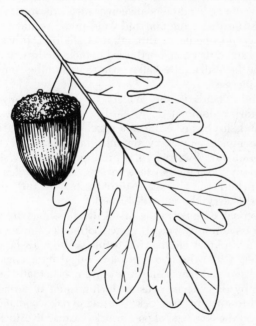

5. Oregon white oak (*Quercus garryana*)

it forms mixed stands with ponderosa pine. Oregon white oaks occur with Oregon ash, red alder, white alder, and bigleaf maple in riparian woodlands in the Willamette Valley.

The dark green, leathery leaves are deeply lobed and about three inches long and five inches wide. The lobe themselves are rounded, whereas those on the leaves of the California black oak, a frequent companion in southwestern Oregon and northwestern California, end in sharp points. The thick, leathery texture helps reduce moisture loss through evaporation during hot, dry summers.

The tree has a short, thick trunk that supports a broad rounded crown. Old trees on fertile valley floors may be 80 to 100 feet tall and more than 350 years of age. Often, one of these old-timers will be surrounded by a thicket of pole sized oaks or a stand of larger oaks, which invaded forme savanna following the suppression of Indian fires.

Oregon white oak produces sizable crops of acorns, which are an important food to western gray squirrels, deer mice pocket gophers, band-tailed pigeons, and acorn woodpeckers. This last bird is a common and widespread resident of oak savannas and woodlands throughout California. It has been able to extend its range northward to include the oak wood lands of the Willamette Valley, where its numbers are now on the increase.

Oak woodlands in the Willamette Valley usually have understories dominated by shrubs. The most common woodland shrubs are California hazelnut, western service berry, common snowberry, the introduced mazzard cherry, and poison-oak. Sword fern is prominent in many stands particularly those on moister sites. Hazelnut, serviceberry and snowberry are characteristic of the least disturbed sites mazzard cherry, the most disturbed.

Poison-oak dominates the driest habitats, many of which have grassy understories. It grows both as a compact shrub and as a vine that climbs tree trunks as high as the upper branches. Often the two types are linked by a single root network, so that plants on the ground may actually be sub sidized by their aerial cousins during times of drought or severe browsing by livestock. Grazing in oak woodlands has increased the coverage of poison-oak because livestock tend to avoid it in favor of other shrubs.

Poison-oak is notorious, of course, for causing severe allergic dermatitis in many people. Within a few days or so of coming into contact with the plant, the unfortunate develop an itchy, festering rash that may persist for a week or two. The agents responsible for this affliction are volatile oils that are present in all parts of the plant during all seasons of the year. The lucky individuals who do not seem allergic to poison-oak should nevertheless avoid touching it, for upon repeated exposure it is possible to develop a sensitivity to the plant.

People who spend much time exploring areas where poison-oak is common should learn to recognize the plant's compound leaves, which consist of three lobed leaflets that individually bear a superficial resemblance to the leaf of the Oregon white oak. Poison-oak is most easily recognized in autumn, when the leaves turn bright red. The new growth of spring is also conspicuous for its pronounced reddish color, the result of pigmentation that protects the tender

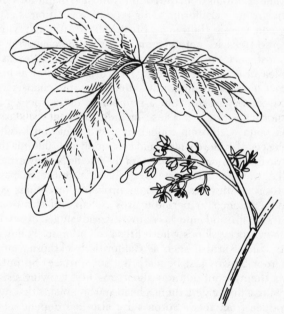

16. Poison-oak (*Rhus diversiloba*)

young leaves from ultraviolet light. The plant bears dangling clusters of small greenish flowers. The fruits, which are eaten by some birds, are dry and inconspicuous.

In the Umpqua and Rogue River valleys of southwestern Oregon, oak woodlands are part of a mosaic that also includes extensive areas of grassland, chaparral, and conifer forest. California black oak and Oregon white oak occur together in many stands. Pacific madrone joins this pair on all but the driest woodland sites. Ponderosa pine, Douglas-fir, and incense-cedar commonly tower over the oaks in cooler, damper northern exposures, the latter often forming a well-developed lower canopy.

The understory on drier sites consists mainly of hard-leaved evergreen shrubs that are also prominent in nearby patches of chaparral. These shrubs include deerbrush, whiteleaf manzanita, and birchleaf mountain-mahogany. These same shrubs are characteristic of California's chaparral and foothill woodland communities.

Patches of chaparral are conspicuous on lower foothills and valley bottoms from the southernmost Willamette Valley southward into California. This type of vegetation is especially common in the Rogue River Valley. Although widely scattered trees are not uncommon within the chaparral, for the most part the community features dense growths of hard-leaved evergreen shrubs. Deerbrush, whiteleaf manzanita, and hoary manzanita dominate the chaparral of southwestern Oregon, but a number of other species are also normally present. These include Fremont's silktassel, yerba santa, California coffeeberry, and squawbush, all of which occur far more widely and commonly in California than they do in Oregon or other parts of the Pacific Northwest.

Like their counterparts in California, most chaparral stands in southwestern Oregon probably owe their continued existence to periodic fires. Chaparral shrubs are adapted to fire and enjoy a competitive advantage over trees on steep, rocky slopes where fires are endemic. Following a fire, some shrubs, such as California buckthorn, sprout from root crowns just beneath the soil surface. Sprouting allows them to put out new shoots the first growing season following a fire, giving them a head start on plants that must reproduce from seed. Sprouts are also less dependent on rain for survival. Buckbrush and manzanita have a different strategy. They produce thousands of seeds, which lie dormant in the soil until their hard coats are weakened by fire. Then, with the first rains, the seeds germinate in such numbers that vast areas may be covered with buckbrush and manzanita seedlings. Individual plants stand less chance of surviving than the new shoots of a sprouting species, but they are nevertheless able to maintain their dominance through sheer numbers.

Fire performs a positive function in chaparral communities beyond merely maintaining them in the face of potential invasion by trees. As chaparral stands mature, diversity declines as the dominant shrubs increase their share of the terrain and less competitive species die out. In addition, individual shrubs lose vigor with increasing age so that beyond a few decades entire stands enter a period of long, gradual decline. Fires remove old plants and thereby make way for young vigorous ones. Moreover, by reducing the coverage of the dominant shrubs, fires open up areas to a greater number of species, including a large number of herbaceous annuals that are absent from mature stands. Following a fire, these ephemeral plants sprout from seeds that may have lain dormant for decades, since the last fire to sweep the area. Fires also improve the soil by returning nutrients bound up in dead plant materials and by evaporating volatile toxins secreted by manzanitas and certain other shrubs. These toxins are one more way in which dominant shrubs are able to eliminate potential competitors from the community.

Grasslands are conspicuous in all of western Oregon's interior valleys. Although many of the early prairies have been replaced by woodlands and forest, grasslands still cover large areas, created and maintained by clearing, burning, or grazing. However, their composition has changed drastically. The original grasslands were dominated by perennial bunchgrasses such as California danthonia and Columbia needlegrass. Today, these have been largely replaced by invasive annuals such as Kentucky bluegrass and wild rye, which were brought into the area by settlers. The same conversion from native bunchgrasses to exotic annuals has occurred throughout the foothills and valleys of California, as well as in the steppes of eastern Washington and Oregon. The annual grasses, which spring anew from seed each year, are better able than the native perennials to withstand the rigorous regime created by the combination of dry summers and overgrazing. More or less native grasslands persist on soils that are too dry or sterile to support trees. These include steep, rocky southern slopes and grass balds on ridgetops with fine-textured soils.

The zone of maximum overlap between Northwestern and Californian floras and plant communities occurs in southwestern Oregon and northwestern California. The region is bounded on the east by the Cascade Range and on the west by the Pacific. The northern and southern boundaries are less exact, but for the sake of discussion they can be considered as two lines drawn on the north between Roseburg and Coos Bay, Oregon, and on the south between Redding and Eureka, California. These lines also more or less mark the northern and southern limits of the Klamath Mountains, which separate the cool, humid coastal zone from the hot, dry interior. Forests on the western side of the Klamaths share many species with the redwood and Northwest coastal forest. Those growing on the eastern sides are more closely allied to that of the Sierra Nevada, albeit with distinctive "Northwestern" touches. In the Cascade Range, which forms the eastern boundary of the region, a mixed conifer forest essentially like that of the Sierra Nevada pushes northward beyond Crater Lake, gradually merging with the Northwest coastal forest.

The Klamath Mountains are home to the most diverse conifer forests in the world, where a dozen or more species of conifers may occur in a single stand. There are several factors contributing to this diversity. Of these the overlapping of Northwestern and Californian, and of coastal and interior, floras has already been mentioned. Northward, the increasing coolness and brevity of the summers and coldness of the winters excludes typically Californian plants. Southward, the increasing heat and drought of summer eliminates Northwestern vegetation. Thanks to the range's intermediate location, it seems to offer plants the best of the Northwestern climate on the one hand and the Californian on the other. Further, the significant height and local relief of the Klamath Mountains, and their position relatively close to the coast, create sharp west-to-east gradients in climate that result in diverse microclimates capable of supporting numerous types of plants in a relatively compact area. Finally, the Klamaths contain a bewildering variety of rock types, each supporting slightly—or sometimes dramatically—different plant communities. Some of these local rock outcrops, notably peridotite and serpentine, yield inhospitable soils that preclude most plants but provide refuges to a few that have been eliminated by competition from other "normal" habitats.

The combination of sharp climatic gradients and varied rock types has also created a variety of very specific habitats that are not reproduced elsewhere in the region. As a result, the Klamaths shelter outposts of several trees that are common in other regions but otherwise not in this one. These trees include Alaska-cedar and Pacific silver fir from the Pacific Northwest, subalpine fir and Engelmann spruce from the intermountain West, and foxtail pine from the Sierra Nevada. The Klamaths have also served as a refuge for a number of plants, such as Port-Orford-cedar and Brewer's spruce, whose ancestors were widespread in North America some 50 million years ago but now occur nowhere else. While varied soils and microclimates no doubt play an important role in explaining the diversity of the conifer forests of the Klamath Mountains, they do not provide the whole answer. For example, it is not at all clear why foxtail pine is abundant in the southern Sierra, only locally present in the Klamaths, and missing everywhere else. A number of plausible suggestions have been offered, but the fact is that nobody knows why for sure. The role of accident cannot be dismissed in some instances, though the high concentration of endemic and relict species in this region is surely due to a combination of environmental and floral factors found nowhere else.

The region's most famous relict—the coast redwood—occurs along the coast rather than in the Klamaths. Fossil redwoods have been recovered across much of the northern hemisphere, but today the tree grows only along the coast of central and northern California and a small corner of southwestern Oregon. The redwood presides over a rich coastal forest that is essentially a southern extension of the Northwest coastal forest. The redwood forest and Northwest coastal forest share a large number of plants and animals in common, including salal, evergreen huckleberry, sword

17. Coast redwood (*Sequoia sempervirens*)

fern, wood sorrel, evergreen violet, vine maple, Douglas-fir
Douglas' squirrel, winter wren, and rough-skinned newt.

Redwoods are limited to a narrow coastal belt extending
450 miles from south of Big Sur, California, to just across
the Oregon border. At the southern end of their range
redwoods occur in isolated groves tucked away in damp
coastal canyons open to invasions of summer fog. Muir
Woods, near San Francisco, and the redwoods of Big Sur
both occur in such situations. Farther north, in Mendocino
Humboldt, and Del Norte counties, redwood forests occur
more or less continuously, growing at elevations from sea
level to about 3,000 feet. The most splendid groves of this
region are found on flats and benches along streams. River
deltas, floodplains, moderately steep slopes facing the sea
and well-watered canyons also support fine groves. At the
northern limits of its range in southwestern Oregon, how
ever, redwoods occur mostly on slopes, possibly because
valley bottoms are too cool.

All these habitats have in common ample, dependable supplies of soil moisture. Redwoods are excluded from drier forest habitats by an evolutionary curiosity—the lack of root hairs. Forming elaborate soil networks, root hairs allow most other conifers to extract soil moisture more efficiently than redwoods are able to do. Redwoods do have mycorrhizae, however, albeit a different type than other Northwestern conifers.

Like the spruce-hemlock forest to the north, the redwood forest is restricted to areas where fog drip offsets summer drought—except that in California the drought is more severe. Where river valleys allow the fog to penetrate inland, redwoods may occur many miles from the sea. Along the famous Avenue of the Giants, south of Eureka, for example, superb specimens grow 50 to 75 miles from the coast. The moisture gradients that far inland are abrupt, however; as a result, redwoods there are largely restricted to river flats and damp lower slopes. Adjacent hillsides support a mosaic in which mixed evergreen forest dominates northern and eastern slopes, while grasslands and oak woodlands occur on southern and western ones.

The coast redwood is the tallest tree in the world and surpasses all other Northwest coastal conifers in girth and age as well. Redwoods routinely exceed 250 feet in height, 10 feet in diameter, and 1,200 years in age. Trees more than 300 feet tall, 15 feet in diameter, and 2,000 years old are not uncommon. The tallest known redwood is a 367-foot specimen in Redwood National Park.

Redwoods have fibrous, reddish-brown bark that is thick and heavily ridged. The leaves are of two kinds. Those on the lower branches are ½- to ¾-inch long, needlelike, and arranged in flattened, two-ranked sprays much like those of true firs. Leaves on the upper branches are less than ½-inch long, awl-shaped, and arranged in tight spirals that completely cloak the twigs. The barrel-shaped cones are ½- to just over 1-inch long and hang in clusters from the ends of branches.

Within their limited habitat and geographic range, redwoods possess a formidable array of traits that make them tough competitors. Of these traits the most important is their combining a degree of shade tolerance exceeded in this region only by western hemlock with the longevity of trees such as Douglas-fir, Sitka spruce, and western redcedar. Tree-ring analysis has revealed that redwoods are able to withstand as much as 400 years of shade and still grow vigorously upon exposure to sunlight. The significance of this figure becomes clearer when one considers that four centuries amount to the normal lifespan of western hemlock, the redwood's only potential competitor for space on shady sites. It may be that the scarcity and sporadic occurrence of western hemlock in the redwood belt is due as much to this disadvantage as to physical environmental factors. At the same time, redwood grows more rapidly and lives longer than Douglas-fir, Sitka spruce, and western redcedar, the longest lived and fastest growing of its associates. Douglas-firs are able to persist alongside redwoods by occupying drier habitats and poorer soils at the fringes of the redwood belt—places where the redwood's normal competitive advantage is diminished. Similarly, Sitka spruce, shore pine, and Bishop pine are able to occupy headlands, coastal bluffs, and other shoreline habitats where the redwood's intolerance of drying winds and salt spray places it at a disadvantage. Within the redwood's favored habitats, however, it has no real competitors, dominating all stages of forest succession.

The redwood's competitive advantage, however, is not limited to shade tolerance and longevity. It is also better adapted to fire than any of its associates. Mature redwoods have thick, resin-free bark and damp wood that burns slowly and coolly if at all. Large, centuries-old redwoods that continue to live even though their trunks have been hollowed out by fire are common sights in old-growth redwood forests. The ability to survive fires—and even continue growing—no doubt is responsible in part for the great age attained by redwoods. High resistance to insect damage and fungal disease is also a factor in the conifer's longevity.

Redwoods also have the ability to reproduce rapidly in the wake of fires, logging, or other disturbance by sprouting readily from still-living root crowns. The sprouts appear within only two or three weeks following a disturbance and may grow to heights of seven feet within a single year, filling the space with young trees while conifers depending solely on seeds for reproduction may have barely gotten started. The ability to sprout from root crowns is a characteristic shared by numerous other trees and shrubs in California, where adaptation to frequent summer fires is mandatory for survival.

Redwoods also have the ability to rapidly sprout new crowns when old ones are broken by lightning, wind, or fire. In this way the trees are able to maintain their height advantage and reclose the forest canopy, depriving potential competitors of necessary sunlight.

Redwoods reproduce from seeds, but not so readily or dependably as from sprouting. Seed crops vary greatly in size and viability and require special conditions for success. Bare mineral soil is necessary for redwoods to reproduce successfully from seed. The seeds are able to germinate in forest duff, but the young seedlings generally succumb rather quickly to damping off and other diseases caused by root fungi. Seedlings in mineral soil do not have to contend with root rot, but they do require ample moisture and some protection from desiccation to survive. One reason for the particular success of redwoods on floodplains and river terraces is that sediments deposited during flood stage provide a nearly ideal environment for seedlings. As a result, redwood reproduction in such stands, unlike that in hillside forests, tends to consist of successive generations of seedlings that correspond to episodes of flooding.

Mature redwoods survive flooding by sprouting new roots farther up the trunk, in the newest layer of sediments. Most other trees and shrubs, however, are unable to do so and must reinvade newly flooded sites from outside. Since the prospects of successfully becoming reestablished beneath mature redwoods are poor, most river-flat groves are pure stands from which other conifers are excluded.

Although the river-flat groves of California's north coast region are the most famous and contain the tallest and oldest trees, they are not typical. Most redwoods grow on hillsides in the company of Douglas-fir, tanoak, and Pacific madrone. Typically northwestern conifers such as western redcedar, grand fir, and western hemlock are present in some redwood stands but not regularly. Sitka spruce occurs in the redwood belt but only in the north and mainly on steep, exposed bluffs and headlands.

Understory vegetation in redwood forests ranges from sparse to dense and lush and many-tiered, depending on the habitat. In shady river-terrace groves, redwoods often form pure stands with understories consisting mainly of small or straggly shrubs and a scattering of ferns and wildflowers. Large shrubs and understory trees are often absent except along the higher, drier margins of the groves because periodic floods occur too frequently to permit their development. On slopes and in other locations where severe flooding is not a problem, a number of understory trees may associate with coast redwood. Deciduous trees such as bigleaf maple and red alder are often found on cool, moist slopes or along streams in company with black cottonwood, white alder, and Sitka willow. On south-facing slopes and other warmer, drier sites, the most common understory trees are drought-tolerant broadleaf evergreens such as tan-oak, Pacific madrone, and California laurel, which is known in southwestern Oregon as Oregon myrtle. Oregon white oak, California black oak, and coast live oak may even be present along dry forest margins, particularly where redwoods tucked away in moist ravines give way suddenly on nearby slopes to oak woodlands or mixed hardwood forests such as those around San Francisco Bay.

Many understory trees become established when a redwood or some other tree falls and creates a sunny opening. In order to claim their share of sunshine, opportunistic broadleaf trees commonly funnel most of their energies into vertical growth, developing long, skinny trunks that angle upward toward the light. Some understory trees, however, are able to tolerate exceedingly low levels of light and consequently retain their normal compact or generally bushy forms. These include Pacific dogwood, vine maple, western yew, and California nutmeg. Vine maple often resembles the pruned Japanese maples of Zen gardens. In shady situations the branches are contorted horizontally, each one supporting a tier of leaves whose upper surfaces are held more or less at right angles to the sky.

Well-watered hillside forests often support healthy growths of understory shrubs. These may include typically Californian species such as poison-oak and blue blossom, especially at the drier margins of the forest. More often, however, the most common shrubs are ones that also occur widely on comparable sites within the Northwest coastal forest. These include evergreen huckleberry, red huckleberry, salal, low Oregon-grape, Pacific rhododendron, thimbleberry, salmonberry, Pacific blackberry, ocean spray, Nootka rose, and common snowberry, among many others.

Ferns constitute an important part of the herb layer, just as they do in the Northwest coastal forest. What is more, many of the same species will be found here as farther north. Sword fern grows thickly on moist, shady slopes while lady ferns flourish on sunny streambanks and mix with skunk-cabbage in poorly drained bottomlands. Licorice ferns festoon the branches of bigleaf maple and other trees, while wood ferns sprout on old stumps and decaying logs. Also contributing to the "Northwestern" look of the redwood forest are the abundant mosses that pad rocks, logs, stumps, and living trees in cool, moist, fog-kissed stands.

Evergreen violet, western trillium, wood sorrel, and false Solomon's seal are among the many wildflowers common to both the redwood forest and Northwest coastal forest. In addition, the redwood forests also feature a number of California specialties such as red clintonia and California toothwort.

Originally, there were some two million acres of old-growth redwood forest. Today only a quarter-million acres of old growth remains, of which less than half is preserved within state and national parks. Many years ago, selective cutting allowed redwoods to regenerate themselves. Today, however, clearcutting is the rule, and the redwoods are not

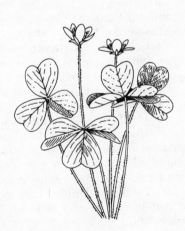

18. Wood sorrel (*Oxalis oregana*)

recovering from the drastic alteration of habitat that this practice represents. The increased heating, desiccation, erosion, and exposure to wind not only discourage regeneration of young redwoods, including those hand-planted on clear-cut plots, but lead—within ten to 15 years—to the death as well of residual old-growth trees. These forlorn giants lose limbs, suffer root decay, and eventually succumb to high winds. This experience teaches us that the redwood forest is not simply a collection of curious individual trees but a superorganism of sorts that can function and sustain itself only so long as all its parts remain healthy.

Inland from the coast, beyond the reach of fog, Douglas-fir and tanoak dominate—and are the climax trees—in a mixed forest in which drought-tolerant broadleaf evergreen trees are common. This forest forms a transition between the redwood forests along the coast, oak woodlands in the interior, and mixed conifer forests at higher elevations in the Klamath Mountains and California North Coast Range. The mixed evergreen forest occurs extensively in the Klamath Mountains and California North Coast Range at elevations between 500 and 4,000 feet, depending on local topography and other factors. The mixed evergreen forest forms a more or less continuous belt southward through the North Coast Range to Napa and Marin counties. It also occurs sporadically in the Berkeley/Oakland Hills east of San Francisco Bay, and southward through the Santa Cruz and Santa Lucia mountains to southern Monterey County.

The inland sections of southwestern Oregon and the north coastal region of California experience winters that are nearly as wet as, but a whole lot warmer than, those of comparable areas in northwestern Oregon and western Washington. As a result, almost all precipitation in the mixed evergreen forest zone falls as rain; snow occurs sparingly, and then mainly at the upper limit of the forest, where it gives way to Sierran mixed conifer forest. Unlike coastal areas farther north, however, summers in southwestern Oregon and northwestern California are a whole lot hotter and drier. As a result, summer moisture stress is the single most critical factor governing plant life in the mixed evergreen forest.

Climates with mild, wet winters and hot, dry summers are called Mediterranean because they are characteristic of that region. Mediterranean climates also occur in California, coastal Chile, western Australia, and south Africa. The predominant vegetation in each of these areas consists of woodland and brush communities dominated by broadleaf evergreens. These plants are known as broadleaf sclerophylls (meaning "hard leaves") for their thick, leathery leaves, which provide protection from heat and reduce moisture loss.

Being evergreen, broadleaf sclerophylls such as tanoak, live oak, manzanita, and Pacific madrone are able to take advantage of mild, wet winters, whereas deciduous plants cannot. At the same time, they are far better able than most conifers to withstand prolonged periods of summer moisture stress. In midsummer they generally become dormant, reducing photosynthesis and respiration to maintenance levels. Many also drop some of their leaves or branches during periods of prolonged drought as a way of reducing the amount of tissue that must be supplied with water. With the first rains of autumn, however, broadleaf sclerophylls resume activity, putting on new leaves and revving up their metabolic engines. Most of them are also capable of quickly resuming photosynthesis during freak periods of summer rain.

Local moisture regimes reflect such factors as slope exposure, local relief, elevation, rock formations, soil types, and distance from the ocean, which commonly change abruptly from place to place. The resulting vegetation is a rich mosaic of forest communities, which merge at the moist end of the spectrum with the redwood and Northwest coastal forests and at the dry end with Oregon oak woodland, chaparral, and grassland.

This same region also features a bewildering assortment of rock types, including large outcrops of peridotite and serpentine. Community surveys in the region have demonstrated distinct associations occurring on (1) steep, rocky slopes, (2) steep slopes with soils derived either from granites or metamorphic-sedimentary rocks, (3) moister, deeper soils of various types, and (4) outcrops of peridotite and serpentine. Adding to the complexity is the regular incidence of summer fires, which has produced a spectrum of successional communities of varying ages and types. Finally, the region has an extremely rich regional flora consisting of elements drawn from both Northwestern and Californian sources.

As a result of all the above factors, the number of plant

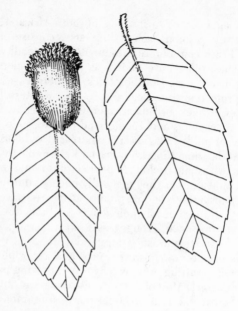

19. Tanoak (*Lithocarpus densiflora*)

associations within this forest and the patterns they form over the landscape are so various as to defy easy summary. The descriptions of the mixed evergreen forest that follow are generalizations that apply mainly to the Klamath Mountains and adjacent areas of California's North Coast Range. The general character and distribution of the forest changes markedly southward in the Coast Range, where it is increasingly allied with Californian woodland, chaparral, and grassland formations.

On more or less typical sites, mature old-growth mixed evergreen forests have a more or less open canopy dominated by 200-foot Douglas-firs and a secondary canopy of 100-foot tanoaks, which occurs beneath and between the conifers. Pacific madrone and canyon live oak occur throughout these forests and even dominate some stands. Generally, the madrone is more common on hot, dry, south-facing slopes while the oak prefers cool, steep, often rocky, north-facing slopes. Golden chinquapin, California laurel, and big-leaf maple are also common members of the forest. The deciduous California black oak may also be present, becoming common on deep, well-drained soils at the upper limit of the forest. Douglas-fir's principal conifer associates in this forest are Sierran species such as sugar pine, ponderosa pine, and incense-cedar, any or all of which may be present on drier sites.

Poison-oak, along with shrubby forms of tanoak and coast live oak, dominate the shrub layer on drier sites. Low Oregon-grape, ocean spray, California hazelnut, and wild roses are sprinkled among the more common shrubs. In coastal areas the understory may consist of little more than extensive, nearly pure stands of evergreen huckleberry. North-facing slopes are denser shrub layers that include Pacific dogwood and Pacific rhododendron in addition to the species listed above.

Western hemlock extends southward into California immediately east of the redwood belt, contributing to a western hemlock phase of the mixed evergreen forest. In areas long free of fire, western hemlock may even be codominant with Douglas-fir and tanoak. Port-Orford-cedar is an important member of this community and may be locally dominant. These woods usually have a well-developed shrub layer in which Pacific rhododendron and salal are prominent. Clumps of common sword fern and bracken commonly flourish among the shrubs. Evergreen violet and wood sorrel are common in mesic habitats, beargrass and vanilla leaf on drier ones.

Port-Orford-cedar and bigleaf maple are characteristic of stream bottoms, cool mesic slopes, and other moister habitats in the Klamaths, where they join Douglas-fir and western white pine. Broadleaf sclerophyll trees are present but not a significant element in these lush canyon-bottom woods. Dense ravine forests often have a well-developed shrub layer dominated by shrubs that also occur within the redwood and Northwest coastal forests. These shrubs include salal, low Oregon-grape, vine maple, western yew, and Pacific blackberry. Sword fern may carpet cool, moist, north-facing slopes. Vanilla leaf, twinflower, and bunchberry are among the more common members of the herb-subshrub layer.

The Klamath Mountains and California North Coast Range contain widespread outcrops of peridotite and serpentine. Peridotite is the dark rock that makes up the earth's mantle;

serpentine is peridotite that has absorbed water in the process of being erupted onto the sea floor along mid-ocean ridges. Large outcrops of peridotite in the Klamaths have weathered to a reddish or pinkish hue. Weathered serpentine is usually greenish and has a greasy feel. Soils derived from these rocks are deficient in essential plant nutrients such as calcium, nitrogen, potassium, and phosphorus; contain toxic metals such as nickel and chromium; and in the process of weathering tend toward extremes of either acidity or alkalinity, depending on the type of plant cover.

Relatively few types of plants tolerate soils derived from serpentine and peridotite. As a result, outcrops of those rocks tend to be sparsely vegetated, and plants growing on them are often stunted. On the other hand, many plants are either endemic to serpentine or do better on it than on normal soils. Plants adapted to serpentine soils have fewer competitors, which seems to be the major reason they are rare or absent elsewhere.

The shift from rich mixed evergreen forest on normal soils to open, scrubby woods on serpentine and peridotite is abrupt and dramatic. Botanists have reason to be fascinated by the unusual flora found on serpentine and peridotite, but most other people find the combination of scrawny, stunted plants, barren soils, and intense heat unattractive. The extensive red peridotite barrens of the Siskiyous, and comparable serpentine outcrops in the North Coast Range, seem like mountain deserts, and hiking through them on a hot summer day is a truly infernal experience. Yes, they have a beauty of their own, but it is a harsh, alien beauty, the appreciation of which takes time to cultivate—if it comes at all.

Peridotite and serpentine forests in the Klamath Mountains and adjacent North Coast Range are very open, with widely scattered and stunted Douglas-fir, sugar pine, Jeffrey pine, and incense-cedar. Port-Orford-cedar is an important tree in cool, moist sites. Jeffrey pine, another Sierran species, is largely restricted to serpentine or peridotite in the Klamaths and North Coast Range, though in the Sierra it occurs on normal soils. The shrub layer consists of drought-tolerant species such as huckleberry oak, Sadler oak, California coffeeberry, hoary manzanita, and buck brush. Herbaceous plant growth is sparse and consists mainly of bunchgrasses. Overll plant coverage is low, and there are large areas of exposed rock or thin, gravelly soils. On mesic sites the coverage increases though the forest remains thin by normal standards. The more common trees in such habitats are Douglas-fir, incense-cedar, Jeffrey pine, lodgepole pine, and knob-cone pine.

In the wake of wildfires, either on normal soils or those derived from peridotite and serpentine, knobcone pine forms pure stands. Areas subjected to repeated fires often host extensive stands of this opportunistic pine. Knobcone pine actually depends on fire to prepare its seed beds and trigger the release of seeds from cones that are tightly sealed with resin. The resin prevents the premature release of seeds or their loss to squirrels and other foragers. Fire melts the resin, thereby releasing the seeds onto ground that has been cleared of potential competitors and fertilized with nutrient-rich ash.

Extensive brush fields occur throughout the Klamath Mountains and North Coast Range. They are composed mainly of broadleaf sclerophyll shrubs that are characteristic of California chaparral, of which greenleaf manzanita, buck brush, and a dwarfed, scrubby form of canyon live oak are most characteristic. Some brush fields probably developed following forest fires and owe their perpetuation to repeated burning. Others occur on steep, dry, rocky, south-facing slopes, where heat and drought would seem to exclude forest plants. These two types of chaparral habitats are characteristic of such vegetation throughout California.

Port-Orford-cedar is endemic to southwestern Oregon and northwestern California, where it grows in numerous forest communities on a wide variety of soils. The tree ranges along the coast from the Mad River southeast of Eureka, California, north to Reedsport, Oregon, and inland as far as the crest of the Oregon Coast Range and the eastern Klamaths. In coastal forests it associates with western hemlock, Sitka spruce, western redcedar, coast redwood, Douglas-fir, grand fir, shore pine, red alder, tanoak, bigleaf maple, and California laurel. Farther inland, at higher elevations, it grows with typically Sierran conifers such as sugar pine, ponderosa pine, Jeffrey pine, and incense-cedar, as well as Douglas-fir, western white pine, Pacific madrone, canyon live oak, and golden chinquapin.

Port-Orford-cedar is among the dominant conifers within three vegetation zones, yet it also is capable of establishing itself on open areas following fire, logging, or other disturbance. Like Douglas-fir, it has thick, fire-resistant bark, and older trees often have conspicuous fire scars. Port-Orford-cedar not only tolerates serpentine, but is the dominant conifer on that rock wherever sufficient moisture is available. Normally, Port-Orford-cedar fares better on north-facing slopes, but it also occurs in mesic habitats on south-facing ones. At the drier fringes of its range, Port-Orford-cedar is largely restricted to streamsides, damp ravines, seepage areas, and other places with reliable moisture during the summer.

Port-Orford-cedar is like Douglas-fir and lodgepole pine in its ability to thrive in a wide variety of habitats, yet unlike those widely distributed conifers it is confined to a relatively small and isolated geographic area. Why this should be remains a puzzle. Even within its present range, Port-Orford-cedar is under siege. *Phytophthora lateralis*, a water-borne root rot, has inflicted heavy damage on the tree in coastal stands and threatens eventually to eliminate the tree throughout its natural range. The fungus is spread by road-building and logging.

In the Cascades of southern Oregon and northern California, areas below 4,000 feet generally support a rich mixed conifer forest that is essentially an extension of that found in the Sierra Nevada. This forest also occurs in the eastern Klamath Mountains in a narrow zone immediately above the mixed evergreen forest. In the Cascades the forest extends northward to the McKenzie River, east of Eugene. As in the Sierra, typical stands in the mixed conifer forest contain ponderosa pine, white fir, incense-cedar, sugar pine, Douglas-fir, and California black oak. Of these, white fir is the most shade tolerant and in mesic habitats would appear to be the climax tree. Douglas-fir is the climax tree in drier habitats, while north of the Umpqua River drainage western hemlock shares climax status with white fir on mesic sites. Frequent wildfires favor the perpetuation of the Douglas-fir, the pines, and incense-cedar in stands where white fir might otherwise eventually shade them out. Ponderosa pine and black oak are intolerant of shade and require periodic burning to maintain their presence in the forest. Douglas-fir, sugar pine, and incense-cedar are somewhat more tolerant and are able to maintain their position on drier sites notwithstanding competition from white fir.

Mixed stands containing all the above species are common, though their relative abundance changes depending on available moisture. Douglas-fir and white fir tend to be most common on mesic sites; incense-cedar, ponderosa pine, and black oak on drier ones. Sugar pine is generally less common than the other conifers regardless of habitat. Western white pine, bigleaf maple, Pacific madrone, and golden chinquapin are scattered through the forest.

The Sierran mixed conifer forest prevails northward to the vicinity of Crater Lake, where it begins to merge gradually with the Northwest coastal forest along the western flank of the Cascades. Over a fairly broad transition zone, the two forest types tend to split the terrain between them, with the Northwestern coastal forest growing in mesic habitats—such as ravines, streambanks, and lower slopes—and the Sierran mixed conifer forest growing on drier sites. Mixed stands are common, however, with Douglas-fir occurring as a prominent member of both forests.

At the upper limits of the mixed conifer forest, deep winter snows and a relatively short growing season favor white fir over its associates. As a result, pure or nearly pure white fir forests occur in a narrow belt between roughly 4,500 and 5,500 feet in the Cascades. Douglas-fir is the most common associate of white fir in these stands; sugar pine, ponderosa pine, and western white pine are present in small numbers. On drier sites within these cool, shady forests, understory vegetation is often quite sparse, consisting of little more than widely scattered shade-tolerant wildflowers and evergreen shrubs. On mesic sites, however, both the herb and shrub covers increase, with the latter mostly consisting of species that are also common in the mixed conifer forest or adjacent open areas. Among the most important herbs are twinflower, vanilla leaf, and prince's pine, all three of which are common in cool, shady montane forests throughout the Northwest.

In the eastern Klamath Mountains, including the Siskiyous, mixed conifer forests much like those in the Cascades occur at elevations between 5,400 and 5,900 feet. Common understory trees include Pacific dogwood, black oak, canyon live oak, bigleaf maple, and western yew. These are replaced in the Western Cascades, at elevations from 4,600 to 5,900 feet, by white fir/Douglas-fir forests with understories of salal, vine maple, evergreen huckleberry, and other coastal plants. In both the Cascades and Klamaths, white fir or mixed conifer forests give way at their upper limits to dense subalpine forests dominated by Shasta red fir.

White fir occurs widely throughout the western United States. It covers hundreds of thousands of acres in the Sierra Nevada, but also ranges northward to central Oregon and south to Baja California. Though perhaps most characteristic of and numerous in mixed conifer forests of the Pacific slope, white fir also ranges through Arizona and New Mexico and northward to Colorado, Utah, and extreme southeastern Idaho. Young white firs are very tolerant of shade. They are able to grow at rates as low as three centimeters a year for periods up to 80 years or more. Even where conditions are ideal, growth is initially slow, then increases to a foot a year thereafter. Before the implementation of fire suppression policies early in this century, periodic wildfires—either natural or man-made—opened up tracts of forest, creating conditions suitable for the regeneration of ponderosa pine and sun-loving shrubs and herbs. The suppression of fires in this century has tended to keep forests closed, a situation

20. Twinflower (*Linnaea borealis*)

that favors the regeneration of white fir and discourages that of ponderosa pine, which requires full sun.

Throughout most of the Pacific Northwest, white fir is replaced by its close cousin, grand fir. In southwestern Oregon, where the ranges of the two species overlap, one may encounter hybrid individuals with characteristics intermediate between the two species. In most instances, however, the two species are fairly easy to distinguish. The needles of white fir are pale blue-green with whitish lines on both surfaces, whereas those of grand fir are dark green above and whitish below. The needles of both firs form two opposite ranks on twigs, but those of grand fir lie flat while those of white fir are twisted at the base, causing them to curve up, if only slightly.

Mature white firs have dark gray, deeply furrowed bark. Seedlings and saplings, however, have smooth white bark. The branches of young white firs are arranged in horizontal whorls on the trunk, gradually decreasing in length from base to crown so that the trees have tidy pyramidal profiles. This regularity, combined with the handsome contrast in color between needles and bark, has made young white firs popular in the Christmas tree trade, where they fetch a pretty price as "silver tips."

The driest habitats within the mixed conifer forest are usually dominated by incense-cedar, which tolerates drought better than all its normal companions save Douglas-fir. At the same time, incense-cedar is moderately tolerant of shade and, with the assistance of occasional disturbances, is therefore able to maintain its numbers in moister habitats where the more tolerant western hemlock, western red-cedar, white fir, or Douglas-fir prevail. Incense-cedar grows abundantly in mixed conifer forests in northwestern California and southwestern Oregon, ranging northward in the Coast Range to near Coos Bay and in the Cascade Range to the east side of Mount Hood.

Like the other so-called "cedars" growing in the Pacific Northwest (western redcedar, Alaska-cedar, and Port-Orford-cedar), incense-cedar is a member of the cypress family, which also includes junipers and cypresses. Incense-cedar, however, belongs in a genus of its own, along with two Asian cousins. The trunks of mature incense-cedars flare at the base but rapidly taper upward to heights between 60 and

21. Incense-cedar (*Calocedrus decurrens*)

150 feet. The bark is bright reddish-brown, fibrous, and deeply furrowed. The leaves are ⅛- to ½-inch long and tightly pressed to their twigs, forming distinctive flat sprays of foliage. The cones resemble small woody flowers and hang from the tips of the sprays. The crowns of mature trees are open and irregular, often with elbowlike branches that grow straight out from the trunk for a short distance then abruptly turn upward. Young incense-cedars form perfect inverted cones, their dense, vivid, yellow-green foliage extending clear to the ground.

The wood of incense-cedar contains aromatic resins that give it a pleasant fragrance. The smell will be familiar to anyone who has ever used a pencil, for incense-cedar provides the wood that sheathes the lead. The wood is also used to make cedar chests for protecting clothing from moths. The heartwood is highly resistant to decay, which makes it valuable as well for posts and shingles.

A flaring base and thick bark provide mature incense-cedars with a measure of protection from fire, which is a fact of forest life throughout its range. The number of living trees with fire scars bears testimony to the effectiveness of the bark in providing fire protection. Yet these same scars provide access for the dry-rot fungus, which riddles the wood with cavities. The resulting "wormwood," however, is valued for decorative panelling.

Among the conifers regularly occurring in the mixed conifer forest, sugar pine is probably the least numerous but most impressive. Nevertheless, its large size and distinctive appearance make it conspicuous wherever it occurs. Mature sugar pines commonly reach 200 feet in height and have trunks six feet in diameter, making them the largest pines in the world. Exceptional trees may be 250 feet tall and ten feet in diameter. The sugar pine's open crown consists of horizontal branches up to 40 feet long, with cones 12 to 18 inches long—or longer—dangling from the ends. These branches occur mostly on the upper half of the trunk and show little inclination to sort themselves out by size, so that the longest may be among the highest, often making the top of the tree appear flattened. The pine's bark is light brown or gray and consists of alternating furrows and scaly ridges. The blue-green needles are about three inches long and grow five to a bundle.

The sugar pine is named for its sugary resin, which was eaten in small doses as a sweet—and in larger ones as a laxative—by various Indian peoples. The white, sugary resin forms scabs over scars on the trunk and seals the cones. When ripe, usually in their third or fourth spring or summer, the cones fall and open, releasing nuts about the size of corn kernels. Western gray squirrels, Steller's jays, and a host of small mammals all relish the large seeds.

Unlike other western pines, sugar pine is capable of reproducing in partial shade, though it faces tough competition in such situations from white fir, Douglas-fir, and incense-cedar. Sugar pines also reproduce in the wake of fire or within small openings that are scattered throughout the mixed conifer forest.

Like the trees, understory vegetation in mixed conifer forests varies greatly between mesic and xeric sites. In drier forests dominated by incense-cedar and Douglas-fir, understory vegetation may consist of little more than the mat-forming shrubs pinemat manzanita and squaw carpet. These same two xerophytic shrublets also occur in forest openings on scree, exposed bedrock, or areas with thin, rocky soil. In mesic habitats the understory vegetation is lusher, of course, but it also features a number of species characteristic of the Northwest coastal forest, including vine maple, Pacific rhododendron, western yew, and twinflower.

Frequently burned areas on the lower western slopes of the Cascades often sustain dense tracts of chaparral or pure stands of knobcone pine. Brush also develops on recently logged lands and on sites too steep, hot, dry, rocky, or thin soiled to support forest. As in the Klamath Mountains, the shrubs making up these mountain brushlands are typical of the California chaparral. They include hoary manzanita, mountain balm, several other species of ceanothus, western serviceberry, and golden chinquapin. Nearly identical brush tracts occur on similar sites throughout the Sierra Nevada. Other open areas feature annual grasslands and rock gardens where wild buckwheats and pussy paws are prominent.

In the Southern Cascades and Klamath Mountains, forests in which Shasta red fir is both the dominant and the climax conifer form a narrow zone above Sierran mixed conifer forests and below subalpine forests dominated by mountain hemlock or lodgepole pine. These forests are essentially northern extensions of the widespread red-fir forests of the Sierra Nevada. Shasta red fir is nearly identical to the Sierran red fir, differing mainly in the cone. That of Shasta red fir has elongated bracts that extend beyond the ends of the scales, giving the cone a fringed appearance. In the Sierran red fir the bracts are shorter than the cone scales and therefore are not apparent. Nevertheless, both populations contain scattered members of the other, and intermediate specimens occur in the California Cascades, where their ranges overlap. Shasta red fir also appears closely related to noble fir, which replaces it in the Cascades of northern Oregon. Noble fir, however, is strictly a seral species requiring fires or other disturbances for regeneration, while Shasta red fir, like Sierran red fir, forms dense, deeply shaded climax forests.

Shasta red fir has thick, deeply furrowed, reddish-brown bark and dark blue-green needles. Mature trees are generally 60 to 120 feet tall and one to four feet thick, though some trees are significantly larger. The pyramidal crown is composed of short, spreading branches, which are arranged in whorls. This trait is particularly apparent in young trees, which also are prized as "silver tips" in the Christmas tree trade. The cones are six to eight inches long, barrel-shaped, and sit erect on the uppermost branches of the tree.

Shasta red fir forests generally occur at elevations between 5,200 and 6,400 feet in the Cascade Range of southern Oregon and 5,800 and 6,600 feet in the Siskiyou Mountains. The composition and density of Shasta red fir stands varies widely. At lower elevations, red fir occurs in mixed forests with white fir, Douglas-fir, and incense-cedar. At higher elevations, mountain hemlock, lodgepole pine, and western white pine are common associates. The two pines are pioneer species that rapidly invade burned areas and other openings but are rarely present in old-growth fir forests on normal sites. Lodgepole pines may persist indefinitely, however, on soggy flats at one extreme or rapidly draining pumice fields at the other.

Pure or nearly pure dense stands of Shasta red fir are common throughout the zone. These stands have sparse understories dominated by prince's pine and a few other shade-tolerant plants. On drier sites, even these plants may be widely scattered amid an understory layer consisting mainly of woody debris and thick mats of needle litter. In dry habitats higher in the zone, more open Shasta red fir forests commonly feature sparse understories dominated by the low, spreading shrubs pinemat manzanita and grouse whortleberry. (The former shrublet covers large areas of dry, open forest in the Sierra Nevada, while the latter occupies similar sites throughout much of the Rocky Mountains.) On moister sites Shasta red firs often preside over lusher understories featuring a rich assortment of deciduous shrubs and herbs. Huckleberries and gooseberries dominate the shrub layer, making this a popular haunt of berry-loving black bears. Thimbleberry may flourish in moist, partly shaded spots. Understory herbs include a number of species common to Northwestern fir and hemlock forests, such as trail plant, vanilla leaf, and starry Solomon's plume.

Openings are numerous within the red-fir zone. Brush fields commonly occur in burned areas or on hot, dry, rocky sites where soils are too thin and poorly developed to support forest. Commonly big huckleberry and mountain balm dominate these tracts in the Cascades, while greenleaf manzanita, big sagebrush, curl-leaf mountain-mahogany, and purple honeysuckle prevail in the Siskiyous. Huckleberry oak and greenleaf manzanita cover large tracts in the Klamath Mountains of northwestern California.

Moist openings within the Shasta red fir zone support flowery meadows dominated by sedges and grasses. In midsummer broadleaf lupine and Bloomer's goldenweed fill these meadows with purple and yellow. Meadows in the upper part of the zone may also contain large numbers of subalpine wildflowers.

Southwestern Oregon and northwestern California have provided a refuge for numerous species of plants that once were widespread but now are rare or absent outside this region. Here, along the foggy coast and in the high mountains, a particularly congenial blend of California sunshine and Northwestern precipitation has created a nearly ideal climate for the proliferation of conifers and the numerous families of plants that are closely associated with them. Until recently, the magnificent forests of the Southern Cascades and especially the Klamath Mountains have been little visited and little known by the general public. Left to the timber industry, much of the region's original forests have already been trucked to the mill, and each year additional old-growth stands are lost to the saw. Unless action is taken soon to preserve at least some of the remaining old growth in the region, the richest, most diverse conifer forests on earth may pass away largely unnoticed and unremembered.

CHAPTER EIGHT

East to the Rockies

THE FORESTS of eastern Washington, eastern Oregon, Idaho, southeastern British Columbia, and northwestern Montana are hybrids compounded of Northwest coastal and Rocky Mountain elements. Coastal conifers, such as western hemlock, western redcedar, mountain hemlock, and grand fir, extend eastward beyond the Cascades to the Continental Divide. Likewise, Rocky Mountain conifers, such as ponderosa pine, Rocky Mountain Douglas-fir, western larch, Engelmann spruce, and subalpine fir, range westward to the eastern flank of the Cascades. East of the Cascade Range, forests dominated by coastal conifers occur on the windward (western) sides of the major mountain ranges, while Rocky Mountain conifers prevail at comparable elevations on the leeward (eastern) slopes.

The coastal influence is greatest along the U.S.–Canadian border, which often falls under the influence of the prevailing westerly storm track. The storm track, of course, fluctuates greatly, both from storm to storm and between summer and winter, in accordance with the ever-shifting position of the jetstream. During the summer, the border region often marks the southern fringe of the storm track, which then lies well to the north. Conversely, in winter the border region lies along the northern fringe of the storm track, the center of which is then most often located over Oregon. As a result of this central position, the border region experiences considerably more cloudiness and rain than areas to the north or south. In addition, the oceanic influence moderates winter and summer temperature extremes, producing an inland version of the Northwest coastal climate.

The coastal element gradually dissipates northward and

southward from the border region. Northward, increasing cold during the growing season is the principal limiting factor for coastal conifers. Southward, increasing heat and drought do the trick. A similar attenuation of coastal influences occurs from west to east, as marine air passes over a series of high ranges, each casting a rainshadow on the next one downwind. As a result, the Rocky Mountain influence is strongest in the southeastern section of the region. In the mountains of central Idaho, for example, only one coastal conifer—grand fir—is present, and it is restricted to the westernmost ranges; elsewhere, Rocky Mountain conifers and communities prevail. Even where the coastal influence is strong, however—say, in northern Idaho or southeastern British Columbia—"coastal" forests are limited to middle to high elevations. Downslope, where summers are hot and dry, coastal conifers are absent, and Rocky Mountain Douglas-fir and ponderosa pine form xerophytic forests just above the grasslands and sagebrush.

The ponderosa pine, also known as western yellow pine, ranges from southern British Columbia to central Mexico and from the coastal mountains of California and Oregon east to the rolling hills of the western Dakotas and Nebraska. Mature trees are commonly between 150 and 230 feet tall and as much as eight feet in diameter. The tree has an open, somewhat irregular crown that from a distance appears to consist of numerous individual, more or less round, clumps of needles. Young ponderosas have dark brown to nearly black bark, but after a century it becomes golden or light reddish-brown, noticeably scaly, and broken into large plates. Its needles grow in bundles of three—at least in the Northwest—and are five to ten inches long. The young cones are bright purple but turn reddish-brown as they ripen. Each of the cone scales is armed with a sharp spine at the tip so that the cones feel prickly when held.

Throughout most of the inland Northwest, ponderosa pine forms pure, open stands on the lowest, hottest, driest sites occupied by montane conifers. Not even Rocky Mountain Douglas-fir, the next most drought-tolerant inland conifer, can endure the infernal conditions tolerated by ponderosa at the lowest extremities of its range. As a result ponderosa pine forests typically form a narrow belt between steppes below and Douglas-fir forests above on the mountain slopes.

bordering the lowlands of the Columbia Basin Province.

Precipitation in the interior ponderosa pine belt ranges from as little as 14 to as much as 30 inches a year, most of it falling as winter snow. Summers are hot and very dry, with rainfall averaging only about an inch for the months of July through September. Most of that falls during brief downpours that accompany thunderstorms. Rather than supplying small amounts of moisture throughout the growing season, these storms drop it all at once, whereupon it either runs off rapidly or evaporates quickly into the atmosphere.

Pines growing in this extreme environment have more difficulty becoming established, grow more slowly than their brethren upslope, and are more subject to infestations of dwarf mistletoe, a debilitating parasite. Reproduction is normally sparse or episodic and the right combination of good seed crops and a succession of favorable years may occur only every couple of decades or so. Coarse soils are generally superior to fine ones for ponderosa pine because the more

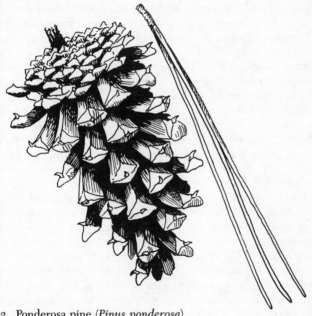

22. Ponderosa pine (*Pinus ponderosa*)

open structure permits greater root penetration and proliferation. This advantage apparently more than offsets the
potential problem posed by faster drainage. Thus in parts
of northeastern Washington, Douglas-firs abut the steppes
on fine-textured soils while ponderosa pines do the same
on coarse, gravelly ones.

Ponderosa pine is missing altogether from southeastern
Idaho, where the lower timberline is formed by Douglas-fir
on cooler, moister sites and limber pine on warmer, drier
ones. In this region—and for that matter throughout the
Middle Rockies—the ponderosa pine is whipsawed by extremes of cold and drought: Places that are warm enough to
support ponderosas are too dry, while places that are moist
enough are too cold. In southern Oregon, east of Crater
Lake, large areas where one would expect to find ponderosa
pines are instead covered by lodgepole pines. The area is
mantled with a deep layer of pumice, which drains poorly
in winter but dries out completely in summer. Lodgepole
pine predominates on poorly drained flats and "frost-pocket"
depressions, while ponderosa pine occupies the higher,
drier ground where somewhat warmer conditions during
the early growing season may favor ponderosa seedlings.

Ponderosa pines also range upslope into forests dominated
by Douglas-fir, grand fir, or white fir, but there they are
able to maintain their presence only in unusually dry locations or through the agency of periodic wildfires, which
open the forest to young seedlings. Even so, the finest
ponderosa stands usually occur in the Douglas-fir zone simply because conditions for growth are so much better there
than downslope. The composition of any particular stand
varies according to the interplay of geographic location,
soils, precipitation, fire history, logging, grazing, and other
more subtle factors.

Stands of ponderosa pine tend to fall in two large groups
according to whether shrubs or grasses are more conspicuous in the understory. All stands have both shrubs and
grasses; the difference among them is one of proportion.
As a rule parklike stands in which trees are widely scattered
over a grassy floor occupy the driest sites while those with
denser, shrubbier understories occur in places where soils
are deeper and more finely textured and retain moisture
longer into the growing season. Repeated burning tends to

avor the grasses, which recover more quickly. Livestock
grazing, however, favors the less palatable shrubs.

The understories of grassy stands are carpeted by one or
rarely more kinds of perennial grasses, chief among which
are bluebunch wheatgrass, pinegrass, Idaho fescue, and
needlegrass, which occur widely throughout the interior
Northwest. Other grasses, or even sedges, may be common
or dominant locally. In the colder northern portion of the
region—eastern Washington, north-central Oregon, and
Idaho—the shrubs are deciduous. The more common ones
include mallow ninebark, common snowberry, antelope bit-
erbrush, and wild roses. In south-central Oregon and north-
astern California, however, the shrub cover is dominated by
greenleaf manzanita and mountain balm. Both are drought-
olerant evergreen sclerophylls that occur widely beneath
ponderosa pines throughout northern California and southward through the Sierra Nevada. In this region, where
winters are mild but wet, evergreenness is an advantage.

Throughout most of the year, herbaceous wildflowers are
ot a conspicuous element in ponderosa pine forests. During
a brief period in spring, however, when warmer weather
and still frequent rainfall combine, sunny slopes may come
live with blossoms. Many of the wildflowers in these open
orests are daisies, whose yellow or white, radially symmet-
ical flower heads are designed to be seen from a great
istance and to be accessible to a wide variety of pollinators.
mong the most conspicuous of these plants is arrowleaf
alsamroot, whose deep yellow flowers are up to four inches
cross. Growing among the daisies may be purple, red, or
lue flowers such as paintbrush, lupine, scarlet gilia, and
arkspur. Herbaceous wildflowers are most numerous along
reams and in other moist places, as well as in rock crevices
rotected from afternoon sun.

Throughout the Northern Rockies and along the east side
f the Cascades southward into northern Oregon, mixed
orests in which Rocky Mountain Douglas-fir is climax form
he next forest belt upslope from ponderosa pine. The upper
nd lower limits of this belt, or zone, vary greatly, depending
n local conditions, but generally range somewhere between
,000 and 4,300 feet in Washington and between 3,000 and
700 feet in central Idaho. The kinds and relative abundance
f conifers in the Douglas-fir forest vary greatly according

to the complex interplay of such factors as geographic location, topography, elevation, soil and moisture conditions, and fire history or other major disturbances. Douglas-fir's most common associates in these forests are grand fir, ponderosa pine, and western larch. Western white pine, western hemlock, and western redcedar are also present in area where the maritime influence is strong. Engelmann spruce, subalpine fir, and lodgepole pine mingle with Douglas-fir at higher elevations.

Rocky Mountain Douglas-fir closely resembles coastal Douglas-fir except that its foliage tends to be bluer green and the distinctive trident-shaped bracts of its cones tend to bend upward. Enduring a colder, drier environment than its coastal cousin, Rocky Mountain Douglas-fir is also significantly smaller, rarely exceeding 130 feet in height. Finally its position in the forest community is significantly different The coastal Douglas-fir is less shade tolerant than all its principal associates and therefore is mainly a seral species, requiring periodic disturbances to maintain its position in the majority of coastal stands. Inland, however, the relationship drastically change. There, Douglas-fir is more shade tolerant than most of the trees with which it associates. As a result Douglas-fir is the climax species on typical mid-mountain sites throughout most of the Rocky Mountain region.

Ponderosa pine is the most frequent companion of Douglas fir at lower elevations, where the ranges of the two species broadly overlap. Although Douglas-fir generally occupies moister sites than ponderosa pine, there is actually often little or no difference in the amount of precipitation falling on places occupied by one or the other. Of greater importance apparently is the degree to which this precipitation which mostly falls during the winter, is conserved through the summer months. Douglas-fir tends to dominate sites where lower air temperatures reduce evaporation or where finer-textured soils prevent the water table from dropping below the level of the roots. Ponderosa pine, on the other hand, prefers coarser soils, where its deeper taproot can pull up water beyond the reach of Douglas-fir.

In areas such as southeastern Idaho, where drought and cold combine, Douglas-firs, rather than ponderosa pines often form a lower timberline at the edge of the steppes In still other places fire has perpetuated the pine at the expense of the fir, so that the former is the more common tree in habitats where one would otherwise expect the latter to prevail. Though Douglas-fir is moderately resistant to fire and regenerates well on recent burns, it is less vigorous in such situations than ponderosa pine. As a result, wildfires have maintained ponderosa pine forests in some areas where moisture conditions would otherwise favor Douglas-fir. The suppression of wildfires during this century, however, has allowed Douglas-firs to reinvade these areas.

On hot, dry, lower slopes, Douglas-fir stands often form savannas, with scattered trees presiding over understories dominated by grasses or shrubs. Ponderosa pine is often present and may dominate stands subjected to frequent fires. Among the more common understory grasses are bluebunch wheatgrass, Idaho fescue, and pinegrass. In some areas elk sedge may be more common than grass. It grows vigorously in the aftermath of fires and may dominate burned areas for decades. Curl-leaf mountain-mahogany,

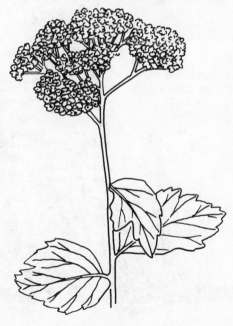

23. White spiraea (*Spiraea betulifolia*)

snowberry, creeping Oregon-grape, white spiraea, and mallow ninebark often form a more or less continuous open cover on gravelly soils.

Almost everywhere in the Rockies, from Canada to New Mexico, Douglas-firs give way upslope to Engelmann spruce and subalpine fir. This relationship remains the case in the mountains of central Idaho and on the eastern flanks of the several ranges along the U.S.–Canadian border. On the western slopes of those same ranges, however, and on the eastern flank of Washington's North Cascades, Douglas-firs are replaced at higher elevation by grand firs, which give way in turn to western redcedars and western hemlocks. To further complicate matters, grand fir and Douglas-fir commonly grow together in the same stands, with the former becoming increasingly important southward. Grand fir forests are the most extensive midslope forests along the east side of the Cascades in southern Washington and Oregon, where they occur at elevations between 3,600 and 4,900 feet. Grand fir

24. Grand fir (*Abies grandis*)

forests also mantle the middle slopes of the Blue Mountains complex of central and eastern Oregon, forming a distinct zone between 4,900 and 6,600 feet.

Like Douglas-fir, grand fir also grows west of the Cascades, where it associates with Sitka spruce, western hemlock, western redcedar, and other coastal conifers. Although it is more shade tolerant than Douglas-fir, it is also more sensitive to temperature extremes and less tolerant of drought. Douglas-fir is therefore the climax species in areas such as central Idaho, where cold, dry conditions favor it over grand fir. The latter replaces Douglas-fir as the climax conifer in the Southern Cascades and central Oregon because there it is favored by a combination of milder temperatures and adequate moisture. In the inland maritime region straddling the Canadian border, a moderate climate extends far enough upslope to permit grand fir to form climax forests above Douglas-fir. In the Cascades of southern Oregon, grand fir is replaced in comparable forests by its close cousin white fir.

Grand fir and Douglas-fir forests are very much alike in both appearance and composition. They generally feature not only the same mix of conifer species—Douglas-fir, grand fir, ponderosa pine, lodgepole pine, and western larch—but also many of the same understory plants—for example, mountain lover and big huckleberry on higher, cooler, moister sites; pinegrass and mallow ninebark on lower, warmer, drier ones. Ponderosa pine, western larch, and lodgepole pine energetically invade recently burned areas and may dominate stands for some time thereafter. Douglas-fir invades more slowly but persists longer in the grand fir zone and indefinitely in the Douglas-fir zone.

In northeastern Washington, northern Idaho, northwestern Montana, and southeastern British Columbia, forests of grand fir, western redcedar, and western hemlock form lush forests reminiscent of those growing west of the Cascades. These forests occur at elevations between roughly 2,500 and 4,000 feet in that part of the inland Northwest where the maritime influence is greatest. They occur along the east flank of the North Cascades and eastward along the U.S.– Canadian border as far as Glacier National Park. These forests range southward in greatly reduced form to the mountains of west-central Idaho and along the east side of the Cascade Range to near Mount Jefferson in Oregon. In British

Columbia, grand fir-western redcedar-western hemlock forests are the principal type in the Columbia Mountain Province, the mountainous region lying west of the Continental Divide and east of the Fraser Plateau. The region is drained by the Columbia River and includes such well-known mountain chains as the Selkirk, Purcell, and Valhalla ranges, all of which are western outliers of the Northern Rocky Mountains. Canadian foresters call this "inland coastal" forest the Columbia Forest, after the great river that drains the entire region, both in Canada and the United States, where this forest occurs. Forest ecologists in the United States know it as the *Tsuga heterophylla* (i.e., western hemlock) series.

The western hemlock series, as it shall be called here, lies between the Douglas-fir forest below and the subalpine fir forest above, occupying a midslope belt that features the mildest, most congenial forest habitats found east of the Cascades. Summers are cooler and bring more cloudiness and precipitation than in the Douglas-fir forest. As a result, soils supporting the western hemlock series dry out only in the upper few centimeters, while those downslope dry out to great depth. At the same time, the growing season is longer and milder, and the winters less snowy and cold, than in the subalpine fir zone upslope. Grand fir, western redcedar, and western hemlock occur together but singly form climax forests in progressively moister habitats, which tend to occur at successively higher elevations. Douglas-fir, western white pine, ponderosa pine, and western larch are among the lower montane conifers that may be present; subalpine fir, Engelmann spruce, and even mountain hemlock can be found growing in frost pockets and other cold habitats. Vast acreages within the region where grand fir, western redcedar, or western hemlock form climax forests instead support stands of western white pine, which vigorously invades open areas following fires. Western larch also pioneers on burned ground but does not persist as long as the more shade-tolerant western white pine. As elsewhere, however, repeated burning can produce nearly pure stands of western larch. Lodgepole pine can be found not only in post-fire stands but also in cold, wet bottomlands, where fluctuating moisture conditions may preclude other conifers. Paper birch grows along streams and invades burned areas.

Forests of the western hemlock series have lush under-stories containing a mix dominated by distinctly coastal shrubs and perennial herbs. Among the more common coastal plants found in these forests are trail plant, lady fern, rattle-snake plantain, starry Solomon's seal, foamflower, western trillium, twinflower, queen's cup bead lily, big huckleberry, and devil's club. Missing from these inland forests, however, are such important coastal species as salal, wood sorrel, and vine maple, while low Oregon-grape and common sword fern are scarce. Mountain lover, Rocky Mountain maple, woods rose, and white spiraea are among the more common Rocky Mountain" shrubs. This large group of understory plants also occurs downslope in the moistest Douglas-fir habitats and upslope in the warmest subalpine fir forests. Wet bottomlands usually feature pure western redcedar for-ests with lush understories of lady fern or devil's club.

The role of fire in the evolution of forests in the inland Northwest can scarcely be overestimated. Dry summers and frequent lightning storms have made this region one of the most fire prone in the West. The region also has a long history of human-caused fires, many of which raged out of control. Long before the arrival of whites, Indians period-ically burned the forest for a number of reasons, chief among which was probably to increase forage for wildlife. In the nineteenth century, prospectors, in their single-minded quest for gold and other metals, used fire to remove vege-tation from areas of mineral outcrops. Settlers set fires to create clearings and improve the range for livestock. Whether human or natural in origin, fires that got out of hand, as many did, burned unchecked until finally quenched by fall rains.

Most of the forest land in the Northern Rockies has burned at one time or another. As a result, climax forests are rela-tively rare. In their place is a rich mosaic of forest types in which seral and climax conifers cohabit in a variety of mixes and proportions. These seral forests often cover huge areas and may be maintained indefinitely by repeated fires. In some cases, the burned areas are so vast that the scarcity of nearby climax conifers to serve as seed sources greatly retards the reestablishment of climax forests. The greatest incidence of fire occurs in northeastern Washington, north-ern Idaho, northwestern Montana, and southeastern British

Columbia, a region that experiences many more lightning storms than elsewhere in the inland Northwest. Lightning, for example, is three times less likely in the mountains of central Idaho or central Oregon and probably even less common along the east side of the Cascade Range.

Depending on geographic location, elevation, fire history, and other conditions, any one of five species—ponderosa pine, Douglas-fir, western larch, western white pine, or lodgepole pine—may dominate post-fire forests in the inland Northwest. Ponderosa pine is the most important seral conifer at lower elevations; western larch, lodgepole pine, and Douglas-fir are preeminent upslope. Western white pine may be found in post-fire forests at middle to upper elevations throughout the region, but it covers vast acreages in the northern half, where the maritime influence is strongest.

Trees, shrubs, and herbs all invade burned areas in the first growing season following a fire, but the first plants to form a conspicuous cover are usually the herbs, which grow rapidly within a single season. The herbs growing on burned ground include plants that were both present in the former forest and those whose seeds were blown into the area from outside sources. Many of the perennial herbs characteristic of the former closed forest spring forth from underground parts and manage to survive, at least for a time, in the shade of tall, aggressive outsiders such as fireweed and bracken fern. Other herbs that rapidly invade burned areas include yarrow, pinegrass, butterweed, and various sedges. Shrubs become established on burned sites as early as herbaceous species but normally take longer to develop. After two or three decades, however, shrub cover may be nearly complete, and most of the herbs present during the first few years following a fire will be gone. Sitka alder, redstem ceanothus, mountain balm, bitter cherry, Scouler's willow, white spiraea, and greenleaf manzanita are among the more common shrubs to be found on post-fire sites in various parts of the inland Northwest.

In central Idaho, westward across central Oregon to the Cascades, and southward, dense fields of mountain balm may form on certain sites in the wake of fire. The seeds of mountain balm have tough coats that do not break open until they have been softened by fire. These seeds are able to lie dormant in the soil for a couple of centuries if necessary. When a fire brings them to life, they may germinate by the tens of thousands, covering an area with young mountain balm plants before potential competitors have barely gotten started. The resulting brush fields are commonly so thick as to prevent the reestablishment of conifers for decades. Among the shrubs that may succeed in joining mountain balm in these post-fire brush fields is greenleaf manzanita, which sprouts vigorously from buried root crowns following destruction of the above-ground portion of the plant by fire.

Eventually, shrubs are shaded out by the young trees, which form dense "dog-hair" stands in which the shading is so complete that the undergrowth consists of little more than woody debris from the trees themselves. Stiff competition soon begins to thin out the young forests, however, allowing increasing amounts of sunlight to penetrate to the forest floor. With the sunlight the shrub and herb cover once again begin to increase. Eventually, the association of herbs and shrubs present in climax stands once again occurs in the understory, often long before the climax conifers have reasserted their dominance.

East of the Continental Divide and southward through the Middle Rocky Mountains, lodgepole pine is the preeminent fire pioneer of mid-slope forests, forming nearly pure stands over vast areas once cleared by flames. The species' strategy is not to survive fires but to quickly reseed burned areas and then outgrow potential competitors. In other words, the emphasis is on youth. Mature lodgepole pines have thin bark that provides little protection even from ground fires; they are expendable. In areas subject to frequent burning, however, many or most of the lodgepoles store their seeds in resin-sealed cones that may remain on the trees for decades. When fire finally occurs, the heat melts the resin and releases the seeds. Fire also removes potential competitors, exposes mineral soil, and reduces the number of rodents that otherwise would gorge on the newly exposed seed crop. In the wake of fire lodgepole pines form dense, pure stands that are gradually invaded by Douglas-fir and other conifers.

Lodgepole pines thrive in burned areas but do not require them. What they do require is little or no competition from other conifers, and they can find that just as well in various

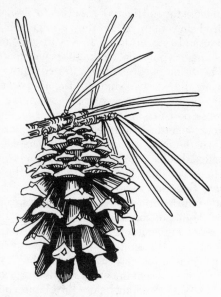

25. Lodgepole pine (*Pinus contorta*)

extreme environments. For example, in the Cascades, lodgepole pines commonly form extensive pure stands on porous
volcanic soils subjected to winter flooding and extreme summer drought. They also form climax stands on the floors of
cold cirque basins, where the combination of soggy soils,
cold-air drainage, and the briefest of sub-timberline growing
seasons is too harsh even for subalpine fir. Similarly, lodgepole pines frequently pioneer on recent glacial moraines,
where they are subjected to icy winds, raw soils, and highly
fluctuating water tables.

Lodgepole pine is a slim tree with a straight trunk and
short branches. As its name suggests, the tree once served
admirably as a source of the supports used for teepees; it
also provided the trailing poles by which Plains Indians
pulled travoises—sledges used for hauling household
goods—behind their horses. Lodgepole pine is most easily
recognized by its needles, which average about two inches
in length and, unlike those of all other western pines, grow
in bundles of two apiece. The bark has the texture of

cornflakes and ranges in color from dull reddish- or golden-brown to plain gray. The cones are up to two inches long and are often—though not always—conspicuous for remaining on the branches.

In the Northern Rockies west of the Continental Divide, lodgepole pine faces stiff competition from western larch and western white pine, which are less able to cope with extremes of heat and cold, flooding and drought, but which are admirably suited to the moist, relatively mild conditions encountered in the mountains of the inland Northwest.

Western larch is a magnificent deciduous conifer, whose new bright yellow-green needles announce the coming of spring throughout the mid-slope forests of the inland Northwest. Like lodgepole pine, it aggressively invades burned areas, but the larch grows faster than the pine and lives twice as long. Moreover, mature western larches have long, clear trunks and thick bark that enable them to survive fires that routinely consume all their associates, including lodgepoles. These surviving larches not only inhibit the success of lodgepole pine seedlings, but they increase their competitive position by continuing to reseed burned areas from year to year thereafter. As a result, western larch frequently forms pure stands on sites subjected to repeated fire.

Western larch thrives on mild, moist, north-facing slopes, where it is eventually shaded out by Douglas-fir, grand fir, and other shade-tolerant conifers. In such situations lodgepole pine competes poorly with western larch. At the same time, it fares much better in places that are too hot, too cold, too wet, or too dry for western larch. This is the case in central Oregon, for example, where warmer temperatures and less reliable summer moisture favor the pine over the larch. Many stands in the inland Northwest, however, will contain both species, with or without a number of other conifers as well.

Western larch, and its timberline cousin alpine larch, are the only two deciduous conifers in western North America. In the fall their needles turn brilliant gold before dropping; in spring their new foliage contrasts vividly with the darker, older greens of their neighboring conifers. The needles are light green, pointed, and about one to 1½ inches long. They first appear singly but later sprout in bundles of 30 to 40 from short, scaly spurs on the twigs.

Mature western larches are commonly 160 to 200 feet in height, of which the first 100 feet or so of trunk is free of branches. Such trees may be more than six feet in diameter and as much as 700 years old. The tall, clear trunk, with its thick bark, is the principal reason that western larches are able to withstand routine ground fires. The bark of mature trees is dull reddish-brown, deeply furrowed, with a zigzag or diamond pattern created by overlapping plates.

The cones of the western larch are egg-shaped and about as long as the needles. Like the cones of Douglas-fir, they have elongated bracts that extend beyond the tips of the scales. The cones open in early fall and drop from the trees shortly thereafter.

Western larch and western white pine are the two most important fire pioneers in forests of the western hemlock series. The larch, however, is much less tolerant of shade than the pine and therefore disappears from the forest mix sooner. Western white pine is able not only to invade newly burned areas but to continue producing successful seedlings even under conditions of moderate shade. As a result, larch is normally absent from old-growth white pine forests, though more shade-tolerant trees such as Douglas-fir, grand fir, western hemlock, and western redcedar are normally present.

Western white pine ranges from southern British Columbia, northwestern Montana, and northern Idaho southward through Washington to the mountains of southern California. It occurs along the coast in Washington and British Columbia but is generally a tree of the high mountains, where cool summers and a lingering snowpack reduce the risk of late-summer soil drought. The white pine reaches its greatest size in northern Idaho, northwestern Montana, and adjacent British Columbia, where it occurs in mixed forests covering millions of acres.

Western white pine is one of three pines in the Pacific Northwest whose needles grow five to a bundle (the others are sugar pine and whitebark pine). These needles are blue-green and two to four inches long. White pine cones are distinctive because they are six to ten inches long and very slim, rather like smaller versions of the cones of the sugar pine. The bark is silvery gray, sometimes purplish, and broken into small, slim, vertical pieces.

26. Mountain lover (*Pachistima myrsinites*)

Western white pine is a rapid grower, exceeded only by lodgepole pine and western larch. The trees are normally about 110 feet tall and three feet thick, though specimens up to 175 feet in height and eight feet in diameter are not uncommon. The trunks show little taper and are usually free of branches for one-half to two-thirds of their length. The crown is symmetrical and rather narrow, with branches seldom exceeding 15 feet in length.

Insects and disease have also played critical roles in the evolution of forests in the inland Northwest. Among the most destructive diseases is white pine blister rust, a fungus that has caused extensive losses of western white pine. The fungus spends part of its life on currant or gooseberry bushes, which grow commonly throughout the West, and part on the so-called white pines, which include whitebark pine and sugar pine, as well as western white pine. Since white pines and currants/gooseberries must both be present for the disease to persist, control efforts in the Northern Rockies used to consist of removing the currants and gooseberries. Western white pine appears to be developing a greater resistance to the disease, however, and the planting of resistant seedlings in clearcuts is likely to continue this trend.

Among the insects that cause significant damage to conifer

forests in the inland Northwest are the Douglas-fir tussock moth, spruce budworm, mountain pine beetle, Douglas-fir beetle, and larch casebearer. Dwarf mistletoe, a parasite on lodgepole pine, ponderosa pine, western larch, and Douglas-fir, rarely kills the host trees but renders them useless as timber. Similarly, Indian paint fungus has rendered 40 percent of the grand firs in the mountains of central Oregon valueless for the market.

CHAPTER NINE

Snow Forests

THE HIGHER MOUNTAIN ranges of the Pacific Northwest support distinctive subalpine forests composed of conifers that are able to withstand long, cold winters; cool, brief summers; and deep, persistent snows. The zone in which these conditions occur is called the subalpine zone. Its upper limit coincides with timberline, the upper limit of tree growth. Its lower boundary, however, is always blurred, blending gradually into upper-montane forest zones dominated by trees such as Shasta red fir, Pacific silver fir, western redcedar, western hemlock, grand fir, or Douglas-fir. The subalpine zone can be divided into two parts: a lower closed-forest subzone and an upper parkland or timberline subzone. The tree species that dominate the closed subalpine forests are normally the same ones found growing in scattered clusters in subalpine meadows and as sprawling shrubs near timberline. Parklands are most extensive in the Cascades and other coastal ranges, where snow is deep and long-lasting. In drier areas or where steep terrain, resistant rock, or inadequate moisture have inhibited soil formation, parks are replaced by open woodlands. With increasing elevations, most forest trees grow smaller in stature, often forming low, wind-pruned shrubs near timberline. Above timberline, alpine communities comprised of tiny mat- or cushion-forming herbs and prostrate shrubs occupy the narrow zone between the highest trees and the lower limits of perennial ice and snow.

The upper and lower elevations of the subalpine zone generally rise from north to south down the Pacific Coast in response to the warming that occurs with decreasing latitude, in particular the increase in average air temperature during the growing season. Alpine timberline occurs at 1,500 feet in south-central Alaska and from there rises to as much as 5,500 feet in southern British Columbia, 6,800 feet on Mount Rainier in Washington, 7,500 feet in southern Oregon, and 9,500 feet on Mount Shasta in northern California. Along the Canadian border, timberline increases from below 4,500 feet on the north flank of Mount Baker to 5,500 feet at Washington Pass, some 30 miles east, and more than 7,000 feet in the Okanogan Highlands and the Northern Rockies. The north-to-south rise in timberline corresponds to the warming that occurs with decreasing latitude, in particular to the increase in average air temperatures during the growing season. The rise in timberline from west to east, however, is less a function of increasing air temperature than of decreasing snowfall combined with summer cloudiness. Extraordinarily heavy winter snows combined with cool, cloudy summers result in a delayed melting of the snowpack at higher elevations west of the Cascade crest. This effectively shortens the period available to conifers for germination and seedling growth.

The subalpine forests of western North America, including the Pacific Northwest, are closely related to the transcontinental boreal forest, or taiga, which extends from New England and Newfoundland across northern Canada to western Alaska. Several conifer species in the two forests share common ancestors and apparently evolved into their present forms in the last 10,000 years, since the close of the Ice Age. For example, the subalpine conifer Engelmann spruce finds its boreal-forest counterpart in white spruce, and where the geographic ranges of the two overlap, in the Canadian Rockies and along the eastern flank of the Coast Mountains of British Columbia, cross pollenation between the two species has produced trees with intermediate characteristics. Other such pairs include alpine larch and tamarack, lodgepole pine and jack pine, and subalpine fir and balsam fir. The boreal forest and subalpine forests also share a number of understory plants, including mountain ash, twinflower, bunchberry, and wintergreens.

During the late Tertiary Period, a mixed subarctic forest containing a wide variety of both conifers and broadleaf deciduous trees stretched across the northern edge of the continent from Alaska to Newfoundland. The climate at that time was steadily growing cooler, a trend that would reach its climax in the Pleistocene Ice Age to follow. In response to the deepening cold, less hardy conifers and broadleaf trees dropped out of the community, and the forest as a whole retreated southward into what is now the northern section of the contiguous United States. Boreal conifers penetrated even farther south along the high ranges of the Rocky Mountains and the Cascade-Sierra chain. At the same time, the formation of alpine glaciers and summit ice fields pushed the boreal conifers downslope, in places even out into the nearby lowlands. Then, about 15,000 years ago, the climate began to grow warmer and drier. Valley glaciers retreated upslope, mountain ice caps shrank, and the great Cordilleran Ice Sheet slowly lurched back into Canada. Everywhere, boreal conifers followed the retreating ice, colonizing newly exposed ground much as conifers do today in southeastern Alaska. At the same time, steppe and desert vegetation marched northward through the intermontane region, largely isolating the forests of the Pacific mountain

27. Mountain hemlock (*Tsuga mertensiana*)

Snow Forests

system from those of the Rockies. Some boreal conifers retreated northward along the Sierra–Cascade axis, fleeing the deepening summer drought that now characterizes the region. Meanwhile, certain lowland and montane conifers were able to advance far upslope, where they managed to become more or less permanent fixtures along the lower boundaries of the subalpine zone. In this way what was once a more or less uniform boreal forest evolved into the distinctive regional subalpine forests that exist today throughout the western United States and Canada.

Ecologists recognize two major subalpine forest zones in the Pacific Northwest: a mountain hemlock zone and a subalpine fir zone. The mountain hemlock zone ranges from Alaska southward to northern California. It forms the highest forest zone on the seaward slopes of the Coast Mountains and Cascade Range, as well as in the Olympic Mountains, Klamath Mountains, and the ranges of Vancouver Island and the Queen Charlotte Islands. The subalpine fir zone is the principal subalpine zone of the Rocky Mountain region. In the Pacific Northwest it occurs along the inland flanks of the southern Coast Mountains* and Cascades and extends eastward to the mountains of northeastern Washington, southeastern British Columbia, central Oregon, Idaho, and Montana. Where the two zones meet along the crests of the Coast Mountains and Cascades, stands containing elements of each are found on both sides of the ranges.

The subalpine forests of southern Oregon and northern California closely resemble those found in the northern Sierra Nevada. In these forests, mountain hemlock and Sierran lodgepole pine occur in closed forests with Shasta red fir and range upslope in open woodlands to timberline with whitebark pine. The subalpine conifer forests of the Klamath Mountains are the most diverse in the world, containing more than a dozen conifer species drawn from Sierran, Northwestern, and even Rocky Mountain sources.

* The eastern slope of the northern Coast Mountains, east of the Alaska Panhandle, lies outside the geographic scope of this book. Its subalpine forest is essentially like that of the far northern, or boreal, Rockies: white spruce and subalpine fir are the principal conifers; balsam poplar and tamarack, both of which range eastward to the Atlantic Ocean, occur locally.

Mountain hemlock is the preeminent subalpine conifer in the high snowy mountain ranges that line the Pacific Coast. At the northern limit of its range, in south-central Alaska, where subalpine conditions occur near sea level, mountain hemlock grows with western hemlock and Sitka spruce in intermittent stands at the very edge of the ocean. The forest extends upslope on the nearby coastal mountains to between 1,000 and 1,500 feet. To the southeast, in the Alaska Panhandle, the upper limit ranges between 2,500 and 4,000 feet. Throughout coastal Alaska, western hemlock and mountain hemlock are the potential climax species along the coast and at higher elevation respectively, but Sitka spruce may dominate stands from tidewater to timberline. It is the first tree to invade areas recently abandoned by retreating glaciers and the most common conifer in the krummholz zone. South of Alaska, Sitka spruce is mainly restricted to coastal lowlands, suggesting that it is able to withstand cold winters only where summers are rainy.

Despite growing at the ocean's edge in Alaska, mountain hemlock, as its name suggests, is normally a tree of the heights, and southward through its range its normal elevation limits rise steadily. From southwestern British Columbia through northwestern Oregon, mountain hemlock generally occurs between 3,500 and 6,000 feet elevation. These limits increase to 5,500 and 7,500 feet in Crater Lake National Park in southern Oregon and 7,000 and 9,000 feet on the flanks of Lassen Peak in northern California. The most extensive stands of this high-country tree occur in the Cascades of central and southern Oregon. Mountain hemlock is also the dominant subalpine conifer in the northern Sierra Nevada, where it occurs in timberline stands as high as 11,000 feet. South of Yosemite, however, increasing rockiness and aridity limit the tree to intermittent stands that are mostly confined to high, cool, snowy basins. It reaches its southern limit in a small spring-watered grove situated near 10,000 feet in Sequoia National Park, near the southern end of the Sierra.

Mountain hemlock is evidently ill suited to the colder, drier conditions that characterize most inland timberlines, for along its entire range it occurs east of the highest coastal mountain chain only in the Pacific Northwest. There, sizable stands occur in southeastern British Columbia's snowy Selkirk

Range and northern Idaho's Bitterroot Mountains. The region's few other inland stands are small and scattered.

In the lower, continuous forest portion of the mountain hemlock zone, mountain hemlocks commonly attain heights of 75 to 80 feet. Trees up to 150 feet tall and three feet in diameter are fairly common in sheltered, old-growth stands. Upslope, in the timberline parkland, the tree assumes a variety of shapes depending upon growing conditions. Upright trees 20 to 30 feet tall, with branches and foliage extending clear to the ground, commonly form the core of tree islands, where they may be joined by Alaska-cedar, Pacific silver fir, subalpine fir, whitebark pine, and other conifers. On exposed sites near timberline, mountain hemlock commonly assumes the form of a huge, sprawling shrub. Small upright trees may have bushy skirts formed by layering. Although young trees have slender, pointed crowns that are admirably suited for shedding snow, mature trees, even those growing in the open, often have long, spreading branches. They are of such flexibility, however, that they can bear heavy loads of wet Pacific snow (locally called Cascade or Sierra "cement") without breaking. In open parklands small trees may become completely clothed in snow. Standing white and still, these trees are called "snow ghosts."

Flexible limbs are characteristic of many subalpine trees (for example, see Alaska-cedar below), which are routinely subjected to high winds and heavy snows. It is particularly important to young hemlocks, which are commonly bent over, like crippled old men, by heavy loads of snow. When released from their white burdens in spring, the young trees, thanks to their flexibility, are able to spring back to an upright posture.

Mountain hemlock has deep reddish-brown or purplish-brown bark and thick, dark blue-green foliage. The plump, flattened, blunt needles vary in length up to about one inch long. The needles differ from those of other hemlocks by having a pair of parallel lines—which are actually stomata—on both surfaces instead of just the lower one. Unlike those of the western hemlock, the needles are arranged spirally so as to stick out from all sides of a twig. This bottle-brush arrangement often causes the tree to be mistaken for a spruce. The confusion is quickly cleared up by testing the tips of the needles. Those of Engelmann and Sitka spruces,

oth of which occur locally with mountain hemlock, end in
noticeably sharp points, while those of the hemlock are
blunt.

The staminate cones are bright purple and hang from the
previous year's twigs. The purple or yellow-green pistillate
cones are usually about two inches long and cluster at the
ends of branches. They begin by growing upright but soon
begin to hang from their increasing weight. Their blunt,
rounded scales and cylindrical shape make them resemble
spruce cones, except that the latter have thin papery scales
whereas the hemlock's are thicker and woody. The small
seeds are borne in pairs beneath each scale. Each seed has
a diaphanous wing, which allows it to ride the wind for
great distances. Although good seed crops occur at roughly
three-year intervals, germination rates are low. Relatively
few young trees are able to survive in the dense, shady
forests formed by this species. Seedling survival dramatically increases, however, where forest yields to parklands.
Once a seedling is established in these high, open meadows,
layering is thereafter more important than seed success as
a means of regeneration.

Throughout its long, narrow range, which spans some
2,000 miles and more than 20 degrees of latitude, mountain
hemlock consorts with more than a dozen species of conifers.
From southern Alaska to central Oregon, its major associates
are Pacific silver fir and Alaska-cedar, either of which may
dominate particular habitats. Both also occur in stands dominated by mountain hemlock and range with it upslope into
timberline parklands. Although mountain hemlock is tolerant of shade, Pacific silver fir is more so. Throughout its
range in northern Oregon and all of Washington, Pacific
silver fir is probably the climax species in old-growth closed
forests in the mountain hemlock zone. Although mature
mountain hemlocks are usually present in these stands,
younger hemlocks are not, while Pacific silver fir is represented by trees of all ages. At higher elevations, however,
seedlings of Pacific silver fir are usually killed by summer
frosts, while those of mountain hemlock routinely survive
them. Young firs are also more vulnerable to limb breakage
as a result of heavy snow loads. Consequently, Pacific silver
fir is able to venture into parklands only in the shelter of
hardier conifers, notably mountain hemlock. (For more in-

formation on Pacific silver fir, see Chapter 6.)

Alaska-cedar occurs with mountain hemlock in southeastern Alaska and ranges southward with it through southern Oregon. South of Mount Hood, however, Alaska-cedar is much less common and does not occur at timberline, as it does farther north. In California the tree is confined only to a few stands in the Klamath Mountains. These would appear to be relicts left over from the Ice Age, when the tree occurred more widely. A couple of other far-flung relict stands occur east of the Cascades, but otherwise Alaska-cedar is even more closely dependent than mountain hemlock on the cold, wet maritime climate of the coastal mountains. This is borne out too by the failure of Alaska-cedar (as well as Pacific silver fir) to accompany mountain hemlock into the drier climes of the Sierra Nevada. In Washington and British Columbia, mixed stands of mountain hemlock, Alaska-cedar, and Pacific silver fir are common, though Alaska-cedar seldom dominates. At lower elevations, Alaska-cedar also mixes with western hemlock, Douglas-fir, and western redcedar.

Alaska-cedar requires abundant moisture throughout the growing season. It is therefore most common on northern slopes, along streams, and in cool, damp ravines and bottoms. In northern British Columbia and southeastern Alaska, the tree ranges down to sea level, but from there southward to northwestern Oregon it is most commonly found at elevations between 3,000 and 6,500 feet.

Alaska-cedar is easily distinguished from its associates by its droopy sprays of blue-green foliage. Its small, flattened, scalelike leaves, like those of western redcedar, grow in opposite overlapping pairs closely pressed to their stems. The leaves of Alaska-cedar end in sharp, flaring points, however, which give the sprays a prickly feeling, unlike those of redcedar. The bark is reddish-brown on younger trees but dark gray and shreddy on older ones. Alaska-cedars commonly live well over 1,000 years, attaining diameters of three to four feet and heights of about 100 feet. The presence of natural fungicides in its wood may partly account for the tree's longevity.

Since Alaska-cedar is less tolerant of shade and grows more slowly than its companions, it is rarely the dominant conifer. It maintains its presence in the forest, however, by outlasting its companions and thriving in habitats where they fare poorly. These include poorly drained areas and poor, wet, mineral soils that form a thin veneer over bedrock. Near timberline, Alaska-cedar forms krummholz on outcrops of bare rock, where fractures provide roots with easy access to deep reservoirs of moisture.

Subalpine fir is a frequent associate of mountain hemlock on parkland sites from Alaska to southern Oregon. The two species commonly occur together in tree islands on both sides of the Cascades and Coast Mountains. Subalpine firs often form closed forests on warm, relatively dry, south-facing slopes in the mountain hemlock zone. In rainshadow areas, such as the northeastern corner of the Olympic Mountains or the northeastern side of Mount Rainier, subalpine fir commonly replaces mountain hemlock as the dominant parkland conifer. At the other extreme, subalpine fir is scarce in the snowiest parts of the zone. For example, relatively few subalpine firs occur on or around Mount Baker, which rises on the western edge of Washington's snowy, cloudy North Cascades. Although subalpine fir is rarely prominent in closed mountain hemlock forests, even in drier areas, it does form closed stands on dry, disturbed sites in Oregon's High Cascades.

Lodgepole pine is also an important pioneer species in the mountain hemlock zone, particularly in Oregon and northern California. It is a prolific seeder that rapidly invades recently burned or otherwise disturbed areas. It is also able to establish itself and persist indefinitely on soils that are poorly drained or otherwise inhospitable to most other conifers. Extensive stands of lodgepole pine occur in the mountain hemlock zone on pumice soils in the High Cascades of southern Washington and Oregon. Throughout much of Oregon and northern California, lodgepole pines are also characteristic of poorly drained flats, meadow margins, and glacially scoured basins.

A number of other conifers also associate with mountain hemlock. Engelmann spruce, which is most common on the east side of the Cascades, occurs sparingly in subalpine parklands and frost pockets on the western slope, as well as in the rainshadow area of the northeastern Olympic Mountains. Except in the snowiest areas, whitebark pine often forms a timberline above mountain hemlock and occurs

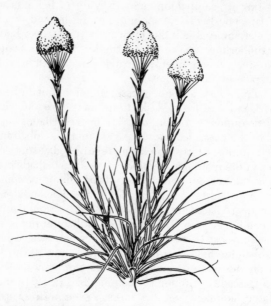

28. Beargrass (*Xerophyllum tenax*)

with it in tree islands. Noble fir is a long-lived seral species on burned sites in the lower mountain hemlock zone of southern Washington and northern Oregon. Shasta red fir occurs with mountain hemlock in southern Oregon and northern California. Coastal conifers such as Douglas-fir, western redcedar, and western hemlock range upslope in small numbers into the lower mountain hemlock zone.

Understory vegetation within the dark interior of the forest can be quite sparse, consisting of a few plants scattered among the fallen limbs and thick carpets of needles. Other stands have ample plant cover beneath the trees but only a few species may be represented. From British Columbia to central Oregon, for example, many stands have understories consisting of big huckleberry or beargrass. Some stands seem to be either all huckleberry or all beargrass, while others contain ample numbers of both. In addition, a few low shade plants such as one-sided wintergreen and dwarf bramble may be present, but that's about all. The low-growing grouse whortleberry is also prominent in the dry, sparse understories characteristic of mountain hemlock forests that occur along the Cascade crest in central and southern Oregon.

Lush, shrubby understories develop in moist habitats, where Alaska-cedar is a prominent member of the forest. The shrub layer is monopolized by the heath family. On northern exposures, spring-watered slopes, and stream-banks, the most prominent shrubs include Cascade azalea, big huckleberry, ovalleaf huckleberry, and fool's huckleberry. Copper bush is the dominant shrub in British Columbia, though it apparently favors somewhat drier habitats. Though not members of the heath family, mountain-ashes are also common. Dwarf bramble and strawberry bramble, which spread by means of runners, occur as low ground covers. Sitka valerian, evergreen violet, and avalanche lily are among the commoner herbs.

Near the upper limits of the closed forest, sunny openings become increasingly common, and these often feature impressive displays of wildflowers. Talus slopes and open areas of bedrock where runoff or springs moisten pockets or crevices of soil host a wide variety of plants, including red columbine, Sitka valerian, stonecrops, red mountain-heather, and rock brake. Cascade huckleberry often forms a low, rather thick ground cover in moist, sunny openings. Showy wildflowers such as broadleaf arnica, glacier lily, and paint-brushes are often plentiful in such places.

Boggy meadows, which are rather common in the mountain hemlock zone, develop on poorly drained valley floors. Small ponds often linger through the summer in the wettest parts of the meadow, while the drier fringes commonly dry out in late summer. Where the water table remains high through the growing season, the vegetation mostly consists of marsh and bog communities dominated by sedges. Grasses and scouring rushes are also prominent. Sphagnum moss forms quaking mats at the margins of ponds. Moisture-loving shrubs such as Sitka alder, willow, high bush cranberry, and blue fly honeysuckle ring the marshes, often forming a thick skirt at the forest's edge.

In southwestern Oregon and northern California, Shasta red fir is the climax species in a zone just below the mountain hemlock zone (see Chapter 7). Mountain hemlock is a major associate in forests dominated by Shasta red fir, and the latter ranges upslope as a minor associate in mountain hemlock forests. These two trees are major elements in the subalpine forests of the Klamath Mountains, which are surely the richest and most diverse conifer forests in the world. More than a dozen different conifers occur in the Klamath forests, including the lovely, weeping Brewer's spruce, which occurs nowhere else in the world. These forests also contain relict stands of subalpine fir, Port-Orford-cedar, Alaska-cedar, noble fir, Engelmann spruce, and Pacific silver fir, all of which are found nowhere else in California. These and other Northwest species ranged as far south as the southern Sierra Nevada as recently as 10,000 years ago. They gradually withdrew northward to their present ranges in response to decreasing summer precipitation. Their persistence in the Klamath Mountains is no doubt a result of the cooler, wetter summer climate of extreme northwestern California and southeastern Oregon.

Along the east side of the Cascades and from there east to the Rocky Mountains, subalpine fir replaces mountain hemlock as the most prominent subalpine conifer both in closed forests and in open parklands near timberline. Its most frequent associate, particularly along streams and in high, moist basins, is Engelmann spruce. Lodgepole pine is the most common and widespread seral conifer in the subalpine fir zone, growing in a variety of habitats from mid-elevation forests to near timberline. Douglas-fir is a frequent associate in the lower, closed-forest portion of the subalpine fir zone, where grand fir, western larch, or western white pine may also be present. Whitebark pine and alpine larch are commonly found in parklands and open woodlands ranging upslope to timberline. Whitebark pine may grow either upright or as a sprawling timberline shrub. Alpine larch remains erect, however, even in the highest, most exposed sites.

Throughout their shared ranges in the Middle and Southern Rockies and the interior Northwest, subalpine fir and Engelmann spruce are considered co-climax species. Pure stands of both trees are common. Mountain hemlock mixes with subalpine fir along the east side of the Cascades and forms scattered climax stands in especially cool, snowy places in the mountains of southeastern British Columbia and northern Idaho and Montana. Throughout the region, subalpine fir ranges above Engelmann spruce to timberline.

The subalpine fir zone occurs above 4,900 feet along the crest and east side of the Cascade Range and 5,500 feet in the northern Rockies. Timberline occurs between 6,000 and 8,000 feet over this same area. Subalpine fir and Engelmann spruce both range farther downslope, however, in canyon bottoms and basin floors where cold air drains and accumulates each night. In these "frost pockets," subalpine fir may occur as low as 2,500 feet and Engelmann spruce down to 1,700 feet.

Subalpine fir has the greatest geographic range of any North American fir: from the Yukon south through the Pacific mountain ranges to southern Oregon and through the Rockies to New Mexico and Arizona. Subalpine firs grow with mountain hemlock in timberline parklands along and west of the Cascade crest. Scattered stands also occur at low to middle elevations along the western side of the Cascades, often on

29. Subalpine fir (*Abies lasiocarpa*)

lava flows. Subalpine fir appears able to grow in the we
maritime climate of the Pacific slope, but it is apparently
unable to compete in closed forests with mountain hemlock
Pacific silver fir, western hemlock, and western redcedar
all of which are more tolerant of shade. Subalpine fir i
common in the parklands of Hurricane Ridge and elsewhere
in the northeastern Olympics, which lie in the rainshadow
of the central Olympic massif to the west. A lot of pure
stands also occur on high, dry, south-facing slopes, such a
Sunrise Ridge, on the northeast side of Mount Rainier.

Subalpine fir is distinctive for its steeplelike crown and
narrowly conical shape, which is quite unlike that of any
other conifer in North America. In open areas at least, the
tree is densely cloaked with deep green needles from the
tip of the leader down to the ground, where brushy skirts
develop beneath the protective cover of the snowpack. I
closed forests the trees normally abandon lower branches
but rarely develop the long, clear trunks so common to
other forest conifers. The fir's short, stiff branches are un
usual among subalpine trees, most of which have flexible
limbs that allow them to bear the weight of snow without
breaking. The tree's slender profile and thick foliage, however, allow it to shed snow rather than bear it.

Subalpine fir has smooth, light gray bark. The needles
are one to 1¾ inches long and flattened, with white stomata
lines on both surfaces. Closely packed, they radiate from
all sides of the twig and usually point upward. The purple
cones are 2¼ to four inches long and grow erect on the
upper branches. Large crops of seeds are produced every
three to four years, but few are viable. Subalpine firs invade
new areas by means of wind-borne seeds, but once established the trees increase their numbers through layering.

Mature subalpine firs 200 years old may be 140 feet tall,
with trunks two to three feet in diameter. More often, however, the trees are less than 100 feet tall with trunks a foot
or so in diameter. Shrubby firs growing on exposed sites
near timberline may be only a couple of feet tall. Like most
subalpine trees, subalpine fir grows slowly. A leisurely rate
of growth is an advantage given the brief amount of time
available each year to subalpine trees for the addition o
new tissue. Slow growth is also an advantage in shady situations, where young trees may have to bide their time before

an opening in the forest canopy triggers a rapid spurt upward. Subalpine firs are often among the first trees to become established in openings in the wake of fire or other disturbance, but they are soon overtopped by such fast-growing opportunists as Douglas-fir, western larch, western white pine, and lodgepole pine.

Engelmann spruce occurs in every western state except Nevada, though it is extremely rare in California, where it is limited to a few cool, moist places in the Klamath Mountains. It also ranges northward into Canada to central British Columbia, where it mingles with white spruce, its analogue in the boreal forest. Where the two species overlap, trees with intermediate characteristics may be encountered.

In the Pacific Northwest, Engelmann spruce is most commonly encountered in stream bottoms or in high, cold basins, where snow melt keeps the soil damp throughout the growing season. Though normally found at elevations between 3,000 and 7,000 feet in the Pacific Northwest, it ranges downslope along streams to as low as 1,700 feet. Engelmann spruce also occurs in smaller numbers in a variety of drier habitats, including exposed places near timberline.

Typical bottomland spruces have slender, dense crowns with branchlets that hang vertically from the main limbs. Such trees are normally three feet thick and between 120 and 140 feet tall. In parklands and other open areas, spruces commonly bear branches clear to the ground. Near timberline they may form sprawling shrubs.

Engelmann spruce grows slowly but not as slowly as subalpine fir. Where the two grow together, the larger and faster-growing spruce usually dominates the canopy, while smaller, repressed firs prevail in the understory. In some stands, however, young spruces may also be present.

Engelmann spruce is readily distinguished from other western conifers by its sharp, stiff, four-sided needles, which radiate from all sides of the twig. The needles are attached to little pegs, which remain intact after the needles have fallen. The bark is thin, purplish or reddish, and broken into loose flakes. The seed-bearing cones hang from the upper branches. Initially bright red in color, the slender one- to 2½-inch-long cones darken to purple then turn light brown when mature. The scales are rounded and papery in texture.

Closed stands of subalpine fir or Engelmann spruce com
monly have brushy understories, but the dominant specie
of shrub varies according to habitat. The lower portion c
the closed spruce-fir forest features the same collection c
understory species that occur in moister habitats withi
adjacent midslope forests dominated by Douglas-fir, gran
fir, western hemlock, or western redcedar. Vine maple
white spiraea, western serviceberry, and western re
baneberry are characteristic of these lower forests but occu
nowhere else in the subalpine fir zone. Wildflowers suc
as queen's cup, bedstraw, heartleaf arnica, trail plant, starr
mitrewort, and white-flowered hawkweed are similarl
restricted.

Forests on higher south-facing slopes and ridgetops
where conditions tend to be warmer and drier, generall
have understories consisting of little other than beargras
or big huckleberry. Except for the dominant conifers, thes
stands are very similar to mountain hemlock forests contain
ing the same understory species.

Closed spruce-fir forests on northern exposures, in well
watered basins, and along the bottoms of damp ravine
commonly feature lush shrub layers in which fool
huckleberry is prominent. Cascade azalea or Labrador-te
may also be present. Similar mountain hemlock communi
ties exist in northern Idaho.

Drier habitats often feature rather open forests in whic
grouse whortleberry forms a low ground cover. Red moun
tain-heather, another ground-hugging shrub, also may b
conspicuous. Common juniper, big huckleberry, and dwar
huckleberry are typical associates. Among the large variet
of wildflowers that grow in this habitat, heartleaf arnica
white-flowered hawkweed, and various asters are common.

Open woodlands in which whitebark pine and subalpin
fir occur together are common in colder, drier portions c
the timberline zone, where moisture and soil are inadequat
for the development of parkland. Whitebark pine and sub
alpine fir also occur together in tree islands within the park
lands, with or without the other usual subalpine conifers.

Lodgepole pine is the most common and widespread c
the several seral conifers found in the subalpine fir zone
Pure, even-aged lodgepole stands occur in burned or logge
areas. Lodgepole pines may form climax stands on soils tha

are too poor, thin, or waterlogged to support fellow conifers. For example, waterlogged soils covering the floors of high cirque basins may support lodgepoles, while forests on adjacent slopes are dominated by subalpine firs. Where conditions are less extreme, lodgepoles may invade new territory only to be supplanted in time by the slower-growing Engelmann spruce and subalpine fir. Lodgepole pine is highly intolerant of shade and cannot maintain its place in dark old-growth spruce or fir stands.

Small meadows that are essentially downslope extensions of subalpine parklands occur on poorly drained sites within the closed forest. Wet meadows, or fens, in which sedges and grasses predominate, occur in poorly drained areas bordering lakes, in basins where former lakes have been replaced by vegetation, and along meandering streams on the flat floors of glaciated valleys. Acidic bogs occur on poorly drained sites at higher, colder elevations. Mountain laurel, bog cranberry, creeping snowberry, the insectivorous sundews, and sphagnum moss are characteristic of true bogs. Delicate bog orchids and the beautiful lady's tresses commonly grow along their margins.

Parks dominated by lowland grasses and shrubs form on ridgetops and adjacent south-facing slopes within the closed-forest portion of the subalpine fir zone. During the winter, these exposed ridges and slopes are commonly stripped of snow by high winds. As a result, conifer seedlings that might become established on such sites are exposed to lethal winter desiccation and wind damage. These high, dry parklands are dominated by bluebunch wheatgrass and Idaho fescue, which are also among the most common perennial bunchgrasses in the lowland steppes of eastern Washington and Oregon. Growing among the grasses are low, fragrant clumps of mountain sagebrush, a high-altitude form of big sagebrush, which covers tens of thousands of acres throughout the intermountain West. Sandberg's bluegrass, yarrow, low sagebrush, and bitter cherry are among the other steppe plants found in these mountain communities.

Scientists often speak of three different kinds of timberlines: arctic timberline, lower timberline, and alpine timberline. In the Far North the arctic timberline designates the northernmost limit of tree growth, the place where stunted spruces yield to arctic tundra. Most western mountain ranges have two timberlines. The lower timberline occurs where trees yield to grassland or scrub in the face of steadily increasing aridity. The upper or alpine timberline is the one most people mean when they use the term. Alpine timberline designates the upper limit of tree growth on a mountainside, the line beyond which conditions are too cold to support upright woody vegetation.

Alpine timberline is actually a broad ecotone, a transitional area between continuous subalpine forests downslope and treeless alpine communities at higher elevations. The forest line divides the lower continuous forest subzone from the upper timberline subzone. The transition from forest to subalpine parkland or woodland may be gradual or rather abrupt, depending on local soils and topography. Subalpine parkland consists of meadow communities dotted with tree islands. Parkland forms where deep, persistent snows preclude the development of forest. The most extensive parklands occur in the Northern Cascades, Olympic Mountains, and other coastal ranges. Subalpine woodland consists of widely scattered trees interspersed with areas of meadow, bare soil, or outcrops of rock. Woodland commonly forms on thin, stony soils, rock outcrops, or steep slopes and may dominate such sites even in areas where parkland is extensive. Woodland is usually most extensive in drier subalpine regions, where soil formation is slower and summer precipitation is minimal.

Woodland and parkland both feature upright trees, though these are often smaller than those of the same species in the continuous forest nearby. Many timberline trees feature multiple trunks or produce shrubby skirts of foliage as well as upright trunks. The upper limit of upright trees, or tree line, is usually hard to trace and commonly zig-zags up and down in response to local topography. Above the tree line lies the krummholz belt, where tree species grow only as prostrate shrubs. The krummholz line marks the upper limit of shrubby trees, as well as of the timberline subzone. Since the other plants growing in the krummholz belt are generally dwarf alpine herbs and shrublets, it is also commonly treated as the lowest part of the alpine zone.

The amount of heat available during the growing season appears to be far more important than winter cold in determining regional timberlines. Timberline trees, after all, remain dormant through the winter. High winds may shear their branches; blowing ice and snow may deform them or stunt their growth; frosts and winter desiccation may wither young shoots—but the trees endure to sprout another season. In fact, timberline trees as a group are among the longest-lived species. Measurements taken along arctic and alpine timberlines in Eurasia as well as North America have shown them both to correspond approximately to the 50°F isotherm for the warmest month, which is normally July. In other words, beyond timberline the average temperature for the warmest month falls below 50°F.

That timberline should be more sensitive to summer than winter temperatures makes sense. The warmer months from late spring through early autumn are the only ones when timberline trees are active, when growth and regeneration occur. Although subalpine conifers are able to carry out photosynthesis and other metabolic processes at lower temperatures than other types of trees, they too have certain minimum heat requirements that must be met. Timberline would appear to be the place where that minimum is reached. Even so, the ways in which plants respond to air temperature, either by itself or in combination with other environmental factors, are various and complex. As a result, while there is broad agreement that summertime warmth is the most important factor governing alpine timberlines, the precise mechanisms involved and their relative importance remain matters of debate.

Numerous hypotheses have been put forward to explain the existence of alpine timberlines. One that was formerly popular but is no longer widely held suggests that timberline occurs at an elevation where there is enough heat to carry out photosynthesis but not enough to add new woody tissue. The extraordinarily slow growth rates of timberline trees, some of whose annual growth rings are so thin that they can be detected only with the assistance of a microscope, would seem to support this view. As some researchers have suggested, however, slow growth seems more like a positive adaptation to timberline than a negative effect. By growing slowly, a tree is more likely to be able to ripen its new shoots before the onset of killing autumn frosts.

According to a more recent hypothesis, timberline occurs where too little warmth is available during the brief growing season for trees to ripen new growth. Ripening is the proces whereby new tissues lose their initial succulence and de velop the woody or cutinized skins of mature stems and leaves. Ripe shoots are more resistant to both frost damage and winter desiccation. Frost damage involves the formation of ice crystals in the interstices of cells. Winter desiccation occurs when shoots are induced to transpire moisture into the atmosphere at a time when frozen roots are unable to replace it from the soil. Shoots that have ripened, or "hardened off," are better able to withstand lower temperatures before freezing, and they have larger intercellular spaces in which ice crystals can form without causing severe damage Ripened tissues are also better able to resist daytime heating during the dead of winter and to control moisture los through the closing of stomates during times of stress.

Frost damage may also play a role in determining upper timberlines. Conifers growing near timberline are most vul nerable to frost damage in midsummer, before the season' new shoots have ripened. Killing frosts may occur at subal pine heights at any time during the summer. Above timber line, summer frosts occur often enough to kill back new growth.

Along the Pacific Coast, increases in air temperature from north to south are reflected in a gradual rise in timberline from as low as 1,000 feet in south-central Alaska to 3,500 feet in the Alaska Panhandle, 6,000 feet in western Washing ton, 7,500 feet in northwestern Oregon, and 9,000 feet in northernmost California.

Variations in regional timberlines occur in response to local conditions of snow, wind, cloudiness, topography, soil and other factors. In the Pacific Northwest heavy winter snowfall combined with frequent summer cloudiness seem to be an especially important factor in lowering the timber line on the western slopes of the coastal mountain ranges Snowfall near timberline in the Washington Cascades aver ages more than 500 inches a year. In many years cool, cloudy summers cause melting to proceed so slowly that the snow pack persists through much or nearly all of the summer Heavy, lingering snows can severely damage young tree and prevent new ones from getting established. A persisten summer cloud cover not only retards melting but, by block ing the sun, creates cooler conditions at all elevations. Both factors working together act to lower timberlines. Along the international border, for example, timberline rises from an elevation of about 6,000 feet in the cool, snowy Mount Baker region to 8,000 feet in the warmer, drier Pasayten Wilderness, which is located 70 miles to the east in the rainshadow of the main peaks. Farther east yet, in the mountains of northwestern Montana, timberline occurs at roughly 9,000 feet. Although the western slopes of these ranges actually receive more snow than the Pasayten, the greater number of sunny days during the late spring and early summer melt the snow pack more quickly.

Timberline areas are subject to high winds throughout the winter, when a succession of storms moves across western North America. Storm winds strike from a southern or southwestern direction as they circulate counterclockwise around their associated low-pressure cells. High winds remove snow from exposed south- and southwest-facing slopes and deposit it in deep drifts on northern and northeastern slopes. Removal of snow from windward slopes may lower timberline by exposing young or prostrate trees to killing frosts, winter desiccation, or physical damage from windblown ice or snow. At the same time, the deep drifts of snow that accumulate on slopes facing away from the wind persist well into summer and may thereby lower timberline in the manner discussed earlier.

Winds are also largely responsible for the appearance of vegetation near timberline. Many trees that grow upright at lower elevations assume prostrate, shrubby forms near timberline. Known as elfinwood or krummholz, these dwarfed trees are characteristic of timberline regions. Ranging from just over one foot to as much as four feet tall, the height of these dwarfed trees corresponds roughly to normal snow depths wherever they happen to be growing. Shoots that stick up above the surface of the snow are quickly pruned back by the wind or succumb to winter desiccation. Since vertical growth is thus discouraged, krummholz trees are, in effect, trained by the wind to grow laterally instead. As the limbs extend outward they sprout new shoots wherever they touch the ground (layering). These new shoots grow upward until they reach the height of the snow-pack surface, whereupon they too are encouraged to change direction. Growth tends to be directed away from the wind, so that the oldest portion of the tree is the one most exposed to the blast. The older, upwind segments of the krummholz colony are generally the first to die, even as the younger, downwind members continue their slow advance into new territory. In this way krummholz stands can creep downwind 50 feet or more.

Below tree limit, one commonly encounters trees with one or more upright trunks and dense, krummholz-like skirts at their bases. The skirts developed under the protective cover of the snow pack. The upright shoots are ones that grew enough during their first summer to lift them well above the snow surface, where abrasion from snow and ice particles is most severe. Not all subalpine conifers, however, grow multiple trunks. Subalpine fir and alpine larch, for example, almost always occur as upright single-trunked trees. Mountain hemlock and whitebark pine, however, may have one or several trunks depending on their circumstances and, to some degree perhaps, their genetic make-up.

Upright timberline trees that grow in places exposed to high winds commonly have no branches on the windward side of their trunks, while the sheltered side may have numerous branches stretching downwind like pennants on a mast. Known as flagging, this asymmetric growth habit occurs when winds persistently break or otherwise kill young branches that sprout on the windward side of the trunk. Where winds are particularly fierce, large areas of bark may also be missing.

Tree islands are widely scattered groves that occur within subalpine parklands and woodlands. Often the groves consist of only a few trees; sometimes they are larger. Each tree island begins with a single tree that through a combination of fortunate circumstances has managed to establish itself out in the open, away from the forest's edge. Knolls, rocky outcrops, and other high ground provide the best chance of success because they generally have better drainage and are free of snow earlier than low-lying areas. The founding trees in tree islands are usually the hardiest species, such as mountain hemlock and whitebark pine. The pioneers not only provide shelter from the wind but act as "black bodies" that absorb solar heat. The result is a warmer microclimate than exists in the open. For example, snow commonly melts completely from around a tree sooner than

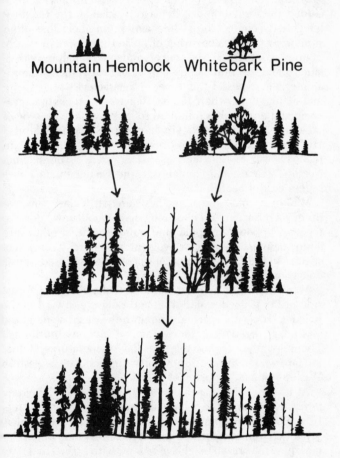

30. Two possible sequences leading to the formation of a tree island (adapted from Franklin and Dyrness, *Natural Vegetation of Oregon and Washington*)

it does in the open, thereby lengthening the growing season for young trees. Tree islands expand as successive generations of young trees become established around the periphery of the older ones. A so-called "timber atoll" occurs when the oldest trees in a tree island die, leaving an opening in the center. The shrubby skirts around the periphery of tree islands are produced through layering.

Where slow soil development or general aridity has precluded the formation of extensive parklands, the territory lying between the forest line and krummholz line often supports a mosaic consisting of pocket meadows in poorly drained basins where soil collects and open subalpine woodlands on high ground, steep slopes, and rock outcrops. Subalpine landscapes of this type are characteristic of granite mountain ranges, where the resistance of the rocks to weathering and erosion has inhibited soil formation. This type of subalpine landscape reaches its finest expression in California's High Sierra but is well represented in the Northwest in Idaho's Sawtooth Mountains and in large areas of Washington's North Cascades, most notably in the Enchantment Lakes region east of Seattle.

Whitebark pine and alpine larch are particularly successful in such terrain, often forming open woodlands, alone or together or with lodgepole pine, subalpine fir, or other subalpine conifers. Understory vegetation generally consists of species found in either adjacent meadows or closed forests downslope.

Whitebark pine is most numerous along the drier east side of the Cascades and on inland ranges eastward to the Rockies. It occurs sparingly along the western slope of the Cascades, becoming increasingly common southward. Though whitebark pine tolerates low temperatures, it does not fare well in the cool, snowy maritime climate of western Washington and British Columbia.

At its lower limits, near the upper margins of the closed forest, whitebark pine commonly grows as a slim forest tree. In sheltered subalpine woodlands, where trees are widely separated and competition is therefore less intense, whitebark pine may reach heights of 80 feet, with a trunk diameter of three to four feet. Near the upper limit of erect trees, it normally develops two or more slim trunks, which rise from a skirt of branches. Above the tree line or in exposed locations this hardy conifer grows as a low, wind-pruned shrub, often forming nearly impenetrable thickets. In the highest, coldest, most wind-blasted sites, whitebark pine may occur as a prostrate mat barely a foot or two high.

Whitebark pine gets its name from the smooth white bark of young trees. As trees mature, the bark turns gray and scaly. Growth is slow, however, and trees may not reach full size for 500 to 700 years. Like western white pine, with which it occurs in some places, whitebark pine bears its yellow-green needles in bundles of five. While those of white pine are slender and flexible, however, the needles of whitebark pine are fat and stiff. The cones are only one to three inches long, more or less spherical, and purplish in hue. Unlike the cones of all other North American pines, they disintegrate on the trees, like fir cones do, rather than falling to the ground first. Before that happens, however, most cones are picked clean by Clark's nutcracker, the large gray, black, and white timberline "jay" that occurs throughout western North America wherever whitebark pines are found.

Whitebark pines ooze with sticky pitch, as anyone who has camped near them can attest. This same pitch makes their branches extremely flexible, which helps the trees bear heavy loads of snow without breaking. Wind-blown snow and ice, however, often blast away the bark of exposed timberline specimens, polishing the inner wood to a rich, warm reddish-brown.

Foxtail pine is the dominant timberline tree in the central and southern Sierra, where it forms open woodlands at elevations as high as 12,000 feet. The only other place in the world this pine occurs is at timberline in the Klamath Mountains, about 300 miles north of its Sierran range. The absence of this tree from the northern Sierra may be the result of increasing summer drought over the past 10,000 years. The Klamath Mountains and southern Sierra both receive greater amounts of summer precipitation than does the northern Sierra.

Unlike most timberline trees, foxtail pine remains upright even in the highest, coldest, most exposed locations. Such specimens are often badly twisted and have been almost entirely stripped of bark and foliage by the wind. Often a narrow ribbon of bark extending up the sheltered, downwind side of the tree will be all that supports the few remaining tufts of foliage. Yet such trees may be more than 2,000 years old. In more sheltered locations, foxtail pine grow up to 60 feet tall and five feet thick at shoulder height. Like the whitebark pine, the foxtail pine bears its needles in bundles of five. Unlike the needles of the whitebark pine, however, those of the foxtail pine are generally less than 1½ inches long and are crowded along the twig, forming a dense bottle-brush or foxtail—hence the name. In contrast, the needles of whitebark pine are usually longer than 1½ inches and tend to be clustered at the end of the twig.

The only tree to rival, indeed surpass, whitebark and foxtail pines in their ability to withstand the highest, coldest, most exposed timberline sites is alpine larch, which forms open woodlands at or above the highest elevations reached by other subalpine trees. Alpine larch rarely occurs below 5,000 feet elevation, and relatively few people have seen it up close because only a few roads venture into its high kingdom. Of these, one of the most frequently traveled is U.S. 12, the North Cascades Highway, which winds through alpine larch country near Washington Pass before winding its way down the eastern slope of the range toward the Methow Valley.

Alpine larch is found only in the high mountains of the interior Northwest. It ranges southward down the eastern side of the North Cascades from Manning Provincial Park in southern British Columbia to the Stuart Range east of Seattle. Alpine larch also occurs widely in the Northern Rockies of southeastern British Columbia, neighboring Alberta, northern Idaho, and western Montana. Between the Cascades and the Rockies is a gap of some 125 miles in which alpine larch does not occur because the mountains there are not high enough to support it.

Alpine larch is one of only two conifers in the Northwest that are deciduous, the other being western larch, which grows at mid-elevations over much of the same range as its timberline cousin. Clusters of needles grow in bundles attached to short spur twigs; individual needles are about one inch long, stiff, bluish-green, and four-angled. In fall they turn a rich burnished yellow that makes the high country glow.

Purplish cones appear with the new needles each June

The cones are about 1½ to two inches long, barrel-shaped, and stand upright on the twigs. In most years, however, the young cones are killed straight away by frosts, which blackens them like a blight. Since alpine larch does not regenerate vegetatively through layering, reproduction most years is negligible. Even when cones do survive, few seeds land in appropriate places for germination to occur. And those that do germinate have little chance of surviving in the harsh timberline habitat. Successful reproduction of alpine larch therefore apparently depends on a combination of large seed crops, warm springs, and suitable conditions for seedling survival thereafter. Since the trees reach 500 to 700 years of age, however, there is plenty of time for such unusual years to occur.

Mature larches often reach three feet in diameter and 70 feet in height. More often, they are 30 to 50 feet tall and one to two feet thick. The bark is thin, dark reddish-brown, and broken into plates. Often it encases a tough shell of outer wood while the heart of the tree is hollow from rot. Even so, larches are rarely toppled by wind or broken by loads of snow.

Larches are timberline pioneers, marching into places too hostile for most other subalpine trees. Once established, however, the larches provide enough protection to allow less hardy types such as subalpine fir and Engelmann spruce to become established beneath them. Eventually, these conifers create a shaded understory in which young larches are unable to survive.

CHAPTER TEN

Living with Conifers

THE CONIFER FORESTS of the Pacific Northwest contain an assortment of plant communities that provide distinctive habitats for numerous species of wildlife. Stands of different ages, structure, and composition are intermingled with meadows, brush fields, cliffs, lakes, streams, and other openings, each providing wildlife with different sources and types of food and opportunities for cover. The greater the diversity of food and cover in a given area, the greater the number of wildlife species that will be present.

The types of food and cover available to wildlife ultimately depend on the structure and composition of the vegetation. While it is true that some creatures—notably butterflies and certain birds—are rather closely tied to particular species or genera of plants, most animals are far less choosy. For example, old-growth western hemlock forests and white fir forests share numerous animals in common because it is far more important to wildlife that both stands are mature conifer formations than that the dominant conifers happen to be different. On the other hand, the assortment of animals found in an open sapling-shrub stand of either type will be different from those of later successional stages. Certain species of wildlife, however, will be found in all stages.

For these reasons the three main forest regions discussed in previous chapters—Northwest Coastal, Rocky Mountain, and Southwest Oregonian/Northwest Californian—are much more alike than different in the types of habitats they provide for animals. This essential similarity is why the majority of wildlife species found in one of the forest regions—black bears, yellow-rumped warblers, and Pacific treefrogs, for example—are also found in one or both of the others. The fact that all the forests are dominated by conifers is far more important to most species of wildlife than are regional differences in the kinds or relative abundance of particular conifer species. Lacking mobility in the normal sense, plants are much more dependent than animals on the physical environment. Animals do respond to local and regional differences in climate and topography, and a few burrowing species, such as pocket gophers or moles, even have soil preferences, but most animals are able simply to move on if conditions don't suit them. As a result, they are rarely restricted to particular habitats. Most wildlife species roam freely among several habitats, and many regularly utilize different ones for different purposes. For example, chipmunks often nest in rock piles, feed among the detritus of the forest floor, and rest atop downed logs on the low branches of living trees. American robins normally nest in tall shrubs or trees, usually near meadows, which they patrol for earthworms and other edibles just as they do on suburban lawns. Animals vary greatly in their versatility, that is, their ability to use more than one habitat, but all possess it to some degree.

Wildlife congregates where appropriate types of food and cover meet, that is, along the edges of habitats. Edges provide easy access to different habitats and a greater variety of plant life than is to be found in either of the bordering communities. Some edges mark important changes in conditions of climate, soil, or topography; others are produced by disturbances such as fire, landslide, or logging. Many species of wildlife are mostly or entirely restricted to edge environments because they require the adjoining habitats for the successful completion of their life cycles.

Different types of edges host different animals. Elk, for example, seek out areas where forest and meadow meet. These large herbivores use meadows for foraging and mating displays and retreat to nearby forested areas for calving, hiding from predators, and relief from excessively hot, cold, or otherwise inclement conditions in the open. Elk also use forested corridors for moving undetected through meadows, brush fields, and other open habitats.

Red-tailed hawks frequent the same forest-meadow edges but use them in rather different ways. The hawks nest in tall trees but soar over adjacent meadows in search of small rodents. Predators such as coyotes and mountain lions survey the open hunting grounds from the obscurity of nearby woods.

Mule deer—including Columbian black-tailed deer—also frequent forest-meadow edges. Since the succulent young leaves of shrubs are the most important single item in the summer diets of these deer, however, they are perhaps even more common along the boundary between forest and brush. In late summer and fall, when huckleberries and gooseberries are ripe, black bears spend most of their time at the forest-brush edge. Numerous birds frequent this edge, and a number occur there more commonly than anywhere else. These include Anna's hummingbird, willow flycatcher, scrub jay, bushtit, Bewick's wren, and fox sparrow.

Jackrabbits and snowshoe hares spend much of their time in places where shrubs and meadow meet. The shrubbery provides excellent cover from predators, while the meadow supplies the succulent herbage that is the main fare of rabbits the world over. Mountain-beaver, a medium-sized rodent that resembles an oversized vole and is only remotely related to the true beaver, prefers moist thickets in close proximity to lush grassy swards or luxuriant stands of broadleaf herbs. A smaller rodent, the long-tailed vole, frequents the margins of wet meadows, where shrubby willows and alder are often thick. Among the birds the song sparrow is one of the most common to use this particular edge, nesting and singing in the shrubbery and prowling through nearby grassy openings for seeds.

Small-scale disturbances, whether natural or human in origin, increase the number of edges and thereby promote diversity in both habitat and wildlife. Disturbances affecting large areas, however, such as extensive fires or vast clearcuts, reduce the number of edges and corresponding diversity. Smaller patchwork clearcuts tend to increase edges, though this advantage is offset if old-growth forest is lost in the process. Disturbances that destroy or eliminate certain types of critical habitat, such as riparian growth, snags, or old-growth forest, also reduce habitat diversity and generally mean the disappearance of wildlife species dependent on them.

The wildlife species that occur in conifer forests vary according to stand condition, which is a product of succes-

sion. Wildlife biologists in the Pacific Northwest have identified six stand conditions or stages of forest succession that
constitute distinctive wildlife habitats. These stages are (1)
grass-forb, (2) shrub-seedling, (3) open sapling, (4) closed
pole, (5) mature, and (6) old growth.

The grass-forb stage is the first one to follow a major
disturbance, such as fire or clearcut logging, that removes
all or nearly all the trees from a site. In the first growing
season following disturbance, the area may have little or no
vegetation. After a year or two, the main vegetation consists
of grasses and forbs whose seeds were blown into the area.
Small shrubs and young trees may be present but they are
not large enough or numerous enough to dominate the vegetation. Relatively few wildlife species breed in these areas
but three to four times as many visit them to feed. Deer,
elk, snowshoe hares, jackrabbits, and other herbaceous
mammals come for the succulent herbs. Mice, salamanders,
and other small creatures find seeds, invertebrates, and
protective cover among the abundant woody debris.
Coyotes, mountain lions, and other large predators follow
the herbivores. The openings are particularly suited to raptors, such as the red-tailed hawk, which soars leisurely overhead in search of rodents. Black bears enter newly vegetated
burns and clearcuts in search of herbage, bulbs, invertebrates, and anything else that might be edible.

The shrub stage replaces the grass-forb stage within two
to five years following a disturbance. As shrubs mature and
tree seedlings grow taller, plant diversity increases but areas
given over to herbs decrease in size and number. The shrubs
attract a number of birds that use them for nesting sites
and that are noticeably less common in both the grass-forb
and later succesional stages. Among these birds are fox
sparrows, green-tailed towhees, mountain bluebirds, and
both Allen's and calliope hummingbirds. Mountain quail
and California quail nest and feed on the ground beneath
the shrubs, the latter species generally occurring at lower
elevations than the former. The cover provided by shrubs
also means that rabbits and hares, rather than merely visiting
the area as they did during the grass-forb stage, now remain
to breed. Small mammal populations increase in general as
a result of better cover and greater habitat diversity.

The open-sapling stage occurs when young trees have

grown tall enough to form a distinct layer above the shrubs, usually five to fifteen years following disturbance. Tree density is low enough that the crowns have not closed. As a result shrubs grow abundantly beneath the saplings. Many of the same birds and mammals that frequent shrub-seedling stands are still to be found in open-sapling stands. Most of the wildlife associated with earlier successional stages also occur in this one. In addition, a number of species appear for the first time as a result of the increased size of the trees. Notable among these are squirrels and a number of tree-nesting birds.

The closed-pole stage begins when the trees are tall and full enough to form a closed canopy, which normally occurs 15 to 35 years following disturbance. Because of the deep shade within the stand, understory vegetation is sparse or nearly absent. The closed-pole stage is therefore the poorest in both habitat diversity and wildlife species of all the stages of forest succession. Numerous birds and mammals use these stands in a casual way or when preferred habitats are unavailable, but few species utilize them regularly and none do so exclusively. West of the Cascades, for example, fewer than 20 species of mammals and five species of birds regularly use closed-pole stands for breeding. Breeding mammals include porcupines, which feed on the tender inner bark of conifers, and Douglas' squirrels, chipmunks, and red-backed voles, all of which eat large quantities of conifer seeds and fungi, both of which are plentiful in closed-pole stands. The northern flying squirrel, however, which glides from branch to branch and down to the ground, rarely occurs in closed-pole stands, where trees are too closely spaced to permit such flights. Deer seek these dark woods as places to rest out of sight of mountain lions and other predators. Bears value the thick stands for denning and resting but usually venture elsewhere to feed. Nesting birds include blue grouse, which feed on seeds and conifer needles, dark-eyed junco, a seed eater, and the calliope hummingbird, which leaves the woods for flowery forest openings. The yellow-rumped warbler visits closed-pole stands to glean insects from conifer foliage, but it breeds in older forests, where it can find the tall, mature conifers that are its preferred nesting sites.

As stands mature, competition among the trees results

in a gradual thinning and opening of the stand and increased accumulations of logs and other woody debris on the forest floor. The canopy is generally more open, as a result of the thinning process, so that one or more layers of understory vegetation are characteristic of normal sites. As a result, mature forests offer more different types of habitats than younger, darker, denser woods and accordingly support significantly more species of wildlife. Mature forests often contain impressively large trees and in most respects resemble old-growth forests, which are generally between 200 and 700 years old, with the dominant trees commonly exceeding 150 to 200 feet in height and four to ten feet in diameter.

Old-growth forests support a number of wildlife species that are rare in mature stands and normally missing from younger successional stages. One important difference for wildlife between merely mature and true old-growth forests is that the large trees in mature forests are mostly standing, while in old-growth forests a good number are lying on the ground. Another difference is that old-growth stands also feature numerous old standing snags in various stages of decay. The presence of the dying ancients, whether erect or reclining, is of critical importance to wildlife because they provide essential habitats to numerous forest species that otherwise would not be present.

Snags are standing dead trees that have lost all their leaves and most of their limbs. The bark is present at first but with time separates from the wood and falls to the ground below. Snags are important components of old-growth forests because they provide food or cover for a large number of forest species. A seminal study of wildlife habitats in the Blue Mountains of Oregon* showed that 39 species of birds and 23 species of mammals used snags of various sizes for nesting or shelter. A similar study conducted in western Oregon and Washington reported that 79 species of birds and mammals use snags for breeding, and 19 use them as feeding sites.**

* *Wildlife Habitats in Managed Forests: The Blue Mountains of Oregon and Washington*, Jack Ward Thomas, ed. U.S. Department of Agriculture Handbook No. 553, 1978.
** *Management of Wildlife and Fish Habitats in Forests of Western Oregon and Washington*, E. Reade Brown, ed., U.S. Department of Agriculture, 1985.

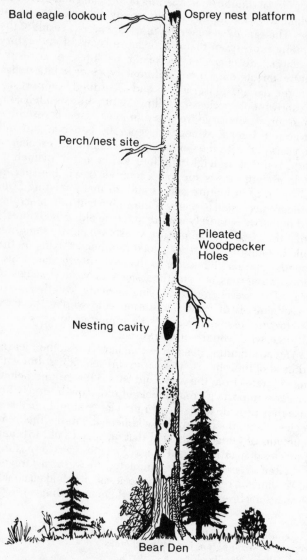

Bald eagle lookout

Osprey nest platform

Perch/nest site

Pileated
Woodpecker
Holes

Nesting cavity

Bear Den

31. Wildlife habitats associated with snags (adapted from Brown, ed., *Management of Wildlife and Fish Habitats in Forests of Western Oregon and Washington*)

Of these, roughly two-thirds depend on cavities for nesting or denning sites. It has been estimated that cavity-nesting birds account for 30 to 45 percent of the total population.

Some birds excavate their own nesting cavities; the majority use natural cavities or holes that have been abandoned by their former occupants. Of the 17 species of birds that excavate their own nesting holes in the Pacific Northwest, 11 are woodpeckers. The red-breasted sapsucker, Williamson's sapsucker, black-backed woodpecker, three-toed woodpecker, and acorn woodpecker primarily excavate sound wood, often in living trees. The downy woodpecker, hairy woodpecker, Lewis' woodpecker, and pileated woodpecker, as well as the northern flicker, all work in wood that has been softened by fungi. Nuthatches and chickadees also excavate their own nesting cavities out of soft wood. Or chickadees may use abandoned woodpecker holes, as do western bluebirds, mountain bluebirds, house wrens, house finches, violet-green swallows, tree swallows, northern pygmy owls, northern saw-whet owls, and several other species. Deer mice, yellow pine chipmunks, and other small mammals also make use of woodpecker holes.

The pileated woodpecker is the primary cavity excavator in old-growth forests. This showy, crow-sized black bird with a long awl-shaped bill and a flaming red crest primarily works in large, old snags with softened wood. It chisels out roomy cavities with distinctive rectangular openings that are large enough to accommodate medium-sized mammals such as red squirrels, flying squirrels, pine martens, and bushy-tailed woodrats. Pileated woodpeckers require large snags, which should be allowed to remain even on clearcut lands if only to preserve these magnificent birds, as well as the various animals that in varying degrees depend on them to provide housing.

Larger birds and mammals sometimes use cavities that have been excavated by pileated woodpeckers and enlarged by subsequent inhabitants. More often, they must rely on natural cavities for suitably capacious quarters. The larger cavity-nesting birds include the wood duck, Barrow's goldeneye, common merganser, great horned owl, and spotted owl. Among the larger mammals that use cavities for breeding or holing up in bad weather are the ringtail, raccoon, fisher, spotted skunk, gray fox, and bobcat.

Living with Conifers

Although the value of snags to wildlife lies primarily in the provision of suitable breeding sites, it does not end there. Woodpeckers regularly probe snags for bark beetles, carpenter ants, and other insects. Bark feeders such as the brown creeper and the nuthatches prefer to forage on living trees but also frequent snags that still retain at least a portion of their bark. Flycatchers often use snags as hunting perches from which to launch repeated aerial forays in pursuit of flying insects. Snags also serve as lookouts or resting places for raptors such as the red-tailed hawk, osprey, and bald eagle. Raccoons, martens, and squirrels also use them as resting places.

Like snags, large downed logs are a characteristic feature of old-growth forests and one of the main reasons that these ancient woods provide greater habitat diversity than closed-pole or even mature stands. When large logs are removed from a forest, as frequently happens in the wake of clearcuts, at least a fifth of the wildlife species go with them. Conversely, if large downed logs are allowed to remain on cut-over stands, they will increase the number of animal species that are able to utilize each successional stage. They can also serve to provide habitat and species continuity that helps to reduce the impact of logging on wildlife habitats.

Large logs provide a variety of habitats. The spaces between loosened bark and the wood provide thermal cover for a large number of invertebrates, as well as small vertebrates such as the Pacific treefrog and various salamanders. The limbs are used as perches by flycatchers, winter wrens, and a large number of other birds. Winter wrens also use the limbs—indeed, the entire log—as a singing perch to declare territorial rights and attract mates. They usually build their nests on or near fallen timber, either in the root wad, in crevices beneath loose bark, or among the woody debris next to the log. The protected areas beneath the logs are used for cover by blue grouse and snowshoe hares. The male grouse also use the tops of the logs during their showy mating display, which includes the oft repeated, deep drumming sound produced by the rapid inflation and collapse of special air sacs. Squirrels use logs as lookouts and feeding sites, where they can dismantle cones while enjoying a good view of their surroundings. They also bury surplus seeds in the soft wood or among the debris beneath the toppled

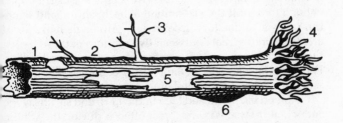

32. Wildlife habitats associated with logs: (1) trunk is food source for woodpeckers; (2) upper surface is used as lookout and feeding site; (3) limbs provide perches; (4) roots are used for perching and nesting; (5) spaces beneath bark are used for cover by invertebrates; (6) areas beneath logs are used for cover by larger animals (adapted from Brown, ed., *Management of Wildlife and Fish Habitats in Forests of Western Oregon and Washington*)

trunk. Northern goshawks use the tops of logs as food-preparation areas where they can pluck fir and feathers from their prey. Mice nest beneath the loose bark and use the soft wood for burrows. The root wad serves as a place for flycatchers to perch, for grouse to dust themselves, and for dark-eyed juncos to nest. Finally, old hollow logs provide denning or resting sites for bears, raccoons, coyotes, foxes, skunks, and many other mammals of sundry stature. In the Blue Mountains, 116 birds, 49 mammals, nine reptiles, and five amphibians use downed timber as habitat. In the forests of western Washington and western Oregon, 130 vertebrate species use fallen timber for breeding, feeding, or resting.

The third distinguishing feature of old-growth forests that sets them off from earlier successional stages is the presence of two or more layers of understory vegetation, each providing distinctive habitats for creatures that otherwise would likely not be present. Layers also increase the number of edges, this time stacked vertically, that are available to wildlife. Although layers are characteristic of many types of vegetation, they find their ultimate expression in old-growth forests, where the vertical dimension is greatest. The number of layers and how well they are developed depends on a variety of factors, including the degree of canopy closure, soil characteristics, and microclimate. On normal sites, however, old-growth stands are usually open enough to permit the elaboration of herb, shrub, and sometimes even understory tree layers. Although most forest creatures move freely between two or more of these layers, they usually favor one for breeding and one for feeding. For some species the feeding and breeding layers are the same; for others, these activities occur in different layers.

Deer and elk breed and feed in the herb and shrub layers, and when browse is scarce, as it often is during the winter, they extend their feeding vertically to include the lower branches of the understory tree layer. Black bears also feed in the two lowest layers, but they use the overstory tree layer to rest and hide from predators. Douglas' squirrels and red squirrels nest and feed in the overstory tree layer but also forage in the understory tree layer and search for fungi in the herb layer. Rufous-sided towhees and dark-eyed juncos nest in the shrub layer but feed in the herb layer. Robins nest in the tree layers but feed mainly on the ground.

The herb layer serves wildlife as a source of nutritious succulent vegetation, plentiful seeds, a wealth of fungi, and invertebrates beyond counting. Deer mice, voles, chipmunks, and other small rodents forage among the litter, prowl about downed logs, and climb into the shrubbery in search of food. Shrews, tiny voracious predators who must eat almost continuously to survive, depend on the abundant insects, spiders, centipedes, and other invertebrates for the greatest part of their diet. The rough-skinned newt, Pacific giant salamander, alligator lizards, and western skinks also feast on the wealth of invertebrates. The numerous small mammals attract a variety of predators, including weasels, foxes, coyotes, bobcats, and snakes. The lynx, whose range formerly coincided closely with that of its chief prey, the snowshoe hare, dens in hollow logs, beneath the upturned root wads of fallen trees, and in other sheltered places. In southwestern Oregon and northern California, the ringtail, a slender, long-tailed cousin of the raccoon, is an efficient predator of woodrats, voles, mice, and other small rodents. Denning in rocky areas, often near water, the ringtail appears at dusk, terrorizes the rodent population until morning, then retires to sleep for the day.

The black bear spends most of its time on the ground but regularly climbs trees to raid bee hives or escape predators. Mother bears send their cubs into the trees upon the approach of predators, including male bears. The ability of black bears to climb trees, while grizzly bears cannot, has suggested that the former developed the ability largely as a way of escaping the latter.

Black bears commonly tear apart old logs and stumps to get at the grubs, bugs, and critters hidden within. Black bears also claw at the bark of certain trees to obtain the soft inner bark and sapwood beneath. Sometimes, bears persist clawing at a tree until they girdle it, whereupon it dies.

The Pacific Northwest is one of the last strongholds of the grizzly bear in the United States south of Canada. Large populations still exist in northwestern Montana and through the Rockies southward to Yellowstone National Park. Smaller populations occur in northern Idaho and northeastern Washington. Unlike the black bear, which is primarily a forest creature, the grizzly prefers open country such as exists at or above timberline. It spends much of its time trying to unearth roots, bulbs, and burrowing rodents. In addition, the seeds of whitebark pine form an important part of the bear's diet in some areas. Grizzly bears will take larger game such as deer and caribou but generally must settle for calves or old or sick animals. It is a scavenger by trade and an opportunistic predator, but one to be treated with great respect and admired from a distance.

Along the major streams of southeastern Alaska and British Columbia, coastal populations of grizzlies, including the huge Alaskan brown bear, congregate in great numbers during the salmon spawning season in late summer and fall. The bears use a variety of techniques to obtain the nutritious oil-rich salmon, including spectacular dives into the streams, but most frequently swat the fish out using their huge well-clawed paws. Unlike the inland grizzlies, these coastal bears are primarily forest animals, foraging along streams and saltwater shores, in alder thickets and berry patches, and wherever succulent herbage, bulbs, or invertebrates are found.

The herb or ground layer also serves as primary breeding habitat for numerous wildlife species, including moles, which burrow beneath the duff. Deer prefer areas of lush vegetation, often near water, for fawning. The snowshoe hare nests in a small depression, or "form," that is located amid dense herbage or shrubbery, often near open areas for foraging. The hermit thrush nests on or just above the ground, where it spends much of its time scratching amid the litter for invertebrates. The dark-eyed junco is perhaps the bird most commonly seen foraging over the forest floor. Its nest is a soft, lined cup placed on or near the ground. The junco also feeds among the shrubs and lower branches of the trees. The blue grouse, the common "chicken" of the western conifer forests, lays its eggs in a shallow depression amidst dense vegetation. It feeds on the ground and among the shrubs for insects, seeds, and berries. In winter, however, it takes to the trees, feeding on conifer needles and using dense foliage for cover during inclement weather.

Among the most commonly heard and seen birds of the forest understory is the tiny winter wren. Just a few inches long, this wonderful singer belts out a complex, melodious song that fairly rings through the forest. And like the song sparrow, it may burst into song any time of year. Its favorite singing perch is an old stump or a branch off a fallen log. Shrubs will do in a pinch. An insect eater, the winter wren commonly nests in, around, and under fallen logs. It is particularly common in the damp coastal forests of western Washington and western Oregon, where it sometimes seems to be the only bird present.

The shrub layer is used in transit by a host of birds and mammals who commute back and forth between the tree-tops and the ground. Shrubs provide browse for deer, berries for numerous birds and mammals, and nesting places for a large number of birds, including song sparrows, orange-crowned warblers, and rufous-sided towhees. The dense vegetation provided by a stand of shrubs provides excellent cover. Moreover, the shrubbery is far enough off the ground to provide a measure of protection from predators yet close enough to it to be convenient for feeding. Even so, snakes often climb into the shrubs seeking eggs and chicks.

The understory tree layer is not always present or well developed in western conifer forests. Where it exists, however, it is often dominated by deciduous trees such as alder, Pacific dogwood, quaking aspen, and bigleaf maple. These trees provide different habitat than the dominant conifer

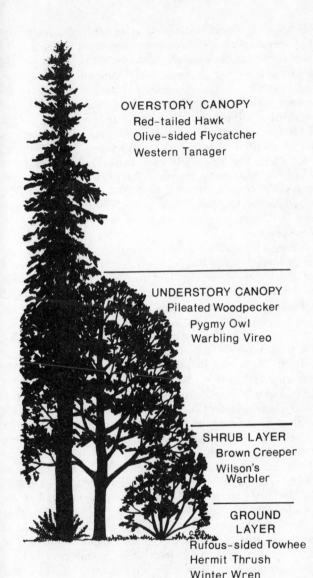

OVERSTORY CANOPY
Red-tailed Hawk
Olive-sided Flycatcher
Western Tanager

UNDERSTORY CANOPY
Pileated Woodpecker
Pygmy Owl
Warbling Vireo

SHRUB LAYER
Brown Creeper
Wilson's
Warbler

GROUND
LAYER
Rufous-sided Towhee
Hermit Thrush
Winter Wren

33. Forest layers and associated birdlife (adapted from Brown, ed., *Management of Wildlife and Fish Habitats in Forests of Western Oregon and Washington*)

Living with Conifers

205

and therefore attract a different group of birds, including some species that are uncommon elsewhere in the forest. Warbling vireos, for example, are most abundant in deciduous trees even though they are also found in conifers. The alder flycatcher and orange-crowned warbler are also more common in deciduous understory trees than elsewhere. The red-breasted sapsucker and yellow-bellied sapsucker, closely related species that live west and east of the Cascades respectively, both prefer groves of aspen and alder for both feeding and nesting. The birds drill rows of small holes in the thin-barked deciduous trees, returning later to feast on the oozing sap and the insects attracted to it. Williamson's sapsucker has similar feeding habits but prefers drilling in whitebark pines, subalpine firs, and other upper montane and subalpine conifers.

The varied thrush is a distinctive member of the coastal conifer forests of the Pacific Northwest, ranging southward into the redwood country and eastward to the Northern Rockies. Closely resembling its cousin the robin, the varied thrush is far more retiring, quickly flying to a hidden perch upon the approach of an intruder. It commonly places its nest in young conifers or even deciduous trees, generally on a branch near where it connects with the trunk. Like the robin, the varied thrush feeds on the ground, searching for worms, millipedes, sowbugs, insects, and other invertebrates, but whereas the robin forages in forest openings the varied thrush prefers the closed forest. More often seen than heard, the haunting song of the varied thrush consists of a series of single, sustained notes, each a different pitch but all in a minor key.

In the mixed conifer and mixed evergreen forests of southwestern Oregon and northwestern California, where Oregon oak, black oak, tanoak, and canyon live oak commonly form an understory tree layer beneath ponderosa pines and other conifers, the large western gray squirrel, a connoisseur of acorns and pine nuts, is the most conspicuous inhabitant of the understory tree layer. In western Washington, where pines and particularly oaks are far less common, so is the gray squirrel. There, Douglas' squirrel, normally a squirrel of fir and hemlock forests, has moved into the oak-pine niche left vacant by the gray squirrel. In the Northern Rockies, where there are plenty of pines but, again, no native pine squirrel, the red squirrel, a close relative of the Douglas' squirrel, has filled the pine-squirrel niche.

The overstory tree layer is the most important in the forest because it ultimately governs the kinds of plants and animals that are able to exist beneath it. It's what makes the forest a forest. In addition, it hosts a number of wildlife species that use it as primary habitat for breeding, feeding, or resting—often all three. Because this layer is so high above the ground and often so thick with branches and foliage, its residents often escape detection even from eager human observers equipped with binoculars. Douglas' squirrels and red squirrels are perhaps the most conspicuous residents partly because they are active during the day and partly because they cannot resist perching on low branches to scold human intruders. The northern flying squirrel is rather common in old-growth conifer forests but is rarely seen because of its nocturnal habits. This small, soft-furred squirrel is uniquely adapted to life in the trees. The flying squirrel has a loose fold of furred skin attached on each side between the fore and hind legs. When outstretched, the folds serve as a cape that allows the squirrel to glide from a higher branch to a lower one or from the latter to a log, stump, or the ground. The squirrel feeds on invertebrates as well as seeds and nuts.

The most unusual and rarely observed arboreal rodent, however, is the red tree vole, which occurs only in western Oregon and northwestern California. It prefers mature or old-growth forests with large Douglas-firs but also occurs in closed-pole stands and in spruce-hemlock and redwood forests. The nest is placed on a branch of a Douglas-fir (less often some other conifer) amid thick foliage, which may be near the trunk on younger trees but is usually toward the tips on large, old-growth specimens. Red tree voles feed mainly on the needles of Douglas-fir, less often those of grand fir, Sitka spruce, or western hemlock. They also feed on the bark and pithy centers of tender, young twigs. Water is obtained from dew and fog that has condensed in the foliage, or from the needles themselves. The red tree vole is an indicator species of old-growth forests, and its numbers are declining as those forests are rapidly destroyed.

The chief predator of the red tree vole is the spotted owl, which has become the symbol of old-growth forests in the

Pacific Northwest. This medium-sized owl nests only in old-growth forests, where large nesting cavities created by heart rot and breakage are abundant. Spotted owls prey on flying squirrels, tree voles, woodrats, and other small mammals. They avoid clearings and rarely venture into pole timber. The steady decline in the numbers of spotted owls in the Pacific Northwest has been linked to the decline in old-growth stands. At the same time, concerted efforts to locate remaining pairs of this endangered species have saved many remaining old-growth stands on our national forests.

The fiercest arboreal predators among the mammals are the marten and its larger, less common cousin, the fisher. The marten and fisher, along with owls, are the scourge of squirrels. It has been said that a marten can run down any squirrel in a treetop chase . . . and that a fisher can run down a marten. It is possible that the gliding ability of the flying squirrel may have evolved as a means of escaping these large, voracious, tree-dwelling weasels. The marten spends winters chasing squirrels through the trees, but during the summer also commonly prowls about talus and other rocky areas in search of pikas, woodrats, and other small rodents. The fisher descends from the trees to prey upon the large, slow porcupine, which depends for protection on its sharp quills rather than speed. Fishers, however, seem little bothered by the quills and are able to quickly flip porcupines on their backs, exposing their soft, vulnerable bellies.

Porcupines feed on buds, tender young twigs, and the bark of young conifers. In some areas the loss of seedlings and saplings that have been girdled by porcupines poses a serious problem for both natural and commercial reforestation. This large rodent normally dens among boulders, but during the winter it commonly retreats to the treetops, feeding on bark and seeking shelter in large cavities.

The treetops, of course, provide nesting sites for numerous birds. Evening grosbeaks nest high in conifers, often placing their fragile twig cups in dense foliage near the ends of branches. These lovely yellow-and-black birds are seed eaters that feed both on cones still in the trees and on seeds that are scattered over the ground. The western tanager, whose red, yellow, black, and white coloring make it one of the most beautiful birds of the western conifer forests, remains high in the trees most of the time. It feeds mostly on flying insects high in the canopy. Other canopy nesters include the yellow-rumped warbler, Townsend's warbler, olive-sided flycatcher, and Cassin's finch. These birds include a number that are brightly colored or boldly patterned or both. Yet they are remarkably difficult to see among the foliage, not only because they are often so high above the ground but also because they blend into the broken pattern of lights and darks created as sunlight filters through the crowns of the conifers. Living high in the trees, these birds have the luxury of bright colors because their nests are well removed from most conifers. Ground-dwelling birds more often tend to be drab so as not to attract attention.

Among the more conspicuous forest birds are the jays. The Steller's jay is a dark-blue bird with a conspicuous black crest. It builds its nest in the branches of conifers and mainly feeds on conifer seeds, particularly those of pines. It also feeds on berries and other seeds, however, and is not above descending into campgrounds for scraps. When nesting, this normally raucous bird is extremely quiet and retiring. At the same time, it raids the nests of other birds in search of eggs and hatchlings. Steller's jay is most common at low to mid elevations and in areas where pines are abundant. At higher elevations it is replaced by the slightly smaller gray jay, also known as the camp robber. The gray jay is an extraordinarily bold bird who will land on one's hand to take proffered tidbits. Unlike most other jays, which have a raucous call that betrays their kinship with crows, the gray jay most often utters a soft, cooing whistle. These birds are more gregarious than the Steller's jay and are often seen swooping through the forest in bands of three or more. Gray jays are normally birds of upper montane and subalpine forests, where Steller's jays are rare. Where the two occur together, Steller's is the larger and more aggressive and will drive the gray jay away from contested campground delicacies.

The goshawk, a relentless predator of forest birds and small mammals, builds a large platform of sticks on a hefty branch of a conifer located far above the ground. The short wings and long tail of this hawk endow it with remarkable maneuverability as it chases fleeing grouse and other birds in a mad scramble through the trees. The goshawk's smaller cousins, the Cooper's hawk and sharp-shinned hawk, are equally agile. The treetop nesting sites of the bald eagle have already been described. Common ravens and American crows also build stick platforms high in the crowns of the dominant conifers. The largest treetop nester is the great blue heron, which builds a huge stick nest in the crown of both conifers and tall deciduous trees. The birds are colonial roosters with a half dozen or more pairs staking out treetop territories within close proximity of one another. A few miles north of San Francisco, a large colony of herons along with great egrets, nest in the tops of old-growth red woods in a moist canyon opening onto a saltwater lagoon. Another notable great blue heron rookery occurs south of Seattle in the tops of red alders on a wooded hillside over looking a pond.

The trunks of the dominant conifers also provide a special habitat for creatures equipped to use them. Trunks are first of all a convenient avenue from canopy to forest floor, with stops at all levels in between. The squirrels are the most accomplished and frequent commuters along this route, but most other mammals use it as well. Several birds have developed adaptations that allow them to forage for bark beetles, carpenter ants, and other insects that infest tree trunks. Woodpeckers use their chisel-like bills to probe for insects. Their feet, consisting of two toes forward and two aft, are well designed for clinging to trunks. The common but seldom noticed brown creeper spirals up trunks, always beginning at the base. Its curved bill allows it to probe bark crevices for spiders and other invertebrates. Its streaky brown plumage makes it difficult to spot against the bark of a tree. The red-breasted nuthatch also forages on tree trunks, working up and down but always head first. It also works along the upper branches, hanging upside-down if necessary to get to a choice morsel. The high, thin metallic note of the red-breasted nuthatch is one of the characteristic—and difficult to locate—sounds of the western conifer forests.

Throughout the world, wildlife is in retreat. As forests are cleared, marshes are drained, and habitats are polluted, the number of wildlife species approaching the brink of extinction increases daily. In the Pacific Northwest, however, most of the animals that were present in the region's coniferous forests at the coming of the first white settlers are till there, albeit often in reduced numbers. The chief danger posed to the region's forest wildlife is not hunting but logging practices that eliminate old-growth forests and disrupt vegetation mosaics that provide essential habitat diversity. Fortunately, recent years have brought a change in logging practices on public lands. The importance of leaving at least a few standing mature trees and large logs in clearcuts is now widely recognized. In addition, concerned foresters and environmentalists have together persuaded timber companies to halt the practice in some areas of clearcutting right down to the edge of lakes and streams. Finally, the uniqueness of old-growth forests and their importance to wildlife is now widely recognized, and the prospect of preserving a significant portion of the old growth that remains in the region is better than it has ever been before.

CHAPTER ELEVEN

High Country Parklands

AFTER THE DARK confines of the midslope forests, the open, sunny expanses of the upper subalpine zone are exhilarating. Backcountry hikers prize the high country near timberline for its picturesque arrangements of rock, ice, water, meadow, and forest; for its panoramic views, its profusion of wildflowers, and its dramatic peaks. Like the ocean shore, this is a landscape that commonly inspires deep abiding affection among those who visit it. Having once experienced its glories, many people are ever after driven to return again and again.

The transition from closed forest to parkland can be abrupt and often coincides with a shift from steep slopes at middle elevations to gentler slopes near timberline. Known as *alp slopes*, after the high pastures of the Alps, these gentle shoulders are characteristic of timberline regions throughout western North America. Views differ as to the origin and significance of alp slopes. Some scientists argue that they are products of timberline, since erosion of originally steep slopes must be greater on exposed timberline terrain than on the densely forested slopes below. Other researchers believe that timberline is a product of the terrain rather than its cause. They point out that poor drainage in a region of maximum snowfall is an important factor restraining the development of dense forest and promoting the establishment of meadows. Yet another view suggests that varied terrain results from the uplift of mountain masses through altitude zones of varying humidity and temperature. Erosion would be greater, of course, in warmer, wetter zones and would decrease in colder or more arid ones. As a mountain mass was uplifted, vestiges of earlier erosional periods might or might not remain.

Whatever their origin, the gently rolling subalpine park-lands of the Pacific Northwest from a landscape of exceptional beauty and great botanical interest. For here, each summer, the region's high meadows put on a flower show equaled only by that of the Southwest deserts after exceptionally wet winters. Well over 150 different kinds of wild-flowers grow in the region's subalpine meadows. Each species follows its own flowering schedule, so that as some are completing their bloom, others are just beginning. The result is a continually changing floral display from the first snows to melt in spring to the first frosts of fall.

The first plants to appear in the high meadows do so in late spring or early summer, depending on when the snow melts from place to place. The parade of bloom begins first on warm, south-facing slopes, which may be free of snow as early as late April or May. Sedges, grasses, and a few hardy wildflowers lead the way. Delicate glacier lilies often poke up through the last lingering inch or two of snow, fueled by nutrients stored in overwintering bulbs. Their clear yellow, nodding flowers quickly appear, often forming profuse displays in places where the soil is saturated. Other early bloomers include western spring beauty, whose small white flowers are lined with candy pink, and, in the interior mountains, yellow bell, which ranges downslope to sage-brush flats. Spreading phlox, a mat-forming perennial with tiny needlelike leaves and pink or pale lavender flowers that often cover the entire plant, is among the first wildflowers to appear on rocky places or exposed southern slopes. In the Olympics, and less commonly elsewhere, it is attended by the lovely red Douglasia and the nodding, pink Olympic onion.

Late-lying snow saturates the parkland soils, which remain wet for several weeks as a result of poor drainage and low evaporation rates. The peak of bloom occurs in late July and early August, when days have warmed up but before soils have dried out. The dominant sedges and grasses mantle the alpine slopes with a brilliant green that reaches upward along snow-melt channels to the realm of rock and ice. Against this emerald ground, red columbine, paint-brush, red mountain-heather, Lewis' monkeyflower, shooting stars, and penstemon provide startling accents of red or magenta. Broadleaf lupine may empurple large flats or entire hillsides. Gentians, larkspurs, and bellflowers supply other shades of blue and purple. Partridgefoot splashes damp gravels with creamy yellow. Cinquefoils, arnicas, and a host of sunflowers are responsible for the more vivid yellows. Mountain bistort, white mountain-heather, western pasqueflower, Sitka valerian, and avalanche lily spangle the parklands with whites from creamy to snow.

In late summer grasses and sedges have grown tall enough to obscure the lower flowers, so that only the taller ones, such as Sitka valerian, cow parsnip, and false-hellebores are conspicuous. As the grasses and sedges begin to fade and wither, however, a host of daisies, asters, and other members of the sunflower family become prominent, sprinkling the meadows with yellow, white, and lavender. The greatest show of color, however, comes in fall, when the grasses turn to bronze and delicious blueberry covers the high country with scarlet and crimson.

Subalpine meadows throughout the Pacific Northwest generally fall into six broad types: (1) heather meadows, (2) lush herbaceous meadows, (3) black sedge meadows, (4) low herbaceous meadows, (5) mountain grasslands, and (6) sagebrush parks. These six basic meadow types, along with islands of trees, form a parkland mosaic that reflects changes

34. Typical parkland plant communities in British Columbia: (1) mountain hemlock/bigleaf huckleberry, (2) dwarf mountain hemlock, (3) delicious blueberry, (4) mountain-heather, (5) black sedge, and (6) snowbed moss (adapted from Krajina, ed., *Ecology of Western North America*)

from site to site in substrate, moisture conditions, and the duration of the snowpack.

Heather communities are characteristic of subalpine and alpine regions in the high mountain ranges of the Pacific Northwest. Heathers, or heaths, are also common in the arctic tundra and in similar arctic and alpine habitats in Northern Europe and Asia. True heathers, or heaths, of the genus *Erica* are restricted to the Old World, but members of the heath family are well represented in North America, where they include rhododendrons and azaleas; mountain laurels; huckleberries, blueberries, and cranberries; manzanitas; madrones; wintergreens; and Indian-teas. In North America, true heathers are found only in cultivated rock gardens. In the wild they are replaced mainly by the rather similar mountain-heathers. Red mountain-heather and white mountain-heather are the most common species. Closely associated with them are the bilberries, dwarf cousins of the large blueberry and huckleberry species of the lower forests.

Mountain-heathers, like the true heaths of Northern Europe, are low, creeping shrublets that form dense ground covers in a variety of habitats. They are exceptionally handsome plants with delicate, nodding, bell- or urn-shaped flowers and needlelike or scalelike leaves that resemble those of conifers. Favoring slightly acidic soils that are moist but not waterlogged, they most commonly occur on gentle slopes and other terrain where snow provides winter protection but melts in late spring or early summer. As a group the heathers have low rates of photosynthesis and respiration, but then, being low or prostrate plants, they do not need to produce much woody tissue. Individual mountain-heather plants may live 20 to 50 years, adding only as little as eight to ten leaf pairs a year.

Dense growths of red mountain-heather, white mountain-heather, and delicious blueberry are a common and widespread element in the parklands of the Cascade Range, Olympic Mountains, and southern Coast Mountains. Mountain-heather communities are also common at the bases of parkland tree groups, along lakeshores, and among boulders. Red mountain-heather and white mountain-heather often occur together, but the former tends to be the more common of the two in the lower parklands, the latter in the upper. Yellow mountain-heather, Alaska mountain-heather, and four-angled mountain-heather are boreal species that range down the Coast Mountains and Canadian Rockies to Washington, Idaho, and Montana, where they are mainly confined to areas near timberline and above. Club-moss mountain-heather grows on thin peat soils in northern British Columbia and southeastern Alaska.

Although delicious blueberry commonly occurs with heathers, it also grows by itself in large patches and swaths. In the drier subalpine areas east of the Cascade crest, delicious blueberry is replaced by grouse whortleberry, which forms a ground cover beneath subalpine firs and extends upslope into parklands to timberline and above. Mountain heathers are present there but generally less abundant than in the coastal mountains. Grouse whortleberry is also found in the High Cascades of central Oregon, where conditions are notably drier than in the Washington Cascades. Still other bilberries occur in sphagnum bogs on cold, poorly drained bottoms and flats, along with other members of the heath family, such as alpine laurel, crowberry, and bog Labrador-tea.

Unlike the evergreen mountain-heathers, the bilberries are deciduous. In fall their leaves turn various shades of brilliant red, and in that season their presence is evident throughout the subalpine parklands and alpine slopes. The bilberries, like their larger huckleberry cousins downslope, bear delicious fruits that are sought after by people and animals alike.

A large number of subalpine herbs, including many of the showier wildflowers, occur commonly in heather-bilberry meadows. As a rule, however, the herbs constitute a minor if sometimes conspicuous component of the communities.

Lush herbaceous meadows featuring many different kinds of plants occur on well-watered, gentle to steep slopes and in avalanche gullies, shallow draws, and ravines. Such meadows are best developed along the west slope of the Coast Mountains and the Cascade Range and in the Olympic Mountains, where lingering snows and deep soils provide perfect conditions. Similar communities occur in the inland ranges, especially in the snowier portions of the Northern Rockies.

Steep, well-watered parkland slopes in the Cascades and

35. Green false-hellebore (*Veratrum viridis*)

Olympics commonly support lush growths of Sitka valerian and green false-hellebore. In the Northern Rockies other valerians, along with green or white false-hellebore, dominate comparable communities. Meadows of this type are characteristic of avalanche tracks, where snow slides eliminate trees and abundant moisture favors tall shrubs that die back in autumn and are therefore invulnerable to slide damage. Valerians may reach heights of three feet, and false-hellebores are even taller, making this the tallest meadow community in the subalpine zone. The valerians have a strong, rather musky smell that pervades the meadows on warm summer days. The false-hellebores are members of the lily family. They have large leaves that sheathe the stem and flowers that grow in tassellike clusters at the end of the stalk. They look something like corn plants, a resemblance that has inspired their alternate name, corn-lily.

Valerian–false-hellebore meadows are the tallest, lushest, and most diverse of all the subalpine meadow communities in the Cascades of Washington and northern Oregon. Early in the summer, before the dominant herbs have reached full size, a variety of other, shorter herbs are conspicuous, including showy sedge, lupines, paintbrushes, dogtooth-violets, pasqueflowers, and mountain bistort. Another common member of the community is cow parsnip, which rivals Valerian and false-hellebores in height and therefore remains conspicuous even after it has attained full stature. In the Olympics, American sawwort is also characteristic of lush meadows. In the High Cascades of central and southern Oregon, arrowhead groundsel dominates a similar lush tall-herb community that also includes western aster, fanleaf cinquefoil, broadleaf lupine, wood violet, Jeffrey's shooting star, and showy sedge.

Lush herbaceous meadows dominated by fireweed, bracken fern, and salmonberry commonly occur on steep, well-watered, often south-facing slopes in the lower mountain hemlock and silver or white fir zones of western Washington and western Oregon. These areas are commonly free of snow by late spring, and from then on support a steady sequence of bloom, beginning with glacier lily and western spring beauty, and ending with goldenrod and wormwood in late summer. By midsummer, the smaller plants are completely obscured by the taller ones, which form a dense tangle shoulder high.

Low lush-herbaceous subalpine meadows are similar to the tall-herb types except that they lack the tall herbs. These shorter communities are usually dominated by showy sedge or black sedge and contain most of the smaller forbs associated with the taller meadow types. Low lush-herb meadows often form a transition between tall-herb meadows on steep slopes and snowbed communities in poorly drained flats and basins.

Dense, flowery turfs commonly line parkland creeks and pools. Although black sedge is often abundant in these communities, the showiest plants are monkeyflowers, which often form massed displays of red and yellow. With their tubular, two-lipped flowers, monkeyflowers resemble wild snapdragons, to which they are, in fact, related. The lower lip commonly protrudes, forming a convenient feeding platform for bumblebees. Red, or pink, monkeyflower is the showiest of the family, featuring dark pink or crimson flowers as much as one inch across and two inches long. Humming-birds, the principal pollinators, can spot these flowers from a great distance. Subalpine monkeyflower is the common yellow monkeyflower of subalpine gardens in the Cascades and Olympics. Several other very similar yellow monkey-flowers occur in sunny, wet habitats from sea level to timber-line. Red and subalpine monkeyflowers both have creeping underground stems—rhizomes—from which new plants sprout at intervals. As a result, large patches of both species are made up of clones, plants that are genetically identical. Many subalpine and alpine plants, including the turf-form-ing grasses and sedges, are rhizomatous. Though most pro-duce viable seed, sprouting from already existing stems is a more reliable method of reproduction in the short, un-predictable growing seasons near timberline.

Though not nearly so showy as the monkeyflowers, alpine willowherb or coltsfoot may also dominate subalpine riparian meadows. Marsh-marigolds, wandering daisy, broadleaf lupine, and red willowherb are among a number of other showy wildflowers found in moist streamside turfs.

Black sedge forms a dense, low turf on poorly drained flats or basin floors, where snows lie long and soils remain cold and wet throughout the growing season. Such places are particularly common on north- and east-facing ridges where wind transfer deposits deep drifts and where cooler temperatures reduce the rate of melting. Snowbed sites are often snow-free less than three months a year. Black sedge begins rapid growth soon after snow has melted, fueling this surge with nutrients stored in underground stems and the bases of shoots.

Avalanche lily, the showy white and yellow flower that has become emblematic of subalpine parklands in the Cas-cades and Olympics, grows most profusely in this commu-nity. This wild lily, also known as dogtooth-violet, does not wait for the snow to disappear. Overwintering in the form of a bulb, the plant pushes new shoots upward through the last few remaining inches of the pack. Small numbers of other subalpine plants also may be found in black sedge meadows. In the High Cascades of central Oregon, for exam-ple, alpine aster commonly grows with black sedge in poorly drained areas. Mountain-heathers or bilberries, for another example, often mantle small rises and slopes, better drained sites that may be scattered like islands amid soggy flats dominated by black sedge.

Several other sedge species dominate communities on wet sites in the Oregon Cascades. Holm's Rocky Mountain sedge, Sitka sedge, woodrush sedge, and beaked sedge are conspicuous in these soggy subalpine marshes. Mountain bistort, Jeffrey's shooting star, twinflower marsh-marigold, Gray's lovage, Oregon saxifrage, bog Labrador-tea, and alpine willowherb are among the forbs commonly found in these various communities.

Diverse communities of widely spaced, low-growing plants develop on bare mineral soils or among outcrops of rock. Saxifrages, with their tiny, exquisitely detailed, jewel-like white flowers, colonize wet gravels and rock crevices. Partridgefoot, a member of the rose family, occurs in most meadow communities but is especially common on moist outcrops or moist but well-drained gravelly soils. Its creamy white flowers with bright yellow stamens are conspicuous.

36. Avalanche lily (*Erythronium montanum*)

Other crevice plants include various blue and purple pen-
stemons, paintbrushes, spreading phlox, mountain lover,
stonecrops, sandworts, knotweeds, wild buckwheats, and
sibbaldia. Mountain lady fern commonly grows in rock
crevices and among talus and scree. Subalpine pussytoes,
a versatile, widely occurring species, may dominate raw
snowbed sites where conditions are somewhat drier than
in black sedge meadows.

A variety of cushion plants form a sparse cover on exposed
ridges and south-facing slopes that high winds keep free of
snow during the winter. Plants growing on such sites must
endure wind abrasion and subfreezing temperatures in
winter and intense sunlight and long periods of drought
during the growing season. Cushion plants, whose tightly
clustered basal leaves form a small rounded cushion rarely
more than a few inches high, are well adapted to these
conditions. Their low stature and rounded form offer minimum wind resistance; in a sense these tiny plants are genetically pre-pruned. By restricting leaf growth to the basal
cushion, these plants also take advantage of the warmer
temperatures found within a few inches of the soil surface.
Their densely packed leaves also trap soil, which helps to
stabilize the plants and enables them to retain moisture
longer than the bare gravels nearby. The leaves of cushion
plants commonly bear coats of fine hairs, which protect
them from both intense sunlight and cold. Moreover, by
keeping surface temperatures low, the hairs help to reduce
moisture losses through evaporation. This is particularly
important during sunny winter days, when rising temperatures at the leaf surface may increase evaporation at a time
when replacement moisture is unavailable because of frozen
soils.

Deep taproots provide cushion plants with strong anchors
as well as moisture. Following germination,, a new plant
concentrates on root growth, so that within a few weeks its
taproot may be several inches long, while the above-ground
portion of the plant is still inconspicuous. Even when mature, cushion plants still consist of far more root than shoot—
as much as six to ten times more by dry weight.

Cushion and mat-forming plants are also conspicuous on
the extensive, nearly barren pumice flats that occur so
widely in the subalpine region of the Oregon Cascades from

Mount Jefferson south. The sparse vegetation on these flats does not seem to be the result of drought, for moisture is generally adequate through the brief growing season. Instead, low soil fertility combined with wide daily fluctuations in temperature are apparently responsible for the dearth of plants.

Subalpine grasslands dominated by green fescue are widespread in the drier interior mountains of the Pacific Northwest. Such meadows are common in the Wallowa and Blue mountains of central and eastern Oregon, the Okanogan Highlands of northeastern Washington, the east side of the Cascades, and drier parts of the Northern Rockies. Green fescue meadows are also common in the warmest, driest habitats within the parklands of the western Cascades and Olympics, especially the rainshadow areas of the northeastern Olympics and the northeastern side of Mount Rainier.

Fescue is a bunchgrass, growing in discrete clumps rather than forming a continuous turf. Where conditions are especially dry there may be considerable bare soil around the plants. On moister sites the clumps of grass may grow closely enough that the intervening spaces are inconspicuous. Pristine green fescue meadows commonly include a number of grass species and a rich variety of showy wildflowers. Since the soils dry out early, the peak flowering period in these meadows extends from shortly after snow has melted to the end of July. In the moister of the green fescue meadows near Sunrise, on the northeastern side of Mount Rainier, blooming broadleaf lupines form great swaths of purple; fanleaf cinquefoil decorates somewhat drier meadows with brilliant yellow; and Cascade aster resumes the purple theme on the driest sites. Similar meadows occur in the Olympics except that the aster is missing and a number of other forbs are either added or more prominent than they are in the Cascades. Pristine green fescue meadows in the Wallowa Mountains include numerous grass species and a large number of wildflowers, of which velvet lupine is the most common.

In the Wallowas and other interior mountain ranges, most green fescue meadows have been badly overgrazed. Since livestock prefer the nutritious fescue, less palatable species gradually replace it. Needlegrass often dominates overgrazed sites, which also feature an increase in both forbs and bare areas. Serious doubt exists about whether these deteriorated meadows can ever return to their pristine state.

The term *alpine* originally referred to the Alps but later was used to describe similar high-mountain terrain around the world. Such terrain is very much like that found in the North Cascades—icy crags presiding over lush green parklands, dark conifer forests, and deep, glacier-scoured valleys. To biologists, however, *alpine* has a more restricted meaning, referring to the treeless zone lying above timberline.

Extensive areas of alpine vegetation do not exist in the Pacific Northwest, as they do in the Colorado Rockies. Rather, the alpine zone exists as widely scattered islands on only the highest mountains. Most massifs in Washington, Oregon, and Idaho are not high enough to support alpine communities at these latitudes. The notable exceptions are the major Cascade volcanoes. Above timberline, however, most of the terrain on these giant cones is either too steep and rocky to support well-developed alpine communities, or it is covered with perennial snow fields or glaciers. Moreover, since these are young volcanoes, the eldest dating back only several thousand years, their upper slopes are mantled with recent deposits of pumice and ash, which are inhospitable surfaces for the development of lush alpine turfs. In the Northern Rockies the situation is much the same. That is, mountains that rise above timberline are rare and those that do are generally too steep, rocky, or ice- and snow-covered to support extensive alpine vegetation.

No single adaptation seems sufficient to account for the success of alpine plants; the two most obvious features are a reduction in plant size and in the amount of energy devoted to woody stems. Low perennial herbs are the most typical alpine plants, and perenniality is an obvious advantage in the harsh alpine zone where the growing season is short. Perennials store the nutrients that will be needed to fuel growth each year in persistent underground parts, such as bulbs, corms, rhizomes, and roots. This allows them to grow rapidly as soon as the ground is free of snow. Perennials are also relieved of the need to produce viable seed each year. Sedges, the grasslike plants that dominate alpine and subalpine turfs, sprout anew each spring from existing networks of underground stems. Many alpine perennials have persistent woody bases or basal stems but ephemeral herbaceous shoots that die back at the end of each growing season. If the presence or absence of woody tissue separates herbs from shrubs, then these tiny plants are technically shrubs. Their soft stems, flowering habits, and general aspect, however, make them more like herbs than shrubs. True shrubs— that is, plants with woody persistent stems—are present in the alpine zone, but they are largely confined to its lower reaches, and they are mainly mat-forming species with stems that hug the ground. There is just not enough time and energy available in the alpine zone to waste it on woody stems whose main purpose anyway is to support upright growth.

The air right next to the ground is generally warmer than that above, so that plants only a few inches tall live in a balmier habitat than exists in the alpine zone as a whole. Prostrate or dwarfed plants also escape the worst of the wind since wind speeds, thanks to friction, are considerably lower next to the ground. Small plants, of course, require less time and energy to reach full size or replace annual leaves, flowers, and fruits thereafter. This is an essential characteristic of plants inhabiting the alpine zone, where the growing season may be less than two months long.

Some alpine plants form tiny cushions whose compact forms shed wind, trap soil, and retain moisture. The radial symmetry of the basal rosettes making up the cushion allow the plants to obtain maximum sunlight with minimum exposure. Other alpine plants form prostrate mats. These plants are as a group less hardy than cushion plants but because of their usual ability to reproduce through layering they are able to form relatively extensive colonies.

Alpine plants may be tiny, but as a group they produce disproportionately large, showy flowers. Moreover, while the leafy portions of the plants are often just an inch or two high, the flowers may be held aloft on stalks several inches tall. Large, brightly colored flowers are more easily noticed by wandering bees and butterflies. Flowerheads that are held aloft better expose their seeds to the scattering alpine winds.

Alpine plants exhibit a number of other specialized features designed to help them survive cold, wind, intense sunlight, and periods of drought. Their stems and leaves are often covered with hairs—fur coats to help protect them from cold. The hairs also filter ultraviolet radiation, which is especially intense in the thin air of the alpine zone. Alpine plants also use carbohydrates stored over the winter to produce anthocyanins, reddish pigments that help protect tender new shoots from burning caused by ultraviolet light. The presence of anthocyanins explains the reddish hue of new shoots and leaves.

Certain alpine plants have tiny leaves that are densely clustered along tiny stems. Such plants save energy because they do not need to form separate stems for the leaves, and the leaves in turn serve to insulate the stems. Succulence is also widespread among alpine plants. The thick, waxy coating of succulent leaves inhibits moisture loss and protects the plants from wind abrasion and cold. Finally, alpine plants as a group have long taproots, which account for a greater portion of the plants by weight than the above-ground parts. Long taproots not only enable tiny cushion plants to probe deep sources of moisture but provide firm anchors that help the plants withstand high winds, soil creep, and churning by frost action.

Alpine communities in the Pacific Northwest fall into three broad types: heath shrub communities, alpine turfs, and fell-field communities.

Heath shrub communities are common only in the coastal ranges of the Pacific Northwest. Heath species occur in the Northern Rockies but mainly as minor components of other communities. In alpine heath shrub communities one or more mountain-heather species, together with showy sedge, form dense green carpets in moist, well-drained alpine habitats. In the Washington Cascades yellow mountain-heather, which has sticky, pale yellow, urn-shaped flowers, is the dominant heath species, though white mountain-heather may also be abundant. Other mountain-heathers are found in Alaska and British Columbia, ranging southward to the North Cascades and Glacier National Park region. In midsummer the showy flowers of several broadleaf herbs are held above the green sward on slim stems that quaver in the slightest breeze. The tiny purple daisies so often found in alpine heaths are alpine aster, a tiny plant with a mere tuft of basal leaves. Alpine lupine, another purple-flowered species, holds its pealike blossoms on a

37. Yellow mountain-heather (*Phyllodoce empetriformis*)

single stem above a flat rosette of leaves. Complementing the purples of aster and lupine is the bright-yellow fanleaf cinquefoil. More restrained are the small white, tightly clustered flowerheads of woolly pussytoes. This common and widely occurring alpine plant has silvery green leaves whose color comes from a dense layer of matted white hairs.

The second major type of alpine community found in the Pacific Northwest is alpine turf. Alpine turf communities are dominated by grasslike plants. The most common of these are the sedges, but various species of rushes and grasses are also usually present. Together, these plants form dense green swards on gentle terrain where late melting snowbanks and poor to moderate drainage keep soils wet throughout the growing season. Rapidly growing sedges are commonly the only plants found growing in places where snows linger into late summer. Elsewhere, a large number of showy wildflowers provide a colorful summer display in alpine turf communities.

Alpine turfs cover large areas in the Colorado Rockies, where high, rolling uplands watered by frequent summer thundershowers characterize the alpine zone. These communities are far less extensive in the Pacific Northwest, however, where alpine terrain tends to be steeper and rockier and where summer rains are rare. Nevertheless, local areas of turf are found in alpine areas throughout the Pacific Northwest, especially in the higher, moister sections of the Okanogan Highlands and the Northern Rockies, where gentle, well-watered uplands are most common. Various sedges dominate these communities; grasses include alpine bluegrass, spike trisetum, and sheep fescue. Alpine pussytoes and snowbed cinquefoil, looking much like their alpine counterparts in the Cascades, are among the more common broadleaf herbs in these alpine meadows. Elkslip marshmarigold may occur in soggy flats, while mats of moss-campion, a widely ranging alpine plant with tiny needlelike leaves and lovely deep pink flowers, favors rocky areas scattered amid the turf. In the Cascades and Olympics, alpine turfs are usually found only in poorly drained depressions or snowbed habitats. Showy and black sedges are the dominant grasslike plants. The more common broadleaf herbs include the odd coil-beaked lousewort, the tiny yellow golden fleabane, woolly pussytoes, alpine lupine, and three-forked wormwood, a tiny herbaceous cousin of big sagebrush.

Fell-field communities occur on dry, shallow, rocky soils where snow melts early or on windswept ridges and south-facing slopes that may be free of snow for most of the winter. Unlike alpine turfs and heaths, where the plant coverage tends to be rather dense, fell-field communities feature large areas of bare rock or thin, gravelly soil inhabited by widely scattered mat-forming and cushion plants. These plants must be able to tolerate poorly developed soils, high winds, possible lack of protective winter snow cover, and prolonged periods of summer drought.

Crowberry, a tiny shrub of the heath family, occurs with alpine lupine, coil-beaked lousewort, and golden fleabane on north-slope fell-fields in the Washington Cascades, where winter snow cover is usually assured. Smooth Douglasia, a mat-forming shrub with bright pink flowers, and subalpine buttercup are characteristic of similar communities in the Olympics. Mat-forming shrubs and shrublets such as kinnikinnick, common juniper, Davidson's penstemon, spreading phlox, and shrubby cinquefoil are conspicuous on drier, more exposed, south-facing slopes in the Cascades. Yarrow, little penstemon, dwarf goldenrod, round-leaved bellflower, and the tufted arctic sandwort are among the more common herbaceous plants. Similar communities occur in the Olympics, the Coast Mountains, and the interior ranges of the Pacific Northwest.

CHAPTER TWELVE

Life at the Top

As THE CLOSED FOREST yields to open parklands, the habitats available to wildlife change dramatically. Animals that rely on closed forest habitats decline in both numbers and kinds while those adapted to meadows, talus, and cliffs increase. As forest dwindles and finally disappears, shelter from predators and inclement weather becomes a greater problem. At the same time, subalpine meadows provide an abundant supply of food in the form of succulent herbs and small shrubs and the host of small mammals that feast upon them. Moreover, in the lower parkland zone the mosaic of meadows and trees provides abundant edges that attract numerous kinds of wildlife, including many forest species.

Animals living at and above timberline must contend with climatic extremes and a scarcity of food during winter. Strategies for coping with these conditions fall into two broad categories: behavioral and morphological/physiological. Behavioral strategies include migration, hibernation, seeking shelter, and timing activities. Morphological/physiological strategies refer to body structures and processes that have evolved in response primarily to extreme cold and low levels of oxygen.

During the summer, timberline regions provide abundant forage and numerous edges, which attract a variety of wildlife. As autumn progresses, air temperature and available food decline steadily. Many animals respond to this annual deterioration of habitat by escaping it altogether through migration or hibernation. Others remain active through the winter in burrows, beneath rock piles, or in other microhabitats that provide shelter from the elements. Because these animals remain active through the winter, they typically rely in whole or part upon foods cached during the summer.

Most predators and all hooved animals remain active throughout the winter. Deer, elk, and moose move to lower elevations. Mountain goats and bighorn sheep, which are better able to move about in the snow, generally remain at somewhat higher elevations but move downslope as food requirements and weather dictate. Predators wander widely in winter. Mountain lions follow their principal prey—mule deer—downslope. Lynxes rely on thick fur to withstand the cold and on large, well-padded paws to move easily across the snow. Their main prey, the snowshoe hare, is comparably equipped. In addition, the hare turns pure white in winter as a means of protective coloration. Weasels turn the tables on their prey by themselves turning completely white, except for the tips of their tails, which remain black. (Such tails provided the familiar black accents in the white ermine robes and stoles that once decked European royalty.)

Timing is critical for animals living at high elevations. The brief summers allow relatively little time to reproduce and rear offspring to the point of independence. In response, birds have evolved a wide variety of behaviors to compensate for short breeding seasons. Many migratory species arrive already paired, and once the young have hatched the male or female may leave the area, possibly as a way of reducing competition. Baby birds typically mature more rapidly than their counterparts at lower elevations and in milder climes, taking days rather than weeks to achieve independence.

Molting, the replacement of old feathers with new ones, is also carefully timed. Generally, high-country birds that migrate long distances leave early in the season and molt on their wintering grounds. In contrast, birds that perhaps only move downslope in winter molt after the young have hatched and remain in the high country as late as possible.

Mammals also show adjustments in breeding habits in response to short reproductive seasons. Most species become sexually active in late winter or spring, when snow is still on the ground, thereby effectively extending the reproductive season. Early pairing also assures that the young will be born shortly after the snowpack disappears, when food is most plentiful. Among deer that frequent the high country, fawning is often postponed until summer, while in bands that remain at lower elevations through the year it more often occurs in spring. In years when food is in short supply, many animals produce fewer offspring or may skip a breeding season entirely. Conversely, abundance of food corresponds with population explosions among small rodents, especially meadow mice and voles, which mature rapidly in any event.

Meadow vegetation is the foundation on which high-country food chains rest. The sedges, grasses, heaths, and other plants that grow in subalpine and alpine meadows are the principal foods not only of animals residing in the meadows but of numerous species that visit them regularly from dens and nests located in adjacent forests or rocky areas. The abundance of food available in meadows tends to concentrate herbivores in these openings, where they attract a large number of predators in turn.

Although meadows are rich sources of food, in and of themselves they offer relatively little cover from predators or the elements. As a result most of the bird and mammal species that feed there depend on nearby tree islands, brush, or rocky areas for protective cover and breeding sites.

Tree islands play a central role in the life of subalpine and timberline animals. The groves provide thermal cover and shelter from inclement weather, a critical service for all animals regardless of season but particularly for those animals that remain active during the winter. The isolated stands of conifers also offer cover from predators and provide sheltered travel corridors across open terrain. Predators, of course, use tree islands for surveying surrounding meadows and ambushing prey. Tree islands also provide breeding habitat for creatures that require woods for that purpose but that rely on nearby energy-rich meadows for food. They also serve as subalpine outposts for a number of species that rarely leave the confines of closed forests. Finally, tree islands are themselves food sources for a number of creatures who feed on conifer seeds, needles, or the foliage or fruit of shrubs growing beneath the trees.

Mountain bluebirds depend heavily on tree islands for nesting and perching habitat. Although the bluebirds require trees for nesting, they forage for insects in nearby meadows. Often they perch on a low branch near the edge of a stand and dart out after insects, taking them on the wing in flycatcher fashion. Or they will hover low over the meadows, alighting to pluck insects from foliage or the ground.

Among the numerous birds that utilize tree islands for nesting, feeding, and cover, none is more closely tied to them than Clark's nutcracker. This large cousin of the jays is gray with black and white wings and tail. Rarely found below the subalpine zone, its bold behavior and raucous call make it one of the more conspicuous parkland residents. The nutcracker feeds on a variety of plant and animal materials, but its chief food is pine nuts, particularly those of the whitebark pine. Indeed, the bird's tie to this single food source is such that except in winter, when it migrates to the lowlands, the bird and the pine are rarely found apart. The nutcracker caches surplus pine nuts for future use, burying them about an inch below the soil surface, usually at some distance from the source trees. Later, cached seeds that are forgotten by the birds may germinate. It is thought

38. Tree islands provide thermal cover for deer and elk.

hat many—perhaps most—groves of whitebark pines originate in this way. In poor seed years, nutcrackers may roam
great distances in search of alternate food sources.

The gray jay can be mistaken for Clark's nutcracker but
is smaller, fluffier in appearance, and lacks the black and
white wings and tail. Often traveling in pairs or small bands,
this scavenger is among the boldest of birds, coming readily
to the hand and frequently visiting campsites to filch un-
guarded food. This behavior has earned the gray jay the
name camp robber, though most people now find the jay's
boldness endearing. The jay's call—often the first sign of
its presence—is a soft cooing whistle that somehow seems
out of character. Among the other birds that frequent tree
islands are the robin, hermit thrush, Hammond's flycatcher,
pine and evening grosbeaks, yellow-rumped warbler, and
rufous hummingbird.

Subalpine parklands are prime habitat for deer and elk.
The meadows supply ample, energy-rich forage; the tree
islands provide convenient thermal cover and places to hide
from predators. The animals generally remain in the high
country until the first deep snows of winter drive them to
wintering grounds in the lowlands. Not all populations of
deer and elk, however, make the annual journey from the
lowlands to the high country. Some, especially along the
coast, remain in the lowlands all year long. Others move
upslope to summer ranges at middle elevations.

The relatively few mammals that breed in meadows tend
to be small or burrowers or both. The most numerous
meadow residents are the various species of meadow mice
and voles. These stout little rodents are prolific breeders
whose populations undergo extraordinary fluctuations, apparently in response to changes in available food supplies.
A single female meadow mouse can have several litters a
year, and the young females of one litter are ready to bear
their own within a few weeks of birth. Population explosions
occur every few years, followed by a sudden crash as predators converge on the meadows. Overcrowding also contributes to the decline, apparently by stimulating the release
of hormones that hasten aging and death.

Meadow mice feed almost entirely on vegetable matter,
eating their own weight in food each day. Grasses, sedges,
rushes, and broadleaf herbs all are important in their diets.

Meadow mice also eat insects and other animal matter, especially during the winter when food plants are scarce. Meadow mice as a rule nest in shallow burrows but spend most of their time above ground scurrying back and forth in well-trodden runways. Some of the mice build their soft globular nests on the surface, amid obscuring vegetation. In winter, however, all meadow mice move their nests above ground, where they remain active beneath an insulating blanket of snow.

Closely related to meadow mice and exhibiting similar behavior are the various voles. The heather vole is the main high-elevation representative of this group in the Pacific Northwest. It inhabits open areas in the subalpine and alpine zones but favors heather meadows where wild huckleberries are abundant. Like meadow mice, it usually nests in a burrow in summer but moves its quarters to the surface in winter.

Many visitors to high meadows are puzzled by the presence of meandering cores of compacted soil running over the surface of the ground. These are the work of pocket gophers, rodents that spend summers below ground and winters on the surface tunneling through the snow pack. In spring, when the animals clean out old tunnels and excavate new ones, they push the dirt up out of the ground and into their abandoned snow tunnels. Melting of the snowpack exposes these soil cores, which are the only contact that most people will have with these seldom-seen rodents.

Pocket gophers are burrowing specialists that exhibit numerous anatomical adaptations to life underground. Their bodies, for example, are compact, and their fur, like that of moles, can be stroked in either direction. When a female pocket gopher is ready to give birth, her pelvis unhinges to widen the birth canal, then returns to its narrower conformation after the process is complete. Pocket gophers are also equipped with long, powerful incisors that enable them to easily snip the tough roots, tubers, and stems that make up the bulk of their diet.

Pocket gophers can be considerable pests in home gardens or agricultural areas, but despite their taste for succulent herbs their overall impact on subalpine and alpine meadows seems positive. Though gophers can cause noticeable damage to plants in some areas, their tunneling aerates and thereby improves the soil. Several studies, including work at Mount St. Helens, have shown that meadow plants re-colonize gopher-disturbed soils more rapidly than other types and grow more vigorously thereafter.

Two species of pocket gophers inhabit the high meadows of the Pacific Northwest: the northern pocket gopher and the western pocket gopher. The former ranges from the Eastern Cascades to the Great Plains and south through the Rockies to the Southwest. The latter is confined to the Western Cascades and the humid coastal region of Oregon, Washington, and British Columbia. The two species are very similar in both appearance and habits.

Ground squirrels constitute a third major group of bur-rowing animals that inhabit the high meadows of the Pacific Northwest. The Columbian ground squirrel inhabits timber-line meadows in the Northern Rockies and outlying ranges such as the Wallowa Mountains and Okanogan Highlands. The smaller Belding's ground squirrel also occurs in the Wallowas. Neither species is to be found in or west of the Cascade Range, where the two closely related species of golden-mantled ground squirrels are the only representa-tives of their clan. These two squirrels, however, prefer wooded, brushy, or rocky areas rather than open meadows. Ground squirrels are missing entirely from the Olympic Mountains and other coastal ranges.

Unlike meadow mice and pocket gophers, which remain active year-round, ground squirrels are hibernators, retiring to their burrow systems each fall and re-emerging in the spring. Often the adults enter hibernation before the young, which need more time to fatten up. Seeds play an important role in the diet of these animals (hence their generic name *Spermophilus,* meaning seed lover), but they feed on a wide variety of other vegetable matter as well.

Among the most characteristic and distinctive alpine birds are the three species of ptarmigans, all of which occur in the Pacific Northwest. The willow ptarmigan and rock ptar-migan range across boreal North America from Alaska to Newfoundland and south down the Coast Mountains to southern British Columbia. The white-tailed ptarmigan, the only one to occur south of Canada, ranges from Alaska and the Yukon through the Rockies and Coast Mountains to Washington and New Mexico. All three ptarmigans prefer open country to woods and rarely venture far below timberline.

The white-tailed ptarmigan feeds mainly on the twigs of dwarf willows but also eats other plant materials as well as insects. It lays its eggs on a sparsely lined scrape amid dwarf willows and heaths. In its open-sky world it relies for protection on camouflage rather than cover. In winter the bird is entirely white; in summer its plumage is a blend of mottled brown and white. Though normally unwary, the ptarmigan freezes when alarmed. At such times it is extremely difficult to detect, resembling either a snow hummock or a rock. If flushed, it prefers to run rather than fly. Aside from serving as camouflage, the ptarmigan's white feathers also provide more efficient insulation. Lacking pigments, white feathers are filled with air instead.

The water pipit is another bird that nests in open alpine meadows, where it normally places a grassy nest in the shelter of a rock or shrub. The pipit is commonly seen along streams, lakes, or ponds foraging for insects. It also frequents snowbanks, where insects blown upslope by valley breezes are stunned by the cold. Unlike the ptarmigan, however, the pipit abandons its birthplace each fall for the milder climes and better pickings to be found in the lowlands along saltwater shores and in plowed fields.

Subalpine parklands offer predators a rich assortment of prey and a variety of cover types suitable for breeding, resting, and hiding from wary prey. As a result, the number and kinds of predators are greater here than in closed forests. Coyotes, red foxes, bobcats, mountain lions, weasels, martens, badgers, wolverines, grizzly bears, and several species of hawks and owls all prowl the parklands. And for grizzly bears, badgers, wolverines, and red foxes the high broken country near timberline is preferred habitat.

The Pacific Northwest is the last stronghold of the grizzly bear in the contiguous United States. Populations still exist in Yellowstone and Glacier national parks, as well as in the Flathead–Beartooth region of western Montana. In addition, grizzlies that wander south from British Columbia are sighted from time to time in Washington and Idaho, where native populations have been eradicated. Grizzly bears still thrive in virtually all mountain areas in British Columbia, as well as along the coast where major salmon streams enter the Pacific.

Unlike the black bear, which visits parklands to harvest huckleberries or harass rodents but is principally a forest creature, the grizzly is a denizen of the high country. Like its smaller forest cousin it feeds on a wide variety of vegetable matter as well as any animals it manages to catch. Although the grizzly is technically a carnivore, its omnivorous habit and lack of specialized hunting skills make it an indifferent predator at best. As a result a large part of its diet consists of roots, tubers, berries, and grasses, on which it seems to thrive.

Though a grizzly bear can run as fast as a horse over short distances, it is rarely able to catch an adult elk or deer. When the opportunity presents itself, however, the bear readily stalks and kills young, old, or sick animals. After eating its fill, a grizzly will cache a large animal for later use by covering it with brush. Anyone who happens upon such a cache should immediately leave the area, as its owner is likely nearby and in no mood to tolerate intruders. Grizzlies also dig up colonies of ground squirrels, in the process often creating pits several feet across.

Grizzlies fear nothing in their domain, though they are intelligent enough to avoid humans when possible. Even so, they will attack readily in the event of threats either real or perceived, and people who out of ignorance or bad luck arouse their anger or defensive response can expect swift, possibly fatal retribution.

The wolverine is much smaller than the grizzly but enjoys an equal reputation for ferocity. Although this largest member of the weasel family is a formidable opponent when cornered or defending its young, it normally avoids confrontations. Like the grizzly, the wolverine is primarily a creature of timberline, preferring the broken country and mosaic of meadows, rocks, and woods. It preys extensively on small mammals, but also feeds on the carcasses of larger animals. Wolverines are incessant wanderers that require huge hunting territories to survive. As a result their population is small under the best of circumstances, and the chance of actually sighting one, at least outside the Far North, is remote. Wolverines have been eliminated from much of their former range in the western United States but persist in the high country of the Cascades, Northern Rockies, and Sierra Nevada.

Cliffs and talus are found at all elevations but are most prominent and widespread at and above timberline, where the erosive action of frost and ice on exposed bedrock slopes favors the development of such terrain. Water that seeps into cracks and crevices within the rocks freezes and expands, gradually wedging rocks farther apart. On a steep slope or cliff, rocks that are eventually dislodged roll or fall to its base, where they accumulate to form sloping fans called talus. As the process continues, the cliff grows steeper and the talus piles deeper.

This single process—the transfer of rocks from the face of a cliff to its base—creates special wildlife habitats in both locations. The ongoing removal of rocks from the face of a cliff produces systems of ledges and shallow caves used by various birds and mammals for resting, nesting, feeding, observing, or getting from place to place. The corresponding accumulation of debris at the base of a cliff amounts to a labyrinthine apartment complex of sorts for small mammals, who find the spaces between the boulders ideal for nesting, hibernating, or seeking refuge from large predators.

Cliffs provide to the wildlife species adapted to use them a degree of protection from predators that is afforded by few other habitats. It is hardly surprising, then, to discover that wildlife favors high cliffs over low ones. Tall cliffs also offer more living space. Similarly, the usefulness of a cliff to wildlife increases with the number of crevices, ledges, and caves on its face. The relative abundance of such features, however, is largely a matter of rock type. Cliffs form only in rocks that are hard enough to resist crumbling, but if the rocks are too hard or massive, there will be few ledges or other irregularities.

Elevation also affects the usefulness of a cliff. Above timberline, lingering ice and snow makes many otherwise suitable cliff nesting sites virtually useless. Still, one of the region's most exciting and distinctive cliff-dwelling animals— the mountain goat—is rarely found at lower elevations.

The mountain goat does not require cliffs but spends most of its time on or near them. The soft pads and wide spacing of the two toes of each hoof enable this relative of Old World antelopes to negotiate seemingly inaccessible cracks and ledges. The young are born in spring on high, protected ledges. During the summer, small bands of females and

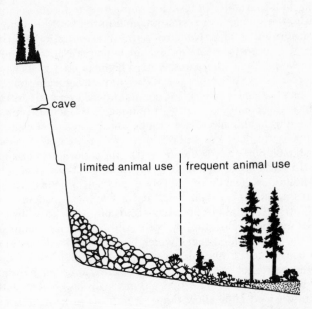

cave

limited animal use | frequent animal use

39. Wildlife habitats associated with cliffs and talus (adapted from Ward, *Wildlife Habitats in Managed Forests, the Blue Mountains of Oregon and Washington*)

kids roam the cliffs, feeding on lichens and succulent vegetation that have rooted among the rocks. Males are generally solitary.

During winter storms, mountain goats commonly abandon exposed cliffs for the shelter of the subalpine forest. Tree islands large enough to provide both thermal cover and protection from icy winds are therefore important to the survival of these animals. In addition, the foliage of the conifers provides an important—sometimes critical—food source during the season of need. Deep snows that impede the goats' movement may force them downslope well below their normal range.

The mountain goat naturally ranges from southeastern Alaska and the Yukon south to the Washington Cascades and the mountains of northern Idaho. Originally, mountain goats were missing from the Olympics, presumably because the hundred miles of lowlands separating those mountains from the species' nearest stronghold in the Cascade Range constituted an effective barrier against colonization. Today, some 700 goats occur throughout Olympic National Park. In the park's northern and eastern high country, goats have become so numerous in places that they are damaging fragile subalpine and alpine plant communities. Proposals to reduce the population through hunting have met stiff resistance from animal welfare groups whose concept of welfare apparently does not extend to the other creatures whose habitat is being adversely affected by the superfluity of goats.

In addition to mountain goats, several other species of wildlife are heavily or entirely dependent on cliffs. These include swifts, certain bats, and a few small rodents. In addition, a number of raptors—birds of prey—use cliffs for nesting sites, lookouts, or both. The most conspicuous of these is the golden eagle, which builds bulky stick nests on broad ledges. From the vantage point of a cliff, eagles and other birds of prey can survey vast expanses of hunting terrain. Moreover, the updrafts normally associated with sun-warmed cliffs allow these large birds to launch themselves into the sky with a minimum expenditure of energy.

The talus slopes at the bases of cliffs provide secure homes for a variety of small mammals. Four factors determine the relative usefulness of talus slopes to wildlife: stability, depth, rock size, and proximity to food sources. Stable talus slopes exhibit dynamic equilibrium between the size and number of constituent rocks and the angle at which they repose. As one might expect, older talus slopes are generally more stable than younger ones, particularly since older slopes often feature accumulations of soil that help bind the mass together. Older slopes may also support scattered shrubs and trees whose roots further increase stability.

Because older talus slopes also tend to be deeper, they more efficiently insulate resident animals from outside temperature extremes. The deepest part of the slope is warmer in winter and cooler in summer than the layer near the surface. By moving up and down through the slope, animals can regulate their environments to minimize gains and losses of body heat. A talus slope that is too shallow affords inadequate insulation from the elements and is therefore of limited use to wildlife.

The size of the rocks making up a talus slope influences the size of the spaces between them. The larger the spaces, the larger the animals that can inhabit the slope. Marmots prefer talus slopes made up of large, angular boulders, beneath which are spacious cavities for nesting and hibernation. Pikas, mice, and woodrats also frequent boulder piles but are more common in talus slopes where smaller rocks create openings that are too small for most predators.

Since talus slopes provide little in the way of food, resident animals normally rely on adjacent plant communities for food. Whether forest, brush, or meadow, the vegetation should be close by the talus slope so that small foraging mammals at the first hint of danger can quickly retreat to the security of the rocks. The liveliest talus slopes are therefore likely to be those where forest, brush, and meadow, as well as a reliable source of water, all exist in close proximity.

Among the mammals that inhabit talus slopes, none is more closely tied to that habitat than the pika, a small chunky member of the rabbit family with large round ears and no tail. Colonies of pikas den within talus slopes and rock piles, each breeding pair staking out a territory from which neighboring pikas are vigorously expelled. Pikas remain active within their talus slopes throughout the eight or nine months when snow lies deep over the high country. Their chief source of food during this period is hay made from a wide variety of plant materials gathered the previous summer. When not harvesting plants, pikas sit on rocks sunning themselves, communicating by means of surprisingly loud, high-pitched nasal barks.

Another talus resident that remains active during the winter is the bushy-tailed woodrat, or packrat. The woodrat sports a luxurious, bushy unratlike tail, as if it were in the process of somehow evolving into a squirrel. Like the pika, the woodrat remains active throughout the winter, feeding on dried vegetation, including fungi, that it gathered and cached especially for that purpose. Most campers meet the woodrat—or packrat—in the middle of the night, when they are awakened by the racket it makes as it rifles among their gear searching for food. For unknown reasons, the rat is attracted to shiny objects, such as coins or silverware, which it will carry off to its den after leaving behind perhaps a stone or twig in trade.

The golden-mantled ground squirrel, which resembles a large chipmunk, commonly winters in rockslides and boulder piles, but unlike the pika and woodrat, it spends the season in a deep slumber from which it occasionally awakens to urinate. During hibernation, it subsists mainly on body fat stored up the previous summer, supplementing this source with a few seeds, nuts, and dried fungi stored in its den just in case. The ground squirrel's nutritional needs are small, however, because during hibernation its metabolism is reduced to a minimum. During the summer, this bold, bright little squirrel is a frequent visitor to campsites.

The largest and normally most conspicuous talus resident is the marmot, a western relative of the eastern woodchuck, or groundhog. Although several species of marmots inhabit the Pacific Northwest, including the woodchuck, the two most common and widespread are the yellow-bellied and hoary marmots. The yellow-bellied marmot ranges from the Eastern Cascades and Canadian Rockies south to California and New Mexico, mostly occurring in the mountains but also inhabiting rocky lowland habitats east of the Cascades. The larger hoary marmot ranges from Alaska south to Washington and east to Montana and is strictly montane in distribution. The Olympic marmot, found only in Washington's Olympic Mountains, is thought by some experts to be a geographic race of the more widely occurring hoary marmot. Two other closely related species occur on Vancouver Island and in Alaska.

Marmots are actually oversized ground squirrels and, like their smaller kin, retire to their dens in fall to spend the winter in deep slumber. They spend the brief summer season fattening themselves on grasses, sedges, and other green vegetation in preparation for their long hibernation. The roly-poly rodents retire to their dens in fall and don't re-emerge until late spring.

Visitors to timberline areas throughout the western United States commonly see marmots scurrying over boulders, feeding in meadows, resting in the sun, or playfully wrestling with their young. In some areas the animals have become quite bold and will allow humans to approach within a foot or two. When alarmed, marmots utter a high, shrill whistle that can be heard for miles.

With succulent pikas, woodrats, ground squirrels, and

armots congregating in and near talus slopes, it is no wonder that these rock slides also attract a large number of predators. Coyotes, foxes, mountain lions, bobcats, wolverines, fishers, and weasels all regularly den among the boulders. Hawks, owls, and eagles nest elsewhere but patrol rock slides for prey.

CHAPTER THIRTEEN

Rainshadow Lands

THE SAGEBRUSH COUNTRY east of the Cascades is popu larly called "desert," particularly by Northwesterners wh live in the damp forest region west of the mountains. Bu plant ecologist Rexford Daubenmire, a recognized authorit on the vegetation of the inland Northwest, argues that "desert is a misnomer in this instance. Although, in Daubenmire words, "a combination of hot dry summers . . . rattlesnakes horned lizards, scorpions, tarantulas and cacti seem to evok this classification,"* the vegetation covering most of easter Washington, central and southeastern Oregon, and souther Idaho is properly termed *steppe*. Plant geographers ar not united in their definitions of desert and steppe, bu Daubenmire's distinction, which is based on the relativ abundance of grasses, is a useful one for the Northwest i particular. By this definition, steppe occurs where precipi tation is too little to support trees but sufficient to maintai a conspicuous cover of grasses. Desert occurs where to little precipitation falls even to support grasses.

Daubenmire's distinction is borne out in the field. Bi sagebrush is the principal shrub throughout most of th intermountain region, from the Cascades and Sierra east t the Rockies and from eastern Washington to souther Nevada. Seen from a distance the sagebrush formations o say, eastern Washington and central Nevada look much th same. In both cases sagebrush and associated shrubs forn a low, nearly uniform (some would say monotonous) cove over vast treeless areas. A closer look, however, reveal:

* Daubenmire, Rexford. *Steppe Vegetation of Washington* Washington Agricultural Experiment Station, Technical Bulleti 62, 1970.

several important differences. First, in Washington's sagebrush steppe, big sagebrush is scattered over an understory of grasses, while in the desert sagebrush scrub of Nevada grasses are normally inconspicuous. Sagebrush steppe occurs in the Great Basin, but it normally is restricted to lower mountain slopes, above the desert sagebrush scrub that covers the region's vast intermontane basins. Second, big sagebrush plants commonly grow to be three or more feet tall in the sagebrush steppe but seldom reach that height in the desert. Third, sagebrush steppe stands normally contain more plants and more species of plants than comparable stands of sagebrush desert scrub. Generally, the desert sagebrush zone of the Great Basin exhibits less diversity, less productivity, and less resilience when disturbed than the moister sagebrush steppe.

Three major types of steppe vegetation occur in the arid lowlands of the inland Northwest: shrub steppe, true steppe, and meadow steppe. Shrub steppe consists of two layers: a canopy layer of widely spaced shrubs and an herbaceous understory layer dominated by grasses. True steppe is an arid grassland that replaces shrub steppe in wetter, warmer areas where the temperature/moisture balance is somehow unsuited to the formation of an extensive shrub cover. Meadow steppe is distinguished by the presence of numerous kinds of grasses and broad-leaved herbs. It may or may not have shrub, though in the Northwest it usually does.

As the above discussion suggests, the terms *meadow steppe* on the one hand and *true steppe* or *shrub steppe* on the other are not mutually exclusive. Rather, they represent two different ways of classifying the vegetation. The terms *true steppe* and *shrub steppe* refer to the appearance—or "physiognomy," as botanists would say—of the vegetation, whereas *meadow steppe* is based on an ecological difference—the greater lushness and species diversity resulting from higher levels of moisture than is characteristic of the other two steppe types. Though not tidy, these categories are widely accepted and correspond to real and recognizable differences in the steppe vegetation of the Pacific Northwest.

Shrub steppe, mostly dominated by big sagebrush, occurs in the central portion of the Columbia Basin, central and southeastern Oregon, and southern Idaho. The largest area of true steppe is the so-called Palouse grassland, which covers a large area in southeastern Washington and north-eastern Oregon. Grassland communities are scarce in south-eastern Oregon and southern Idaho, where they are small in extent and generally confined to areas where moisture is locally more plentiful. Meadow steppe occurs along the moist northern or eastern periphery of the steppe region, from the foothills of the North Cascades eastward along the base of the Okanogan Highlands to the Idaho Panhandle.

The climate of the steppe region of the Pacific Northwest is a product of its northerly latitude and its position in the rainshadow cast by the Cascade Range to the west. The Cascades deprive the region of much of the moderating influence of the Pacific Ocean and wring nearly dry the storms that pass eastward over its crest. As a result, eastern Washington, central and southeastern Oregon, and southern Idaho share an arid continental climate that is modified somewhat by incursions of moist marine air during the winter months. Despite the region's obvious aridity, how-ever, plants are subjected to far less moisture stress here than in the Great Basin. The steppe region's northerly posi-tion means that summers are cooler than those of the Great Basin, while winters are wetter and scarcely colder thanks to the seemingly endless procession of storms characteristic of this latitude. Moreover, the Cascade Range presents a less formidable barrier than the Sierra Nevada to the inland movement of moist marine air. With the exception of the major volcanoes, the Cascades are about half as high as the Sierra, and the Columbia River Gorge provides a major avenue through the range.

As a consequence the steppe region of Washington, Oregon, and Idaho experiences moderately cold winters, warm to hot summers, and somewhat more rainfall than received by desert regions to the south. In the steppes of eastern Washington the mean temperature ranges between 22° and 36°F (−5.5° and 1.5°C) for the coldest month; 65° and 76°F (18.5° and 24.5°C) for the warmest.

Rainfall ranges from as little as six inches at the base of the Cascades to nearly 22 inches in the northeast, where steppe merges into forest. Most of the steppe region aver-ages ten to 15 inches of rain a year. These amounts are comparable to those received by the shortgrass prairie of the High Plains. The major difference is that the prairie receives most of its rain during the growing season, while precipitation on the steppe is mostly confined to the cold season, when most plants are inactive. The driest sections of the steppe region receive only about one inch of rain from June through August. The wetter portion of the steppes, in northeastern Washington, receives only two inches during that same period.

The climates of southeastern Oregon and southern Idaho are comparable to that of eastern Washington. There is a slight decline in precipitation from north to south, enough so that true steppe and meadow steppe are poorly represented south of the Blue Mountains, but overall rainfall totals for the southern portion of the steppe region are not significantly lower than for the driest portion of the Columbia Basin. Similarly, mean and extreme air temperatures for each season vary little over the entire Northwestern steppe region. Southeastern Oregon and southern Idaho are slightly hotter and even less humid in the summer than eastern Washington and experience somewhat lower temperatures in winter. But the differences are far less than those that distinguish the steppe region as a whole from either the Pacific coastal region west of the Cascades or the High Plains east of the Rockies.

Although the climate of the steppe region is neither as hot and dry as that of true desert nor as cold as that of the mountains that surround it, in its blend of winter cold, summer heat, and drought during the season of greatest plant activity it embodies an extreme of its own, one that relatively few kinds of plants can tolerate. Fewer kinds of plants grow in the steppes, for example, than in the various conifer forests that surround them, and the great majority of plants that do grow there are represented by relatively small, thinly scattered populations. Perhaps a half dozen species of shrubs and a roughly equal number of grasses account for the great majority of plant cover over more than 10,000 square miles of territory. Changes in habitat within the steppe more often than not result merely in shifts in the relative numbers of the same few species. Even the shift from shrub steppe to true steppe consists of little more than a loss of the dominant shrubs; the grass species in both types of vegetation are essentially the same. The steppes are ruled by an oligarchy of plants.

The permutations possible even with a relatively small number of species are nevertheless great. Nine climax plant associations corresponding to measurable changes in climate have been identified for Washington alone. Several more that are not found in Washington have been identified in Oregon and Idaho. An even larger number of climax associations occur in response to local variations in topography and soil. Finally, human disturbances—in particular, grazing and agriculture—have produced so-called zootic climaxes: stable, apparently permanent plant associations that have developed in response to the activities of humans and animals. In fact, disturbance in the steppe region has been so widespread and severe that zootic climax associations have replaced native communities throughout most of the region.

Although steppe vegetation covers most of the region between the Cascades and the Northern Rockies, other types of vegetation can be found in special habitats. Embedded within the steppes are a variety of deciduous woodland types that occur along streams, in damp bottomlands, and other places where large amounts of reliable moisture are available throughout the growing season. In southeastern Oregon and southern Idaho, open woodlands of western juniper occupy a zone between the hotter, drier steppe zones and the cooler, moister forest zones. Southeastern Oregon and southern Idaho also contain areas of true desert scrub that are large enough to show up on vegetation maps. This type of vegetation tends to occur on the floors of old, dry lake basins—playas—where evaporation has resulted in high concentrations of salts on and just below the soil surface.

Steppes dominated by big sagebrush occupy the heart of the Columbia Basin, from the base of the Cascade Range eastward as far as Ritzville and south to the Columbia River. In northern Oregon, sagebrush steppe generally occurs on the hot, lower slopes flanking the Columbia, Deschutes, and John Day rivers. Sagebrush steppe also covers most of the southeastern quarter of Oregon, as well as the greater part of southern Idaho.

Well-developed stands of sagebrush steppe have four distinct layers of vegetation: the canopy, or shrub layer; the perennial grass layer; the annual layer; and the moss/lichen layer.

The canopy consists mainly of widely scattered big sage-

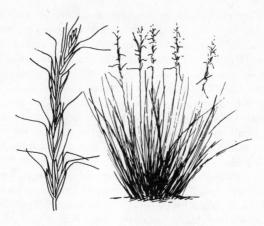

40. Bluebunch wheatgrass (*Agropyron spicatum*)

brush plants averaging about three feet in height. Small numbers of several other smaller shrub species may be found with it. Depending on locale and habitat, these may include rabbitbrush, antelope bitterbrush, spiny hopsage, winter fat, gray horsebrush, low sagebrush, or cutleaf sagebrush, among others.

The perennial grass layer is dominated throughout most of the region by bluebunch wheatgrass. Idaho fescue, Cusick's bluegrass, and needle-and-thread are often present and may dominate special habitats. These grasses, rather than forming a continuous turf, grow in large bunches a foot or more apart and a couple of feet in height. Idaho fescue becomes prominent in sagebrush steppe stands in the east-central portion of the Columbia Basin. The grass coverage is greater in these stands than in those to the west, apparently in response to cooler, moister conditions. The hottest, driest habitats in the Columbia Basin, where surface moisture is scant, feature abundant sagebrush and a sparse understory consisting of little other than a thin cover of the short, tufted Sandberg's bluegrass. In southeastern Oregon relatively moist alluvial bottomlands often support stands of big sagebrush and tall green rabbitbrush, with an understory of tall wild rye.

A variety of low forbs and low, tufted grasses form a sparse as the dominant shrub by other species. Even on what would appear to be normal soils, however, there is wide variation cover beneath and between the larger shrubs and perennial grasses. The layer is dominated by Sandberg's bluegrass, which is a nearly universal component of the sagebrush steppe. Other low grasses are far less common and may be absent entirely. Many different species of either annual or perennial forbs occur in the sagebrush steppe, but none are found in all stands and as a group they account for a small fraction of the total plant coverage. The more common perennials include yarrow, locoweeds, mariposa lilies, balsamroot, shaggy fleabane, desert parsley, false agoseris, lupines, and phloxes. Among the more common annuals are western stickseed, spring whitlow-grass, tansy mustard, small-flowered blue-eyed Mary, small-flowered willowherb, Microsteris, mousetail, Indian wheat, and small-flowered gilia.

Repeated cycles of freezing and thawing, wetting and drying, have broken the soil into irregular hexagons separated by cracks. Annuals are often confined to the cracks, which trap and hold moisture better and are warmer than the exposed ground surface. The cracks also offer seeds protection from foraging mice and birds and pose little resistance to rapid root penetration.

The harsh, exposed soil surface between the cracks is the province of drought-resistant lichens and mosses, which make up the cryptogam layer. (Cryptogams are plants such as ferns, mosses, and fungi, which reproduce by means of spores rather than seeds.) The lichens and mosses of the steppe thrive when moisture is available and become dormant when it isn't. Some mosses die back as early as April. The cryptogam layer is very thin, and noticeable mainly after rains, which wash away the cover of dust that normally obscures it. Epiphytic lichens and a few mosses also grow on the lower stems of big sagebrush and other shrubs.

Sagebrush steppe occupies the hottest, driest sections of the steppe region, where precipitation rarely exceeds ten inches a year, of which two inches or less fall during the summer months. Sagebrush survives the hot, dry summers by tapping reservoirs of moisture several feet beneath the soil surface. The shrub therefore grows poorly in shallow or rocky soils where root penetration is difficult. Wherever such substrates occur, big sagebrush is commonly replaced of sagebrush coverage, even though the grass cover remains more or less the same. The reasons for the variation are obscure but probably lie in deep soil conditions to which the shrub is sensitive but shallow-rooted grasses are not. Sagebrush is moderately tolerant of salt, which it excludes from water taken up by its roots, but it is replaced on excessively salty or alkaline soils by shadscale, winter fat, and other desert shrubs.

Throughout the steppe region, the rains begin in autumn, about the same time as the first frosts. Most forbs and all low shrubs are dormant during the season of cold. Winters are mild enough, however, that big sagebrush can intermittently carry out photosynthesis and sustain brief, slow episodes of growth. The great majority of steppe shrubs, however, are deciduous, which may put them at something

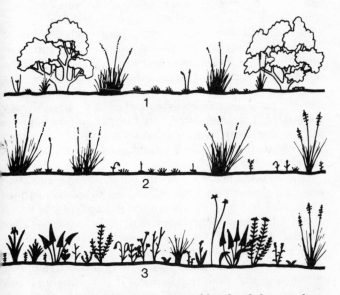

41. Profiles showing relative spacing and height of plants in three major steppe types: (1) sagebrush steppe, (2) bunchgrass steppe, and (3) meadow steppe (adapted from Daubenmire, *Steppe Vegetation of Washington*)

Rainshadow Lands

of a disadvantage. Since rainfall rapidly tapers off in spring—just as these plants are putting on new crops of leaves—they must rely during the long, dry summer on deep reservoirs of moisture that are recharged each winter. Big sagebrush is particularly effective in tapping this resource, but unlike most other shrubs in the region it is also able to supplement photosynthesis and growth during spring and summer with periods of activity during fall and winter. Even so, since relatively little photosynthesis occurs during the winter, evergreenness would seem to confer less of an advantage on big sagebrush than it does, for example, on the conifers of the Northwest coastal forest. Therefore the chief advantage of the evergreen habit may be that it allows big sagebrush to commence photosynthesis as early in spring as conditions permit and to concentrate a greater part of the products of photosynthesis in root growth rather than leaf production.

Root growth among steppe shrubs begins early in spring before any vegetative growth is apparent, and continues well into fall, long after flowers have fallen and fruit has set. This sustained growth is possible partly because steppe shrubs are able to continue photosynthesis even when moisture levels fall far below those tolerated by most other plants. Moreover, throughout the summer their roots probe ever more deeply for water and extract virtually all the moisture there is from the soil levels into which they have already penetrated. Extracting every last drop of moisture from the soil, however, may be more valuable as a way of eliminating competitors than for whatever additional photosynthesis is thereby enabled.

Grasses are able to coexist with the shrubs by elaborating extensive shallow root systems that allow the plants to utilize even small amounts of surface moisture, such as that which might fall during a brief spring shower. Even so, native bunchgrasses do not form continuous turfs but grow in isolated tufts. Perennial grasses germinate in the fall, grow slowly through the winter, then turn up production during the spring. After flowering in May and June, they gradually die back to their underground parts as the season of drought progresses. Most perennial forbs lie dormant all winter, then burst forth in spring before they too, like the grasses, die back over the course of the summer. Perennials are able by irtue of their small size to thrive on spring rains. Moreover, ince the carbohydrates needed to fuel new growth in the pring are stored in bulbs, corms, and overwintering buds, erennials are ready to go as soon as conditions permit. nnuals must germinate and grow rapidly to take advantage f the narrow window of opportunity that spring presents. s a result there are far fewer annuals than perennials in he steppes, though among the annuals are two of the most uccessful and widespread grasses in the region. Some an- uals germinate in autumn and grow slowly through the vinter, but most wait until spring. Even so, seed dormancy s common among annuals of the sagebrush steppe, and ears may pass before the right combination of cir- umstances triggers germination. As a result, given species f annuals do not reliably reappear every year in the same ocation, but their conservative approach to germination ncreases their survival chances in the years they do appear.

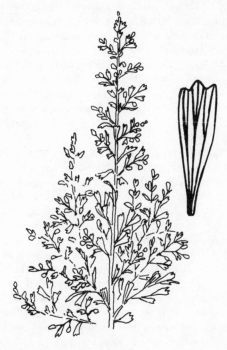

2. Big sagebrush (*Artemisia tridentata*)

Of course, annuals simply avoid the problem of summer drought by dying before it affects them.

Anyone who spends much time in the steppe country of the Pacific Northwest soon learns to recognize big sagebrush. The plants range from 16 inches to more than six feet in height, but most are around three feet tall. They have compact, intricately branched crowns and gray shreddy bark. The leaves are slender, about ½ to 1½ inches long, and are often clustered in small bunches of two or more. They are broader at the tip than the base and culminate in three shallow teeth, which gives the shrub its specific name, *tridentata* ("three toothed"). Soft white hairs on both surfaces of the leaves are responsible for the grayish-green color of the foliage. Aromatic resins within the leaves give the plants a distinctive pungent fragrance that is reminiscent of culinary sage, an unrelated herb.

The leaves of big sagebrush in their size and hairiness are typical of those found on many plants growing in hot, arid environments. Small leaves offer minimum surface area to the sun so that they absorb heat more slowly than larger leaves. Hairs trap a layer of still air next to the leaf surfaces, thereby insulating the leaves and protecting them from the drying effects of wind. Many other steppe plants, such as horsebrush, winter fat, and rabbitbrush, also are covered with pale hairs. This community tendency toward hirsuteness is responsible for the overall grayish coloration of the sagebrush steppe.

The sagebrush steppes of the Pacific Northwest have been subjected to heavy grazing for more than a century. The result has been an overall increase in sagebrush as compared to understory grasses and the replacement of perennial bunchgrasses by alien annual grasses. Since sagebrush is browsed only as a last resort, the reduction of competing grasses favors sagebrush seedlings, which are ignored.

Studies in the Great Basin suggest that range fires increase the abundance of big sagebrush over grasses. This does not appear to be the case in the Pacific Northwest, where range fires are usually hot enough to kill big sagebrush, burning even the main root mass below the surface of the ground. The grasses, however, suffer little permanent damage and commonly invade burned areas for many years. Although a few sagebrush seedlings are usually present during the first year following a fire, full-scale reinvasion of lost ground must wait for a time when a number of favorable conditions coincide.

Although big sagebrush is the most prominent shrub in the shrub steppes of eastern Washington, eastern Oregon, and southern Idaho, it does not dominate all shrub-steppe formations. In Oregon, three other species of sagebrush dominate communities found on particular types of soils. Low sagebrush often replaces big sagebrush on stony soils. Stands of this sort also occur as parks within the ponderosa pine and lower Douglas-fir forests of central and southeastern Oregon. Though resembling big sagebrush, low sagebrush is only four to 16 inches tall. Bluebunch wheatgrass, Idaho fescue, and Sandberg's bluegrass dominate the understory. A large number of perennial forbs also occur in these communities. On even thinner, drier, rockier soils, stiff sagebrush and Sandberg's bluegrass form a sparse cover. No other shrubs are normally present. Communities dominated by silver sagebrush occur on moister sites. Shrub-steppe communities dominated by curl-leaf mountain-mahogany are found in the foothills of the Oregon Cascades and other mountain ranges in the region, where they occur along the broad ecotone between steppe and forest.

At the time of the first white settlers, about 150 years ago, the Palouse region of southeastern Washington, as well as adjacent parts of northeastern Oregon, were covered almost entirely by arid grasslands. Bluebunch wheatgrass and Idaho fescue were the principal grasses on the rolling Palouse hills. On terraces along the Snake River and in the eastern end of the Columbia River Gorge, Sandberg's bluegrass replaced the fescue. Several other bunchgrasses, including Cusick's bluegrass, needle-and-thread, and sand dropseed, also occurred in the grasslands but were not nearly so common. Gray rabbitbrush was widely scattered through the grasslands, but shrubs were generally inconspicuous.

Today, only a few widely scattered stands of pristine Palouse grassland remain. Most of the region has long been converted to agriculture, originally winter wheat, more recently split peas and lentils. Abandoned croplands have been invaded by downy cheatgrass and are unlikely to revert to their climax vegetation.

Climax Palouse grasslands differ from sagebrush steppes

only in the absence of the shrub layer. The same association of annual and perennial herbs occur in both communities. The climate in the Palouse grassland region is slightly warmer and wetter than in the sagebrush-steppe zone to the west. The Palouse is also covered by a thick blanket of loess—wind-blown dust that was deposited there in dry interglacial periods during the Ice Age. The combination of fine soils and increased surface moisture is ideal for grasses. The fierce competition from grasses experienced by steppe shrubs during the seedling stage may account, at least in part, for their absence from these grasslands.

Bluebunch wheatgrass was once the most common and widespread grass in the steppe region of the inland Northwest, occurring in all but the driest or wettest habitats. Its range and abundance have been greatly reduced during this century through overgrazing. Bluebunch wheatgrass has densely clustered blue-green leaves. Its flowering stalks are stiff, straight, and up to 40 inches tall. The flower spikes, which are 3½ to six inches tall, appear June through August.

Idaho fescue is less widespread than bluebunch wheatgrass, generally occurring in moister steppe communities. Together, these two grasses, along with mountain sagebrush, a high-altitude cousin of big sagebrush, range upslope nearly to timberline, where they often form open parks on relatively warm, dry, south-facing slopes and ridgetops. Mountain sagebrush steppe is also widespread in southern Idaho. Idaho fescue has rough, threadlike leaves up to 40 inches tall and flower stems as much as twice that height. The flower spikes are four to eight inches long and appear May through August.

Sandberg's bluegrass is considerably smaller than the two previous species. Its soft, flat leaves grow in a dense tuft. The flower stems are normally about a foot long, but sometimes reach twice that length. Sandberg's bluegrass may be found in all steppe habitats and may also range upward through the forest zones to high elevations, but it favors warmer, drier sites. On thin, dry, rocky soils it may be the only grass present.

Where conversion to crops has not destroyed the original grasslands, overgrazing often has. Livestock favor Cusick's bluegrass over the other species, followed by bluebunch wheatgrass and Sandberg's bluegrass. Only when these species are not available do they turn to less palatable annuals such as downy cheatgrass. Overgrazing results in a conversion from native perennials to cheatgrass within just a few years, and once that transformation has occurred a reversion to native grasses is highly unlikely, even when grazing is halted. Cheatgrass, a rapid grower that each year sprouts anew from seeds produced the previous year, is admirably suited to the region's cold, wet winters and hot, dry summers. Once established, its abundance and vigor prevent native perennials from reclaiming the lost ground.

Along the northern margin of the Columbia Basin, where lava plateaus and coulees give way to the rolling foothills of the Okanogan Highlands, cooler, moister conditions have produced steppe communities characterized by an abundance of grasses and forbs. Deciduous shrubs also occur in these communities, but rather than being more or less evenly distributed, as in shrub-steppe types, they occur as scattered patches or thickets. In their lushness, species diversity, and general aspect these northern steppelands are more reminiscent of mountain meadows than they are of sagebrush steppe or Palouse grassland. The term *meadow steppe*, which is generally applied to moister steppe communities, expresses this similarity.

Idaho fescue and bluebunch wheatgrass are, once again, the two most common grasses in these communities. Joining them are several cold-weather grasses that are not found in the shrub steppe or Palouse grasslands. These include prairie junegrass, alpine bluegrass, and Columbia needlegrass, which are present in small numbers.

The grass layer in meadow-steppe communities consists of dense turf rather than scattered bunches, as in drier steppe types, even though the dominant species remain the same. The difference lies in the existence of two genetically different populations—or ecotypes—of bluebunch wheatgrass that have evolved in response to different habitats. The dry-steppe ecotype is a typical bunchgrass, growing in individual clumps rather than forming a continuous turf. The meadow-steppe ecotype, however, is able to form turfs by sprouting from underground stems, or rhizomes. Wheatgrass seedlings in meadow-steppe communities apparently retain the bunchgrass habit whether or not they later become rhizomatous, growing in clumps on recently invaded bare ground but becoming rhizomatous once a stand is well established.

The turf-forming ability of bluebunch wheatgrass, along with an abundance of showy spring wildflowers, accounts for the lush meadowy appearance of meadow-steppe communities. Although a few of the wildflower species are annuals, the vast majority are perennial herbs. A large number of species occur through most or all of the meadow steppes, though their relative abundance varies widely and often over short distances. Yellow "daisies" or "sunflowers" of several species grow abundantly in the meadow steppes. Of these, arrowleaf balsamroot and little sunflower are undoubtedly the showiest. Both have bright yellow flowerheads that are four to five inches in diameter. The balsamroot also has large leaves that are shaped like an arrowhead. On deep, sandy soils, colonies of balsamroot provide a spectacular display in midsummer. Slender cinquefoil is another common yellow-flowered herb. It is not a sunflower, but rather a member of the rose family. Its flowers are bright yellow, with five petals and sepals. The blossoms are borne in clusters above dense growths of leaves. Less conspicuous but also common is old man's beard, which has soft fernlike leaves and unusual nodding, pink, bowl-shaped flowers that grow in sets of three at the ends of leafless stems. The white plumelike styles of mature fruits resemble an old man's beard. Many other perennial forbs are present in most or nearly all stands, though normally not in large numbers. These include Douglas' brodiaea, which resembles tiny purple lilies; prairie star, which bears tiny bulbs in the axils of its leaves; the spectacular western iris; and the tall, purple-flowered silky lupine.

The meadow-steppe communities of eastern Washington and neighboring areas all look pretty much alike—irregular patches of shrubs scattered over low, dense, flowery turfs. And the turfs feature more or less the same grasses and forbs. Where the communities differ most notably is in their shrub component.

Along the east side of the Cascades from the Columbia River northward to Canada, the only common shrub in the foothill meadow-steppe is antelope bitterbrush. This type is well represented in the foothills near Goldendale, Ellensburg, Wenatchee, and Lake Chelan. The shrubs are 4½ to 6½ feet tall and rather evenly distributed, so that the community superficially resembles sagebrush steppe, with which it merges downslope. Bitterbrush steppe also occurs within the sagebrush steppe zone on cool, moist, north-facing slopes. Upslope, bitterbrush steppe merges with ponderosa pine forest over a broad ecotone in which pines are often scattered through the steppe. Bitterbrush steppe also occurs on disturbed soils or other habitats within the pine forest on sites where conifers are momentarily or indefinitely excluded. Similar bitterbrush communities also occur in the foothills of the Oregon Cascades, the Blue and Wallowa mountains, southern Idaho, and Utah.

From the Wenatchee region and Okanogan Valley eastward through the southern foothills of the Okanogan Highlands, to near Spokane and Ritzville, the chief meadow-steppe shrub is threetip sagebrush. This plant resembles big sagebrush except that it is only eight to 24 inches tall, and the three lobes at the tips of its leaves may themselves be divided into three smaller segments. The shrubs are widely scattered, but their small stature and the density of the grass layer make this community much different in appearance from big sagebrush steppe. Threetip-sagebrush steppe is the type found in the Grand Coulee region and on the tops of the lava plateaus bordering the Columbia and Spokane rivers. It also occurs in southern Idaho, notably near Craters of the Moon National Monument.

In the foothills extending southward from Spokane to Pullman, and eastward into Idaho, the lush turf contains not only the usual grasses and wildflowers but also dwarfed roses and snowberry. Similar meadow-steppe associations occur as far east as Bozeman, Montana, southward along the northern base of the Blue Mountains, and northward into the Columbia River valley in British Columbia.

The usual steppe shrubs, notably big sagebrush, rabbitbrush, and antelope brush, are all missing from the snowberry steppe. Patches of low shrubs, however, are characteristic of the community. An interesting feature of this community is that the dwarfed shrubs—common snowberry, Nootka rose, and woods rose—are all represented in patches and nearby thickets by specimens two to ten feet tall. Differences in available moisture or soil do not seem to explain either the distribution of the shrub patches or, by extension, the differences in the stature of these shrubs. Moreover, the mosaic of thickets and steppe appears to be stable.

Tall thickets dominated by black hawthorn occur throughout the snowberry steppe region along moist hillside ravines and on even damper flats bordering streams. Common snowberry and white spiraea are common understory shrubs in ravine thickets. Lush herbaceous undergrowth dominated by cow parsnip and stinging nettle are characteristic of valley-floor sites. Black cottonwoods in some places tower above the thickets, joined perhaps by quaking aspens or mountain alders. In drier steppe regions, riparian woodlands dominated by black cottonwood commonly line streams. White alder and cottonwood occur together along streams emptying into the Snake River.

Western junipers form open savannalike woodlands over large areas on the high lava plateaus of central Oregon and northeastern California, occupying a zone that has more moisture than the steppes but less than adjacent pine forests. The zone occurs at elevations between 2,500 and 4,600 feet in Oregon and 4,500 and 5,800 feet in northeastern California. Western juniper woodlands also occur in southeastern Washington, southeastern Oregon, southwestern Idaho, and northern Nevada. The trees are widely spaced, with an understory containing shrubs and grasses mainly drawn from adjacent steppe communities. Big sagebrush is usually the dominant understory shrub, though other steppe species, such as low sagebrush, rabbitbrush, horsebrush, and spiny hopsage may be present in small numbers. The main grasses are—of course—bluebunch wheatgrass and Idaho fescue. Forbs are not well represented in these woodlands.

Western juniper is a stout, long-lived tree with dense scaly foliage and a broadly conical shape. The bark is fibrous and rich reddish-brown. In the dry uplands where this tree is often the only type present it is normally short and stocky, rarely exceeding 20 feet in height. Old trees growing in more favorable habitats may reach heights of 50 feet or more, with trunks more than six feet thick. Western junipers commonly reach ages of 500 years or more. Although these trees can tolerate as little as eight inches of rain a year, they are unable to withstand the intense heat and drought of the sagebrush steppe. Nevertheless, isolated junipers commonly occur on rocky sites within the steppe, where roots can probe crevices to reach deep reservoirs of moisture.

True desert shrub communities occur in scattered locations in extreme southeastern Oregon, usually on saline soils that have formed through evaporation on old dry lakebeds, or playas. The Alvord Desert, which occupies the valley immediately east of Steens Mountain in southeastern Oregon, provides an excellent example of the habitat. Typical desert shrub communities feature widely spaced shrubs in which grasses are sparse and large areas of bare ground are common. The most important shrubs are Great Basin species, most of which belong to the goosefoot family. These include spiny hopsage, shadscale, saltsage, winter fat, and greasewood. Spiny sagebrush, which belongs to the sunflower family, is also present. In eastern Washington, communities dominated by spiny hopsage or winter fat, with a sparse understory of Sandberg's bluegrass, commonly replace big sagebrush stands on thin, dry, stony soils.

Plants able to grow in salty or alkaline soils are called *halophytes*. The goosefoot family has specialized in halophytism and therefore dominates large areas of alkaline soil throughout the Great Basin and other desert regions. Saltsage, for example, is able to grow in soils with salt content as high as three percent. Halophytes, however, even those in the goosefoot family, vary in their tolerance for salt. As a result, highly alkaline dry lakebeds often show distinct radial zonation corresponding to gradients in salinity. The low center of a lakebed is normally so saline that no plants whatsoever can survive. It forms a bullseye surrounded by successively less saline zones. In southeastern Oregon the first circle of plants around the barren center of a playa features highly salt-tolerant plants such as greasewood and saltsage. Above them, in the next ring, shadscale is usually the dominant plant. Winter fat and spiny hopsage prefer even less salty soils. Finally, in the outermost ring, where salinity is minimal, big sagebrush takes over.

The steppelands of eastern Washington and Oregon support distinctive communities of wildlife whose livelihood is based on the annual growth cycles of the dominant grasses and shrubs. Grasses and other herbaceous plants offer highly nutritious growth in certain seasons. Annual herbs are most valuable in early spring, when new shoots are most vigorous. By late spring, however, they have mostly died back, and as a food source have been largely replaced by the perennial herbs, which continue growth through midsummer. Herbs also produce valuable forage after fall rains. Deciduous trees and shrubs are heavily crowded in spring and early summer, before nutritious new growth has hardened. Evergreen shrubs such as big sagebrush provide a broad, stable food base throughout the year.

Big sagebrush is valuable both as food and cover. Though unpalatable to livestock, it is an important source of food for mule deer, elk, and pronghorn. In fact, the tender green shoots are higher in nutrients than alfalfa. Sagebrush is particularly valuable because it is both abundant and evergreen. Wintering herds of elk and deer rely heavily on it, particularly during winters when other forage is scarce. Sage grouse use the shrub for both food and cover and may travel long distances in winter to find stands uncovered by snow.

Small animals such as rabbits depend on big sagebrush and other steppe shrubs for thermal cover. During hot weather, they may spend most of the daylight hours in the relatively cool shade beneath the shrubs, emerging only at dusk to forage. In cold weather, the same shrubs protect the animals from chilling winds and driven snow. Reptiles such as the Pacific rattlesnake and leopard lizard also escape the heat of the day by resting in the shade of shrubs, though in particularly hot weather they retire to burrows.

The thick foliage of sagebrush and other steppe shrubs provides excellent cover for nesting birds. Some species of birds nest within the shrubs; others, on the ground beneath them. Among the former are three species—the gray flycatcher, sage thrasher, and sage sparrow—that are rarely found outside sagebrush country. The gray flycatcher places its nest low to the ground but forages for insects in the open areas between the bushes. It also sits atop the shrubs and flies out to catch insects in mid-air. In contrast, the sage thrasher usually nests higher in a bush but forages on the ground for beetles and locusts. Both birds leave the steppe region each fall to winter in southern California and northern Mexico. The sage sparrow hides its nest well within the interior of a sagebrush plant or some other bush. A normally retiring bird, it feeds on the ground and generally restricts its movements to walking or flying in the corridors between the shrubs. In fall, however, the birds take to the air to migrate to wintering grounds in the deserts of the Southwest.

Among the bird species that nest on the ground beneath sagebrush is the sage grouse. This large native pheasant of the intermountain west feeds on the leaves and buds of big sagebrush and builds its nest at its base. In spring, groups of male grouse gather in traditional large openings—called leks—to put on their courtship display. Kept free of shrubs by annual use, these areas often host herbaceous plants that are less common in closed portions of the shrub steppes.

During their courtship displays, male grouse strut about, showing their fancy plumage and engaging in mock battles with one another. They fan their tail feathers, let their wings droop, fluff up their breast feathers, and inflate the pair of bright yellow air sacs at the base of their beaks. By inflating and then explosively expelling air from the sacs, they produce a distinctive thumping sound that can be heard from some distance. Over a period of weeks, the birds establish

43. Wildlife use the upper branches (1) of sagebrush for lookouts; the inner branches (2) for nesting; and the space beneath (3) for cover and feeding.

a hierarchy consisting of a master cock, a subordinate cock, and a few guard cocks. The master cock mates with all the females; the subleader with fewer. The guard cocks mate on the sly, when the two dominant males aren't looking. This monopolization of mating by one or a few dominant males is characteristic of many creatures, including deer, elk, and bighorn sheep. The purpose of such behavior is to concentrate in offspring the qualities of strength, boldness, and general fitness that the dominant males possess to a greater degree than their less effective competitors.

Bunchgrasses also provide protective cover for smaller ground-nesting birds. The lark sparrow, for instance, often places its nest at the base of a bunchgrass tussock behind the obscuring cover provided by overhanging leaves. This bird, however, will also nest beneath or even within sagebrush and other shrubs. At the same time, the horned lark prefers to place its nest in the open in a shallow depression next to a stone or small clump of vegetation, relying on camouflage to protect its eggs and young from predators.

The deep, well-drained soils associated with big sagebrush are ideal for burrowing animals such as horned lizards, voles, kangaroo rats, pocket mice, ground squirrels, and badgers. Burrows, of course, provide excellent thermal and hiding cover, as well as places for hibernation.

The short-horned lizard inhabits steppe, woodland, and desert communities. It also ranges upslope into ponderosa pine forests. During the summer, this flat-bodied reptile is active mainly in the morning, when it forages for ants. In late morning it burrows into the sand to escape the heat of midday. Like other Northwest lizards, the short-horned lizard spends the winter in hibernation. The large, aggressive, long-nosed leopard lizard also frequents sandy areas, often near sagebrush or greasewood. Rather than digging its own burrows, it uses one excavated by kangaroo rats, pocket mice, or other rodents.

The Great Basin pocket mouse may be the most numerous and widespread mammal in the shrub steppes of the Pacific Northwest. Even so, this silky-haired rodent is seldom seen because it is strictly nocturnal, spending daylight hours in its burrow. Emerging at dusk to forage for seed, it also feeds on succulent green vegetation and insects. It returns to its burrow, however, to eat whatever it finds. By restricting its ctivities to the cooler nighttime hours, the pocket mouse onserves water and prevents overheating.

The pocket mouse is a cousin to the larger and more amiliar kangaroo rat, which is also strictly nocturnal, primarily a seed eater, and a burrower. Ord's kangaroo rat is he most wide-ranging of three species found in the Pacific Northwest, ranging northward to south-central Washington. Like the pocket mouse, the kangaroo rat spends the entire winter in its burrow.

Several ground squirrels frequent various parts of the steppe region of the Pacific Northwest. The three most characteristic steppe species are Townsend's ground squirrel, the Washington ground squirrel, and the Columbian ground squirrel. Townsend's ground squirrel inhabits the sagebrush steppe of eastern Oregon, southern Idaho, and south-central Washington west of the Columbia River. The Washington ground squirrel lives east of the Columbia, in the Palouse grasslands of southeastern Washington and the adjacent corner of northeastern Oregon. The large Columbian ground squirrel, which may be nearly twice the size of the two preceding species, is the common representative of the tribe in the meadow steppes of northeastern Washington. It is not restricted to that community or region, however, ranging through a variety of open habitats from lowlands to timberline and from northernmost British Columbia to southeastern Oregon and central Idaho. Six other ground squirrels inhabit the fringes of the steppe region or local pockets within it. In addition, the yellow-bellied marmot, which like all marmots is actually just a giant ground squirrel, inhabits rocky areas within the steppes.

Ground squirrels inhabiting the steppe region of the Pacific Northwest are active only four or five months a year. They avoid the heat and drought of summer and the food shortages and cold of winter by spending those seasons (as well as the intervening autumns) in a torpid sleeplike state deep within their burrows. The animals emerge in late winter or early spring, when the first new green shoots appear, and return to dormancy in late spring or early summer, as the last grasses turn brown.

By virtue of their burrowing habit, ground squirrels are restricted to areas where soils are deep and friable enough to support their extensive tunnel systems. In the scablands of eastern Washington, where glacial floods removed much of the soil, ground squirrel colonies are confined to areas where wind-blown loess has accumulated to sufficient depth. The animals are far more common in the deep soil of the Palouse and in the undisturbed soils of eastern Oregon.

The scourge of ground squirrels is the American badger, a powerful digger that excavates ground squirrels within their burrows. Badgers often remain in an area until they have virtually wiped out the local squirrel population, then move on to the next area and repeat the process. Meanwhile, ground squirrels aggressively reinvade areas where badgers have depleted their population. In addition to ground squirrels, badgers also prey on other burrowing mammals, including pocket mice, kangaroo rats, and pocket gophers.

The burrowing owl commonly inhabits old ground-squirrel burrows that have been enlarged by badgers. Like the original tenants, the burrowing owl is more likely to live in open steppes than in areas dominated by shrubs. Where abandoned burrows are unavailable, the owl digs its own. Active near dawn and dusk, as well as during the night, the burrowing owl often stands at the mouth of its burrow, moving its head in wide circles scanning for prey, which consists mainly of insects but may also include occasional small birds or rodents.

Another characteristic burrower of the steppe country is the Great Basin spadefoot toad. Like most amphibians, the spadefoot breeds in bodies of water, but as befits an amphibian living in an arid land it is not choosy about what kind of bodies they may be. Lakes, reservoirs, ponds, ephemeral puddles, rivers, creeks, and flooded roadside ditches are all acceptable habitats for reproduction. The small toad escapes the dry season by retiring to mammal burrows or by digging its own, where it may remain for up to several months, if necessary. The vibrations of raindrops hitting the soil, however, are enough to bring the toad to the surface.

The number and variety of burrowing animals in the steppe region attests to the importance of burrows as refuges in an open land. Even so, some mammals rely on speed and keen vision, rather than cover, to escape their predators. One such animal is the pronghorn, which is capable of speeds up to 70 miles per hour for three or four minutes at a stretch. Pronghorns can easily outrun coyotes, their most numerous predator. They also use their great speed and endurance to travel over large areas in search of suitable forage or to escape deep snows. As might be expected, the pronghorn prefers level or slightly rolling terrain with low vegetation that affords few hiding places for predators. The fleet herbivore summers in areas where low sagebrush is common and winters where shadscale, saltbush, black sagebrush, and winter fat are dominant. The scarcity of these plants in Washington, combined with normally rugged terrain, probably explains why the pronghorn is not native to that state.

The black-tailed jackrabbit is a common and widespread speedster of the steppes. It feeds on a wide variety of plant materials but has rather strict cover requirements. Ideal jackrabbit habitat includes large open areas where the animal can forage without fear of sudden ambush by predators, along with widely scattered shrubs that are large enough to provide effective cover from intense heat, cold, and wind, as well as good places to hide from predators.

As in forests, the greatest variety of wildlife occurs near the edges of habitats rather than in their interiors. Thus, as important as steppe shrubs are to wildlife, vast monotonous tracts of shrub steppe support fewer animal species than sites where brushy vegetation abuts cliffs, talus, wetlands, juniper woods, or open grasslands. In fact, many of the animals that forage in the shrub steppe nest in adjacent habitats. Edges attract wildlife because they feature greater diversity in nesting sites, thermal and hiding cover, and foods than do areas of uniform vegetation.

Cliffs and rocky areas provide wildlife with secure nesting or denning sites as well as escape habitat for wildlife as diverse as eagles, rattlesnakes, bats, woodrats, marmots, and bighorn sheep. Coyotes, bobcats, and mountain lions also den among the rocks. Most creatures that use cliffs and rocks for reproduction and cover, however, must venture into nearby areas to feed. Bighorn sheep, for example, forage in open areas where grasses and low brush are abundant. But such forage areas must be close to steep, rocky terrain, where the animals reproduce, rear their young, and rest, and to which they quickly flee when a predator appears. Similarly, the large, aggressive Mohave black-collared lizard, which occurs in southeastern Oregon and southern Idaho, forages among the sagebrush for smaller animals and green vegetation but only where rocks are nearby.

Unlike most other rock-dwelling animals in the region, the rock wren rarely ventures far from cliffs, talus slopes, or boulder piles. Placing its nest in crevices between the rocks, the bird forages on their surfaces for spiders, insects, and other invertebrates.

Like rocky terrain, juniper and riparian woodlands provide valuable thermal cover and escape terrain for wildlife of the open steppes. In the meadow steppes of northeastern Washington, hawthorn and snowberry thickets serve the same function. Deer, elk, pronghorn, and bighorn all may retreat to woodlands and thickets to escape the scorching heat of summer afternoons or the fierce cold of winter storms. Wintering populations of birds also depend heavily on woodlands as places to flee wind, cold, and driven snow. In addition large crops of juniper berries (actually fleshy cones) provide an important winter food source for numerous birds and mammals, including the coyote. By virtue of their three-tiered structure, woodlands offer niches that are simply unavailable in steppe communities. This structural variety is particularly important to birds, many of which depend on particular layers or combinations of layers. Altogether, 83 species of birds and 23 species of mammals regularly utilize juniper woodlands in eastern Oregon.

Stands containing old trees are particularly valuable because they provide special habitats for cavity nesters. For example, the bushy-tailed woodrat finds the large cavities in old junipers to be acceptable substitutes for the rock crevices in which it normally places its bulky nest. Cavity nesting birds that frequent juniper woodlands but otherwise would find little suitable habitat in the steppe region include the northern flicker, yellow-bellied sapsucker, Williamson's sapsucker, hairy woodpecker, white-breasted nuthatch, and red-breasted nuthatch.

Riparian woodlands, which are dominated by deciduous trees such as black cottonwood, quaking aspen, and white alder, also support a large number of birds that otherwise would be scarce or absent in eastern Washington and Oregon. These include the northern oriole, red-eyed vireo, yellow-breasted chat, and black-throated gray warbler. In addition, the black-tailed magpie, which ranges widely over steppe and farmland, prefers streamside willow thickets for its nest. (For a brief description of riparian woodlands and other wetland communities east of the Cascades, see the following chapter.)

The steppelands of eastern Washington and Oregon are not what most people have in mind when they picture the Pacific Northwest. Yet these vast open spaces where sunlight and sagebrush reign are as important to and characteristic of the region as the misty rain forests west of the Cascades. Converted steppelands produce bumper crops of wheat, wine grapes, apples, and cherries and provide valuable range for livestock. The steppes also supply critical habitat for numerous species of wildlife, including the tens of millions of ducks, geese, and swans that each spring and fall stop over at the marshes scattered throughout the region. Yet it is all too easy, when contemplating seemingly endless miles of sagebrush, to dismiss the land and its vegetation as monotonous and unproductive, to conclude that they would be better converted to other purposes. Thousands of acres of sagebrush have already been lost to agriculture and to conversion programs designed to increase shrub species that are more palatable to livestock. In addition, overgrazing of the rangelands has caused native bunch-grasses to be widely replaced by exotic annuals that are less palatable and nutritious to both wildlife and livestock. While farming and ranching are undeniably critical to the economy and culture of the inland Northwest, so are its diverse scenic, recreational, and wildlife resources. Preserving those resources for future generations will require that residents and visitors alike recognize the distinctive character and value of the steppelands.

CHAPTER FOURTEEN

At Water's Edge

IT SEEMS IRONIC that wetlands are but a minor element in the landscape of a region so closely identified with rain as the Pacific Northwest. The reason for this seeming contradiction is that the existence of wetlands depends less on total rainfall than on terrain. Wetlands by definition are places where the land is low and gentle enough for standing water to collect for most or all of the year. Such places are relatively scarce in the Pacific Northwest, where the topography tends to be elevated and uneven. Most of the coastal areas that are low enough to support salt marsh are small in area and occur mainly at the mouths of rivers. Inland, areas at once flat enough and wet enough to support wetlands are confined mainly to glacial valleys and lake basins, river floodplains, and high-desert basins with internal drainage. There are numerous such places, but few are extensive. Again, it seems ironic that the largest areas of freshwater wetlands in the region occur not in the humid coastal region, where rainfall is abundant, but in south-central Oregon and northeastern California, the areas with the lowest rainfall in the Pacific Northwest.

The oldest wetlands in the region date back to the close of the last Ice Age, 10,000 to 15,000 years ago. Along the coast as far south as the Olympic Peninsula, glaciers deepened and steepened the valleys of rivers entering the Pacific. When the ice retreated, these valleys were invaded by the sea to create the fiords that line this coast. Salt marshes developed at the heads of the fiords, where stream sediments were deposited in deltas. Coastal river valleys in southern Washington, Oregon, and northern California were not invaded by ice during the Pleistocene Epoch.

Rather, the lower sea level of that period no doubt resulted in the development of far more extensive salt marshes along the Pacific Coast than exist today. When sea level rose at the end of the Ice Age, the lower reaches of these marshes were drowned. Since then, river deposition has gradually reclaimed new terrain from the sea.

The Cordilleran Ice Sheet scoured out basins, large and small, that subsequently filled with runoff and rain to form the countless ponds and lakes of the Puget Sound region. Freshwater marshes developed along the shallower margins of these basins and grew in extent as stream deposits and organic materials continued to accumulate. As the shallowing process continued, bogs formed as many of the smaller ponds were filled in completely.

In the mountains, the gradual filling of glaciated basins and valleys led to the evolution of wet meadows in many low-lying areas once occupied by lakes or ponds and along the margins of meandering streams. In areas where lake basins lay in resistant bedrock, as in the granitic terrains of Idaho's Sawtooth Mountains and Washington's Alpine Lakes region, the process of filling in was retarded so that today lakes and ponds remain numerous while marginal wetlands are severely restricted in occurrence and extent.

East of the Cascades and south of the Cordilleran Ice Sheet, the heavy precipitation that allowed glacier formation also filled the region's interior basins with rainwater, creating vast lakes. In the drier climate of the past 10,000 years, these lakes have either disappeared entirely or greatly diminished in size. Such lakes are scattered throughout the Great Basin, the most notable being Utah's Great Salt Lake. Malheur, Klamath, Tule, and Goose lakes, in south-central Oregon and northeastern California, are smaller examples. Today, the region's largest freshwater marshes are to be found fringing these lakes, or what remains of them.

Floodplain marshes and distinctive riparian woodlands occur along major rivers throughout the Pacific Northwest. Since river channels in the region are so often steep and narrow, however, floodplain wetlands are far less extensive and well developed here than they are in the East, Midwest, or even the Central Valley of California. Wetlands form on floodplains as a normal consequence of river evolution. During floods, which occur annually in wetter parts of the Pacific

Northwest, rivers cover their floodplains with layers of silt that provide a rich rooting medium for wetland plants. When drained, these same alluvial soils are excellent for growing crops or pasturing cattle. This has led to the construction of levees and dikes in the floodplains of most rivers in the region. As a result, the rich sediments are usually washed out to sea rather than spread over the floodplain.

There are many types of wetlands, including marshes, bogs, swamps, wet meadows, and riparian forests and woodlands. Some wetlands are irrigated by the sea. Others develop only in freshwater habitats. Some are dominated by soft-stemmed herbaceous plants; others by shrubs or trees. All wetlands, however, share one critical feature in common: soils that are saturated, either from flooding or tidal inundation, for all or part of the year. Consequently, wetland plants, whatever else they may do, must be able to cope with soils that are waterlogged at least part of the time.

Soils, of course, whether fine- or coarse-grained, are aggregations of particles, between which are spaces that may be filled either with water or air. Well-drained soils allow water to move down slowly enough that individual particles are moistened but fast enough that the spaces between them are not filled with water for prolonged periods. When drainage is poor or soils are flooded—both conditions that typify wetlands—plant roots are deprived of the oxygen they require for carrying out essential metabolic functions. Wetlands are such desirable habitats for plants in other ways, however, that it is not surprising that numerous species have managed to evolve various mechanisms and strategies for getting around this basic difficulty.

Emergent plants such as cattails and bulrushes, which are rooted in submerged soils but whose stems extend well above the water surface, have networks of empty spaces between their cells connecting the roots to pores (stomates) on the leaves through which gas exchange occurs. The root systems themselves are rather small since nutrient-rich water is readily available and gas exchange mainly occurs elsewhere. Water-lilies, as an adaptation to their floating habit, have stomates on the upper surface of their leaves, rather than on the lower, as is generally the case with green plants. The submerged stems of aquatic plants are often slender and thin-walled, allowing oxygen to pass easily from the water into the plant. Submergent plants such as bladder-wort and water-milfoil often have fernlike leaves whose myriad divisions facilitate gas exchange by exposing the maximum amount of surface to the water. Underwater stems and roots of both emergent and submergent plants are typically thin-walled for the same reason.

Willows and Oregon ash, which commonly border lakes and streams in the Northwest, grow new air-filled roots to replace those killed by periodic flooding. The bark of birches and bitter cherry and a number of other wetland trees has obvious horizontal bands of pores (lenticels) through which gas exchange occurs. Black cottonwoods respond to soil saturation by lifting large quantities of water upward to their foliage, where it is transpired into the air. Some wetland trees are able to carry out respiration in the absence of oxygen.

Salt Marshes

Along the Pacific Northwest Coast, where wave-battered cliffs line most of the shore, salt marshes are restricted to protected areas along the lower reaches of coastal rivers and behind bars that extend across the mouths of bays. At one time, salt marshes extended many miles up coastal rivers, but the higher marshes have largely been diked for agricultural purposes. Both types of salt-marsh habitat are associated throughout the region with estuaries, such as Nehalem Bay, the Columbia River delta, and Puget Sound. Estuaries are more or less protected bodies where ocean water circulated by tidal action is diluted with fresh water supplied by streams and runoff.

There are 21 major estuaries in Oregon and 34 in Washington. Many times that number occur along the coasts of British Columbia and southeast Alaska. These estuaries are mainly of three types: (1) bar-built, (2) drowned-river, and (3) fiord. Bar-built estuaries are embayments created by the formation of sand bars at the mouths of rivers. Examples include Netarts Bay and Sand Lake in Oregon and Willapa Bay and Gray's Harbor in Washington. If the bar closes an estuary's outlet to the sea, as has occurred, for example, at

the mouths of Oregon's Elk, Sixes, and Winchuck rivers
the result is a so-called blind estuary. Drowned-river estuaries
were formed about 10,000 years ago at the end of the last
Ice Age, when rising sea levels caused the ocean to flood
the lower reaches of coastal rivers. Examples include Coos
and Yaquina bays in Oregon. Fjords also date back to the
close of the Pleistocene Epoch. They are drowned glacial
valleys that were invaded by the rising seas that followed
on the heels of the retreating ice. The coasts of southeast
Alaska and British Columbia comprise a succession of classic
and spectacular fjords that surpass in number, size, and
general scenic splendor even those of Norway. Washington's
Hood Canal is the southernmost fiord on the Pacific Coast
of North America. Puget Sound is a composite fiord with
many arms and numerous tributary rivers. Within its boundaries can be found small subsidiary estuaries of both the
bar-built and drowned-river variety.

44. Saltmarsh gum plant (*Grindelia integrifolia*) is one of the
showiest wildflowers found in the high salt marshes of the Pacific
Northwest. The flower heads appear from June through November.

orming a transition between land and sea, estuaries offer rich, protected habitat for marine life and a number of dges that attract a large number of animals from adjacent errestrial communities. Marine fish such as herring spawn, ed, and rear young in estuaries. In addition, populations f anadromous fish such as salmon, sturgeon, and shad use uiet estuarine waters as resting areas before undertaking ae final push upstream to their spawning grounds. The oung of these species also spend time in estuaries before aoving out to sea. During the winter, freshwater fishes may aove downstream into estuaries to escape the fast, turbulent oodwaters. Birds also depend heavily on estuarine environents. Huge numbers of waders, waterfowl, and other quatic species depend on estuaries as resting places during pring and fall migrations or as wintering grounds. Many f these species feed on the mudflats associated with salt aarshes.

Salt marshes are transitional communities that occur along entle shores subject to periodic tidal inundation. Salt aarshes occupy ground that is too high and dry for subaerged estuarine communities dominated by eelgrass and eaweeds and too wet and saline for upland plants. Saltaarsh vegetation begins about halfway between the mean ow and mean high tides, where wave action and tidal inunation have declined enough to permit the establishment f essentially terrestrial plants. Low salt marshes may be aundated during each high tide. High marshes may be avaded by the sea only a few times during the year.

Salt marshes are characterized by saline soils that inhibit he establishment of most upland plants. The degree of alinity, however, varies widely from marsh to marsh and ven within individual marshes. Salinity also varies during he year as a natural consequence of seasonal climatic flucuations. In the Pacific Northwest, salinity is lowest during he winter, when salt concentrations are diluted by precipiation and runoff, and highest in summer, when precipitation alls off and warmer weather promotes increased evaporation.

The soils of Pacific Northwest salt marshes are more or ess like those of marshes at comparable latitudes on the tlantic Coast. Depending on the amount and type of sedients supplied by contributing rivers, the marsh soils range om silt or peat to sand. Soil texture helps to determine

salinity, with fine, slowly draining soils accumulating mo
salts than coarser ones through which seawater passes mo
rapidly. Average tidal heights also affect salinity since, obv
ously, the more times an area is bathed in seawater th
higher its levels of salt are likely to be.

Salt marshes are among the most productive plant com
munities in the world, producing larger crops of vegetatio
than most agricultural fields and forests. This high produ
tivity is due to a combination of several factors. First, sa
marshes, like open prairies, are able to capture and stor
maximum amounts of incoming solar radiation. Second
marsh plants are rarely subjected to water deficits that i
other habitats often place a lid on growth. Third, tides an
tributary streams subsidize salt-marsh productivity by reg
larly contributing nutrients derived from other areas. Alon
the Pacific Coast, this subsidy includes nutrients broug
to the ocean surface by upswelling waters off the coast.
addition, driven by prevailing winds, the nutrient-ric
waters of the Columbia River spread out along the coast-
southward in summer, northward in winter—entering est
aries by means of tidal flow. As a result of such subsidie
estuaries commonly have higher levels of nutrients tha
either adjacent marine or terrestrial habitats. Finally, tid
influxes help to maintain high oxygen levels essential
vigorous growth.

In the Pacific Northwest, unlike most other parts of th
world, mature coastal forests are generally more productiv
than local salt marshes. This anomaly seems attributable
the coastal region's cool, cloudy climate, which seems t
inhibit production in salt marshes while maximizing it i
adjacent conifer forests.

Viewed from above, well-developed salt marshes resem
ble mosaics comprising numerous islands ringed by narro
waterways. These tidal creeks provide several importan
services to salt-marsh communities. First, the creeks circu
late saltwater, with its subsidy of oxygen and nutrient
throughout the marshes. Salt-marsh sedges grow more vigo
ously along the creeks than they do in the interior of th
marshes. Second, these waterways provide access fc
marine animals that use the marshes as nurseries or rearin
grounds. Third, tidal creeks help to flush impurities fro
the marsh by transporting detritus to deeper waters.

The plants that inhabit salt marshes are classified as halo-phytes, literally "salt lovers." These are specialists, plants that have carved niches for themselves by evolving methods of utilizing a habitat that most other plants cannot tolerate. As a reward for specialization, halophytes are freed from competition; that is, relatively few species grow in saline habitats compared to normal soils. The goosefoot family contains numerous halophytes, including salt-marsh species such as pickleweed and orache and residents of alkali deserts such as winter fat and greasewood.

One of the chief difficulties faced by halophytes is the potential loss of water to the soil as a result of osmotic imbalances induced by high salt concentrations. During osmosis, water passes through cell walls from low to high concentrations. Normally, water in root cells is more concentrated than that in the soil, but in salt marshes soil concentrations are so high that plants must take extraordinary measures to prevent loss of water to the soil. Halophytes ward off water loss by concentrating salts in their roots. In addition, these plants may also possess other methods for coping with salinity. Saltgrass, for example, has glands on its leaves that remove salts and deposit them as a white film on the leaves. Milkwort concentrates salts in special glands, excreting it through roots or shedding leaves where salt concentrations are highest. Pickleweed, a low leafless succulent, stores fresh water in its fleshy stems. This reserve not only dilutes incoming salt solutions but allows the plant to reduce water uptake during prolonged periods of heat and drought, when soil salinity is highest.

Within a typical estuary along the coasts of Oregon and Washington there may be as many as eight distinctive salt-marsh communities. These are low sandy marshes, low silty marshes, sedge marshes, immature high marshes, mature high marshes, bulrush-sedge marshes, intertidal gravel marshes, and diked marshes. Each type of marsh occurs in a particular habitat and features a distinctive assemblage of plants.

Low marshes occur on nearly level terrain at the edge of mudflats just above the low tide line. They are flooded by nearly all high tides, so the plants growing there must be able to withstand long periods of submersion. Low sandy marshes, as the name suggests, develop on sandy soils, often on the protected side of bay-mouth sand spits. They also fringe tidewater islands composed of coarse sediments. Vegetation typically consists of scattered clumps of pickle-weed, three-square, saltgrass, Jaumea, seaside plantain, sandspurry, Lyngbye's sedge, and milkwort. Alkaligrass is common in this type of marsh from Washington northward. Low silty marshes occur in similar terrain as low sandy marshes except that they occur on fine-grained rather than sandy soils. In these saline, oxygen-poor muds, vegetation is scantier and less varied than in low sandy marshes, consisting mainly of circular patches of arrowgrass and clumps of pickleweed. Scattered growths of spike-rush and sand-spurry may also be found.

Sedge marshes consist of often extensive, pure stands of Lyngbye's sedge, which resembles a tall, coarse grass except that the stems are angled rather than round. This type of marsh is often found along tidal creeks at slightly higher elevations than low marshes. Even so, it too floods during most high tides. Sedge marsh also occurs at the edge of deltas and islands. The sedge plants produce enormous amounts of organic material, which forms the base of salt-marsh/estuarine food chains. The sedges grow more vigorously along tidal creeks, where they are washed constantly by the nutrient-rich waters, than they do in the inner marsh.

Bulrush-sedge marshes are transitional communities that develop on either silty or sandy soils in the low, brackish backwaters of an estuary where saltwater and freshwater habitats meet. These marshes are regularly covered by high tides, but tidal action is less vigorous and the role of fresh-water is more important than in other salt-marsh communities. As the name suggests, the dominant plants in these marshes are softstem bulrush and Lyngbye's sedge. These plants form a more or less continuous meadow, with the sedge dominating saltier soils and bulrush the less saline habitats. Extensive bulrush-sedge marshes border the Columbia River estuary.

Intertidal gravel marshes are rare because they are restricted to an unusual habitat. They form on bars of sand or gravel near the mouths of estuaries where tidal exchange and river discharge are both high. Large contributions of fresh water combined with a rapidly draining substrate create less saline conditions than exist in other low-marsh ypes. Vegetation is generally discontinuous and dominated by the grasslike spike-rush.

High marshes occur at or below the mean high-tide line on flats at least 16 inches higher than adjacent sedge and ow marshes. A conspicuous step often marks the transition. Many high tides cover the marshes, but they also experience longer periods when they are not submerged than any other ypes of marsh. As a result, salinity fluctuates widely, depending on rainfall, tides, and evaporation rates. Shallow saline pools, called pans, are common in high marshes and may become very salty and dry when tides are low and warm weather increases evaporation rates. Well-developed networks of tidal creeks both flood the marshes and carry away the organic detritus they produce. On their landward sides high marshes often border dune grasses, tidewater forests, and other strictly terrestrial vegetation.

High marshes are generally dominated by grasses and resemble lush seaside meadows. Immature high marshes feature extensive stands of tufted hairgrass or saltgrass. Mature high marshes are characterized by tufted hairgrass, Baltic rush, and creeping bentgrass. High marshes are the least saline and are submerged for the shortest periods of all the naturally occurring marsh types. As a result they support the greatest number of plant species, including several with showy flowers. These include Pacific silverweed, gum plant, paintbrush owl's clover—all of which have yellow flowers—and marsh clover, whose blossoms are reddish or purplish pink.

As the name indicates, diked marshes are created when high marshes are diked in order to keep out the tides. Although diked marshes contain a greater number of upland plants than other types of salt marshes, they still feature a high water table, abundant seepage, and traces of salinity. The tidal creeks so characteristic of unaltered high marshes, however, are no longer active. Vegetation is meadowlike and more or less continuous. The dominant plants are saltmarsh grasses such as tufted hairgrass and creeping bentgrass. The grasslike Baltic rush, gum plant, Pacific silverweed, and orache are also present.

Upstream from marshlands, Sitka spruce, also known as tideland spruce, lines tidal creeks from Alaska south to northern California. In such creeks the fluctuation of tides produces a regular rise and fall in water levels, but salinity levels are minimal owing to the greater proportion of fresh water this far above the high tide level. Riparian woodland trees such as red alder or black cottonwood less commonly occur along tidal channels and become steadily more common upstream. Shrubs such as red osier and various willows form dense tangles beneath the trees.

Estuarine food chains, including those of the salt marsh, are either detritus-based or grazer-based. Both begin with organic materials carried into estuaries as detritus and dissolved matter derived from living or dead plants. Bacteria and fungi break down these materials to form inorganic compounds that fuel the growth of estuarine plants. These plants include phytoplankton in deep waters, eelgrass and other submergents in subtidal areas, and salt-marsh plants in the intertidal zone. In detritus-based food chains, invertebrates that feed on detritus in turn provide food for fish, shorebirds, seabirds, and even some mammals. Grazer-based food chains begin with phytoplankton, which is eaten by fish that provide food for various birds and for mammals such as harbor seals, bears, and humans.

Estuarine consumers include both aquatic and terrestrial animals. The latter are those creatures that cannot withstand prolonged submersion and that move to intertidal areas only during low tides. These include invertebrates such as leaf hoppers, flies, bees, wasps, ants, and spiders, which are eaten by larger animals. For example, chinook salmon and steelhead during their sojourns in estuaries feed heavily on insects. Shorebirds such as plovers and various sandpipers also feed on insects but specialize in worms, amphipods, insect larvae, and other invertebrates buried in the exposed tidal muds.

Salt marshes are prime habitat for feeding and wintering birds. Approximately 350,000 birds each year winter in Washington estuaries, and another 50,000 winter in the less extensive estuarine habitats of Oregon. In addition, thousands of additional migrants use the estuaries and associated marshes as resting grounds during migration. Large concentrations of shorebirds are particularly evident in spring and fall, in transit to and from breeding grounds in the arctic and wintering grounds in California and points south.

Two dozen or more bird species regularly use the tidal

marshes of the Pacific Northwest. Though not restricted to salt marshes, the song sparrow is probably their most numerous resident bird, nesting among marsh plants, in snags within the marsh, or in neighboring upland shrubbery. The song sparrow probes the mud for worms and feeds on marsh insects. The other characteristic songbird of the salt marsh is the marsh wren, which nests among the tall grasses of high marshes and feeds on insects and spiders. The marsh wren's rough song, which makes up in energy what it lacks in melody, is frequently heard over the high marshes even when the tiny singers cannot be seen.

The Virginia rail is a frequent but seldom-seen salt-marsh resident. Resembling a cross between a chicken and a sandpiper, this rail uses its long bill to probe marsh mud for worms, snails, larvae, and other invertebrates. It builds its nest close to the ground among dense marsh vegetation. A reclusive bird, the Virginia rail is most often observed foraging along the banks of tidal creeks. The sora, a smaller, less common rail, is also a resident of Northwest salt marshes.

One of the most conspicuous salt-marsh birds is the great blue heron, which is commonly seen foraging for fish in tidal creeks or other shallow waters. Although herons are known to rest on old pilings or other structures within the marsh, they prefer nearby trees for that purpose. Actually, this heron is a marsh visitor rather than resident, for it nests in colonies high in alders, cottonwoods, Douglas-firs, redwoods, and other trees. In spring, as the young mature, heron parents make frequent trips back and forth between their forest rookeries and nearby estuarine fishing grounds, where they obtain food for the chicks.

Another large bird that nests high in forest trees but frequently visits estuarine shores is the bald eagle. This magnificent predator patrols the waters for salmon and the shores for dead fish or other edibles that may have washed up. Bald eagles also take small resident mammals.

The characteristic hawk of the marshes is the northern harrier, which nests among high-marsh plants and patrols the entire marsh for mice and shrews. Easily distinguished by its long wings, the conspicuous patch of white at the base of the tail, and its habit of gliding low over the marsh, this hawk is one of the community's top predators. Other hawks that feed in the marshes or nearby waters from time to time include the osprey, red-tailed hawk, and peregrine falcon.

The vagrant shrew and deer mouse are the two most common small mammals in Northwest marshes. Others include the Oregon vole, Trowbridge shrew, and black rat. The deer mouse nests in shrubbery and trees at the fringe of the high marsh but visits the marsh in great numbers to feed on plant detritus, seeds, and insects. The vagrant shrew actually nests within the marsh, preferring the dense meadowlike vegetation of sedge and high marshes. It builds its nest on the highest ground in each area, placed beyond the reach of most high tides. During tidal inundations, it commonly retreats to the tops of logs or vegetation.

Numerous larger animals regularly visit tidal marshes to feed and rest. The raccoon, which fancies the snails and clams found in the tidelands, is the most frequent marsh visitor. Deer sometimes feed on marsh grasses and regularly use the tall, dense salt meadows for cover. Beavers and muskrats frequent freshwater areas near coastal marshes. Most of the region's mammal predators, including mink, gray fox, coyote, bobcat, and weasel, forage in tidal marshes from time to time.

Freshwater Marshes

Freshwater marshes are dominated by emergent, soft-stemmed herbaceous plants such as cattail, bulrush, wapato, and various grasses and sedges. Emergent plants are rooted in submerged soil but the greater portion of their stems extends above the water surface. Some marshes are dominated by cattails; others by bulrushes or other plants. Shallow marshes are those with standing water up to six inches deep. Deep marshes may have as much as two or three feet of water and in addition to emergent plants often feature floating species such as water-lilies and pondweeds.

Some marshes originate as shallow lakes or ponds that gradually fill in as a result of accumulating sediments and organic detritus. Other marshes develop along the shallow margins of rivers and sloughs. Both types of situations occur commonly in the Pacific Northwest.

Freshwater marshes are not subjected to such great fluctuations in water level as salt marshes; nonetheless, water levels commonly fall during the summer and some marshes may dry out completely for a time. Floodplain marshes experience periodic flooding when swollen rivers overflow their banks. However destructive such floods may be to human life or property, they enrich wetlands by spreading nutrient-rich silts over the marshes. Through providing this nutrient subsidy, such floods play a similar, albeit less critical, role in the life of freshwater marshes as tides do in that of coastal salt marshes. Wet meadows are closely related to marshes, differing from them mainly in that the soil while always saturated is rarely covered with standing water for prolonged periods.

Cattails are classic emergents and probably the most widely known marsh plants. Although there are several species, all are very similar, featuring the familiar brown flower spikes resembling frankfurters on the ends of sticks. The familiar cattail of the Pacific Northwest is the common cattail, which ranges through most of North America. Although cattails reproduce sexually from seed, the extensive pure colonies formed by these plants are clones made up of genetically identical plants that sprouted from a single network of spreading underground stems, or rhizomes. Cattails are perennials. Their underground stems persist from year to year while their upright, emergent stems die back at the end of each growing season and sprout anew each spring. To fuel each spring's new growth these plants store large amounts of nutrients in their underground parts.

Hardstem bulrush dominates extensive marshes in the inland Northwest, including those of the Malheur and Klamath basins in south-central Oregon and northeastern California. Also known as tule, hardstem bulrush superficially resembles grass but is actually a member of the sedge family. While most sedges have three-angled rather than round stems, hardstem bulrush has round stems, as do grasses. As the name suggests, however, its stems are hard and difficult to crush between the fingers. Like many grasses and cattails, hardstem bulrush reproduces mainly by sprouting from rhizomes and in this way forms extensive clonal stands. Hardstem bulrush is tolerant of alkaline conditions, which often exist in interior marshes subject to high evaporation rates. As a result this species is the most common and widespread marsh plant in the western United States, particularly in the Great Basin and central California, where such conditions are typical. West of the Cascades, however, the smaller, softer-stemmed, small-flowered bulrush is more common.

Other grasslike plants found in Northwestern marshes include true rushes, spike-rushes, and true sedges. Several dozen species of true rushes grow in the Pacific Northwest, occupying a variety of wetland habitats, particularly salt marshes, freshwater marshes, and wet meadows. Soft rush is one of the most common and widespread species both in our region and throughout North America and Europe. It grows in great dark green clumps a foot or more tall, with numerous hollow, round, pointed stems radiating from a single base. The stems have taken over the job of photosynthesis, and the leaves when present resemble bristles.

Spike-rushes are actually members of the sedge family. Several species occur in the Pacific Northwest, all of which feature slender stems topped by scaly flower spikes. Most species reproduce by sprouting from rhizomes. True sedges of the genus *Carex* are numerous both in number and variety in the Pacific Northwest, where they occur in virtually all wetland habitats. True sedges are particularly characteristic of wet mountain meadows, where they may form nearly pure stands. Among the more common and widespread marsh species are slough sedge and water sedge, both of which tolerate standing water.

A number of grasses also occur in Northwest marshes. One of the most common is reed canary grass, which is found in Eurasia and throughout North America except in the southeastern United States. It grows in marshes and on damp shores lining sloughs, streams, ponds, and rivers. This and other grasses can be distinguished from sedges by their round hollow stems with solid joints. Grass leaves are also distinctive, consisting of a flat blade and a basal portion that sheathes the stem. Other marsh grasses occurring in the region include rice cutgrass, mannagrasses, water foxtail, and sloughgrass, all of which occur widely in North America. Marsh grasses are valuable to wildlife both for the seed they produce and the cover they provide.

Broadleaf emergent plants include wapato, water-plantain, and water-parsley. Also known as arrowhead for the shape of its leaves, wapato is one of several rather similar species growing in our area. All bear starchy tubers that are eaten by ducks and muskrats. Local Indians also harvested the tubers, giving rise to the other name for this plant, "Indian potato." Wapato grows in marshes and in the shallow margins of sloughs, streams, ponds, and lakes. Related to wapato, water-plantain is a many-branched plant up to three feet tall whose lower part is often submerged. While leaves that emerge from the water are elliptical, those growing beneath the surface are ribbonlike. The edible rhizome of this species is also a source of food for wildlife. Water-parsley grows profusely in shallow, slow-moving streams and marshes. Though not a true parsley, it belongs to the same family (Umbelliferae) and shows two of its classic traits: small white flowers arranged in nearly flat clusters (umbels) and leaves that are finely and deeply dissected into numerous leaflets and segments.

Floating plants include the water-lilies and duckweeds. Floating plants are able to do without stiff supporting stems and therefore save the energy that otherwise would be invested in their manufacture. Primitive floating plants such as the duckweeds lack anchored roots and therefore don't bother with stems at all. Instead, each plant consists of a single floating green segment only a few millimeters across with a single tiny rootlet hanging from it. The floating portion of the plant is the site of both photosynthesis and reproduction, which occurs vegetatively by simply growing new segments that eventually split away from the parent. Through this process, duckweed is able to form dense colonies that can entirely cover a small pond.

The floating habit allows more advanced plants such as water-lilies to grow large leaves without having to expend energy to physically support them. Two types of water-lilies are common in the Northwest. The native pond-lily has large heart-shaped leaves and yellow bowl-shaped flowers. It grows in shallow ponds and lake margins. The common white water-lily of urban and suburban lakes and ponds is an import from the East Coast. Its leaves are round and its flowers are white and fragrant. The water-lilies are unusual for having stomata on the upper rather than lower surfaces of their leaves.

Growing entirely beneath the water surface, submergent plants are restricted to deep marshes and open water. As a group they tend to have slender, much divided leaves that maximize the surface available for photosynthesis while minimizing water resistance. One of the more familiar—and despised—submergents is water-milfoil, an invasive European species that has clogged many Northwestern lakes and ponds. Among the more interesting submergent plants are the carnivorous bladderworts, whose tiny air sacs not only keep the leaves near the water surface but double as fly traps.

Marsh plants form the base of the food chain. Muskrats, mice, and ducks are among the primary consumers. In some marshes, algae and phytoplankton are also significant producers. They are devoured by zooplankton, crustaceans, tadpoles, and various aquatic invertebrates, which are eaten in turn by fish, snakes, and turtles. Muskrats play an important role in recycling the nutrients bound up in plant materials. In the process of building their lodges, they shred large amounts of vegetation, thereby preparing it for more rapid decomposition by bacteria and other decomposers. In the course of decomposition, some nutrients leach into the water, where they are absorbed by plankton and other aquatic organisms and thereby returned to the system. The rest are incorporated into the marsh muck, where they are available to cattails, bulrushes, and other marsh plants.

Muskrats are characteristic of marshes throughout North America. Their lodges are built from cattails, bulrushes, and other marsh vegetation and may be as much as ten feet in diameter. These aquatic rodents feed entirely on the leaves, stems, and roots of various marsh plants and, as summarized above, play an important role in the recycling of nutrients. Muskrats are essentially large aquatic meadow mice and, like their smaller cousins, are given to periodic population explosions. When this occurs, muskrats may seem to be everywhere, and even terrestrial predators such as coyotes and bobcats may enjoy their fill. But where it still survives, the chief predator of the muskrat is the mink, a large aquatic weasel. Minks also feed on fish, frogs, birds, and other small mammals that live in or on the fringes of marshes and other wetlands.

The freshwater marshes of the Pacific Northwest lie within the Pacific Flyway, the great corridor used by migrating birds in their travels between nesting grounds in the north and wintering grounds to the south. In October and November, millions of waterfowl use the bulrush marshes of Oregon's Malheur and Klamath basins as resting places in their journey southward to wintering grounds in central and southern California, Mexico, and Central America. In a typical autumn Malheur National Wildlife Refuge may host as many as 100,000 snow geese and more than 250,000 ducks. To the south, in the Klamath Basin, several million ducks and geese use the network of refuges associated with Upper Klamath, Lower Klamath, and Tule lakes. In addition, more than 500 bald eagles winter in the Klamath Basin, one of the largest congregations of the national symbol outside Alaska.

During the summer, more than a dozen species of waterfowl nest in the freshwater marshes of the Pacific Northwest. Gadwall, mallard, cinnamon teal, ruddy duck, and northern shoveler are regular nesters in freshwater marshes west of the Cascades. These species also nest in the extensive marshes east of the mountains, along with blue-winged teal, pintail, American wigeon, and green-winged teal.

Common birds of the region's freshwater marshes also include several species discussed above in connection with salt marshes: the song sparrow, marsh wren, great blue heron, Virginia rail, sora, and northern harrier. Aside from the ducks, however, among the most conspicuous marsh residents are the red-winged and yellow-headed blackbirds. Red-winged blackbirds occur throughout the region; yellow-headed blackbirds are mainly restricted to marshes east of the Cascades. Where the two occur together, the redwings arrive first and stake out nesting territories. Then the larger yellowheads arrive and proceed to evict the redwings from choice protected real estate in the interior of the marshes. The redwings are left with sites along the marsh fringes, where they are more vulnerable to predators.

Red-winged blackbirds occur in a variety of marsh habitats, including salt marsh, or even in vegetation along roadside drainage ditches, but they prefer cattail marshes above all others. The males perch atop the tall stems to proclaim their territories and attract females, which arrive a week or two after the males. Since the birds normally arrive before the year's new growth of cattails has appeared, they attach their nests to the dried stalks of the previous year.

Several distinctive species and subspecies of garter snakes are found in and along freshwater marshes and other wetlands in the Northwest. Depending on the species, they feed on small birds, eggs, frogs, salamanders, and fishes. The common native frog of Northwestern marshes is the spotted frog, which occurs on both sides of the Cascades. In western Oregon, however, this species has largely been replaced by the larger, more aggressive bullfrog, an introduced species that is native to eastern North America. The red-legged frog occurs only west of the Cascades but prefers the edges of streams and ponds to extensive marshes. When not breeding it often ventures far from water. Like the spotted frog, its numbers have been greatly reduced as a result of competition from the bullfrog.

The Pacific Northwest is home to many kinds of salamanders, including several that breed in freshwater marshes. These include the rough-skinned newt and the three large mole salamanders. These animals are terrestrial for most of the year, holing up in trees, in rodent burrows, or beneath logs, rocks, and other debris, but return to lakes and ponds in late winter and spring to breed.

Wooded Wetlands

People generally use the terms *marsh, bog,* and *swamp* interchangeably, yet they actually designate distinct types of wetlands. Marshes are wetlands dominated by soft-stemmed emergent vegetation, swamps are dominated by trees and shrubs. Riparian woodlands, the distinctive communities that occur along freshwater shorelines, may or may not be swamps, depending on whether or not the trees normally grow in standing water. Bogs are wetlands that form on peat. They may not support trees but almost always feature a cover of shrubs.

Bogs and fens are varieties of a type of vegetation known as mire, or moor, which develops on wet peat, often at the margins of old, gradually filling lakes and ponds. Peat consists of undecomposed vegetable matter that accumulates in cool, highly acidic, poorly drained areas where bacteria and other decomposers do not thrive. Because peat is not broken down by bacteria and other decomposers, the nutrients bound up in the dead materials are not recycled back to the community. Moreover, the peat itself, for the same reason, is an inhospitable rooting medium for most plants. Therefore, bogs and fens support fewer types of plants than upland areas.

Bogs occur widely in Alaska and Canada, as well as northern Eurasia. In the continental United States they are mainly confined to New England, the Great Lake states, and the humid coastal region of the Pacific Northwest. While large tracts of land in Canada are given over to muskeg—the Algonquin word for bog—bogs are relatively uncommon south of the border. In the Puget Sound region, for example, they have developed mainly in once-glaciated basins that cradle, or cradled, lakes and ponds.

In Ireland peat is still an important source of fuel, though the Irish government, recognizing the need to preserve bogs, now discourages the practice of cutting peat. In Scotland, distillers use peat fires to impart the distinctive smoky flavor to Scotch whisky. In North America, peat is harvested mainly for sale as peat moss, a popular soil conditioner for gardens and potted plants.

Bogs are peatlands that form in poorly drained basins where precipitation is the main source of water. Since rainwater contains few minerals, bogs are generally deficient in nutrients and therefore support relatively few types of plants. Fens are peatlands that form in areas watered by streams or runoff. Because these waters have been in contact with mineral soil, they contain more dissolved minerals than rainwater. As a result, fens are more fertile and host a wider variety of plants than do bogs, though they are less productive than nearby uplands.

Fens often develop at the margins of lakes and ponds, as the build-up of peat near the shore creates a tangled mat that supports new vegetation. Some of the mats are anchored as a result of the complete filling in of the area beneath them. Others float on the surface of the water and may extend for several yards toward the center of the pond. Where inflowing water contributes nutrients and keeps acidity relatively low, mats are commonly dominated by emergent plants such as true sedges. The resulting vegetation is a fen. However, if the pond receives too little water from runoff or streamflow to lower acidity and replenish the nutrients used by plants, sphagnum moss will dominate the mat and the resulting community will be a bog. Bogs may succeed fens, as the accumulation of peat proceeds to a point where the mat vegetation surface sits too high to receive runoff or stream water.

In the Pacific Northwest the same trees dominate both upland forests and bogs: western hemlock, Sitka spruce, and western redcedar. Douglas-fir won't appear in the heart of a bog but may lurk about its drier fringes. The presence of these conifers in bogs indicates that they are able to tolerate levels of acidity far higher than those to which they are normally subjected. At the same time, the growth of these trees may be severely stunted if nutrient levels are too low.

While the same trees occupy Northwest bogs and uplands, the understory vegetation in the two habitats is markedly different. Bogs feature a distinctive assemblage of shrubs and herbs consisting of species that are particularly tolerant of high acidity and low fertility. The shrub layer is dominated by members of the heath family, which also dominate other inhospitable environments in the region. The largest of the bog heaths is Labrador-tea, which attains heights of three feet or more. It is readily distinguished by its whorls of droopy, leathery leaves whose margins are rolled under and whose undersides are matted with rust-colored hairs. A similar species occurs in bogs and poor soils in southern Oregon and northern California. The native bog cranberry is a low creeping shrublet whose stems intertwine with sphagnum moss, forming thick, tangled mats. A relative of the cultivated cranberry of East Coast bogs, the bog cranberry has fruits that are smaller and rather more sour than bitter, though quite palatable. Frequently found along with the cranberry is swamp laurel, also a low heath shrub, whose delicate, pink, saucer-shaped flowers are surprisingly large for so tiny a plant.

Two common shrubs of the bog community are not heaths. Sweet gale is a deciduous shrub with waxy leaves and flowers. Commonly invading sphagnum mats, it may attain heights up to five feet. Bog birch is a shrub or small tree with oval leaves about the size of a quarter. It grows in bogs, swamps, and bottomland woods in Alaska, across Canada, and southward in the Cascades and Rocky Mountains.

Bogs are also noted for their unusual herbaceous vegetation, including orchids and rare carnivorous plants such as sundews and pitcher plants. The round-leaved sundew has a rosette of basal leaves that are covered with knobby glandular hairs, each tipped with a drop of sticky fluid. Insects attracted to the secretion adhere to it and are enfolded by the leaf, whereupon they are digested by means of powerful enzymes that render them into nutrient broth that is absorbed by the plant. The California pitcher plant is found in bogs that occur in the Siskiyou Mountains and along the coast to a few miles north of Florence, Oregon. The leaves of this plant are tubular and terminate in a hood of sorts from which dangles an appendage resembling the tail of a fish. Nectar secreted by glands on the appendage attracts insects, which are drawn into the leaf by additional secretions within. The interior of the leaf is lined with downward-pointing hairs that allow hungry insects to crawl downward but prevent them from escaping. The insects drown in the pool of secreted fluid that lies at the bottom of each leaf, where their remains are decomposed by bacteria. Soluble proteins and other nutrients are then absorbed by the plant. Carnivorousness is a clever, though disconcerting, adaptation to the inadequate nutrient regimes characteristic of bogs.

Swamps are wetlands dominated by trees or, less commonly, shrubs. The presence of standing water during most of the year separates swamps from other wooded wetlands. Two types of swamps occur in the Pacific Northwest: conifer swamps and deciduous swamps.

Swamps dominated by western redcedar or red alder occur widely throughout the coastal forest region of the Pacific Northwest. They are probably best developed on the broad coastal plain that runs along the western edge of the Olympic Peninsula. They are also common, however, on low, poorly drained flats along the entire Northwest coast and in the glaciated lowlands of the Puget Sound region.

Red alder is normally a seral tree, one that succeeds conifers in the wake of fire, logging, or other disruption and is eventually succeeded by them in turn. In some Northwest swamps, however, this common and widespread deciduous tree seems to be a climax species, that is, it appears able to occupy such sites more or less indefinitely. Though cedar and alder are the most common swamp trees by a large margin, Sitka spruce, western white pine, shore pine, and western hemlock may also be present.

Understory vegetation in coastal swamps is normally dense, with tangles of salmonberry or other shrubs giving way in places to stands of skunk cabbage or devil's club. Though normally dominated by one or two species, a large variety of herbs and shrubs may actually be present. Clumps of lady fern, a large, showy species that dies back in fall, lend a lush tropical aspect to the swamps. Slough sedge, false lily-of-the-valley, youth-on-age, mitreworts, water-parsley, and Cooley's hedgenettle are among the other soft-stemmed plants characteristic of this community.

West of the Cascades, bottomlands are subjected to seasonal flooding, but where standing water is temporary, they commonly support distinctive woodlands dominated by one or more deciduous trees. Red alder is, again, an important member of this community, but black cottonwood, Oregon ash, and Pacific willow may be more common locally. White alder and Oregon white oak occur with the ash in the Willamette Valley and areas to the south. Paper birch occurs in this community from the Seattle area northward. Bitter cherry, Pacific crabapple, cascara, Pacific dogwood, and a host of willow species also occur in these floodplain woods.

In a region where conifers reign, bottomland woods provide havens for deciduous trees, which require a reliable source of water to sustain them through the normally dry growing season. Deciduous trees of several species are sprinkled through the conifer forests, particularly second-growth stands near city and suburb, but only in the bottom-lands can one find extensive deciduous forests where conifers are often a minor element. At the same time, many bottom-land woods in the Puget Sound region are essentially man-made, created from conifer swamps either through selective logging of cedar and spruce or as a result of water projects that either flooded forests or exposed new lands to invasion by deciduous trees. In Seattle, for example, completion of construction of the locks connecting Puget Sound to Lake Washington in 1917 caused the water level of the lake to drop nine feet, exposing new shoreline that was invaded by cottonwoods, ashes, alders, and willows. Eventually, these shoreline deciduous woods will be invaded by conifers.

Bottomland deciduous woods contain most of the same understory herbs and shrubs found in conifer swamps. The trees change in the course of succession, but the regime of abundant shade and water that supports the understory plants remains more or less the same regardless of the particular species forming the canopy. Various shrubby willows and red osier may form dense thickets in bottomland woods. Hardhack, a tall coarse shrub with spikes of pink flowers, often grows in impenetrable stands where the woods give way to marsh or wet meadow. Creeping buttercup, youth-on-age, lady fern, bedstraw, water-parsley, and large-leaved avens are among the more common and conspicuous bottomland herbs.

Riparian woodlands east of the Cascades form corridors of trees in a landscape dominated by brush and agricultural fields. As a result, riparian woodlands are particularly conspicuous in this largely unforested region. In northeastern Washington, tall thickets dominated by black hawthorn occur among moist hillside ravines and in bottomlands. Common snowberry and white spiraea are common understory shrubs in ravine thickets. Lush herbaceous undergrowth dominated by cow parsnip and stinging nettle are characteristic of valley-floor woodlands. Black cottonwoods in some places tower above the thickets, joined perhaps by quaking aspens or mountain alders. In drier steppe regions, riparian woodlands dominated by black cottonwoods commonly line streams. White alder and cottonwood occur together along streams emptying into the Snake River. Riparian bottomlands in Oregon feature thickets of cherry, hawthorn, and willow.

Riparian woodlands provide dramatically different habitats for wildlife than does adjacent upland. The presence of water and cover attracts wildlife from adjacent communities, and the rather different vegetation provides a home for animals that otherwise might be absent from a region. Most of the wildlife living within forest and steppe at one time or another visit lakes and streams for water or to feed on vegetation that may be found there but not elsewhere in an area. In addition, numerous species of wildlife, including elk, deer, coyotes, bears, mountain lions, and a variety of birds, use riparian zones as corridors for moving undetected through meadows, brush, and other open areas. Mule deer prefer riparian areas for fawning because water is close and the rank growths of shrubbery or succulent herbs provide excellent food and cover for fawns.

In addition to visitors from surrounding forests, meadows, and brush, riparian zones also support a rich assortment of wildlife that rarely occurs elsewhere. The most famous of these is the beaver, whose valuable pelts provided much of the economic incentive behind the early exploration and settlement of western North America. Astoria, Oregon, the oldest settlement in the Pacific Northwest, was established in 1811 as a fur trading post, and the fur most eagerly sought was that of the beaver. Beavers were trapped nearly to extinction, but have since made a remarkable comeback

45. Vegetation profile of riparian woodland (adapted from Brown, ed., *Management of Wildlife and Fish Habitats in Forests of Western Oregon and Washington*)

throughout their former range. They now occur commonly throughout the Northwest and are known to exist even within the city limits of Seattle.

Beavers are known to live along large rivers, where they dig burrows with underground entrances in soft riverbanks. Their preferred habitat, however, is a quiet pond surrounded by deciduous trees such as birch, aspen, cottonwood, willow, or alder. Beavers feed on the soft inner bark of these and other trees, including young conifers if deciduous trees aren't available. Where small ponds don't exist, beavers will, if possible, create them by damming small streams with pole-sized trees felled expressly for this purpose. Beavers also use the timber to create dome-shaped lodges, which may be incorporated into the dam. The lodges have underwater entrances, which means that the beavers will be locked inside if the pond freezes over. Much of the industry for which beavers are credited is directed toward stockpiling food to guard against this possibility.

Except for humans, beavers alter their environment more profoundly than any other animal in North America. Creating and maintaining ponds where none existed before, they provide habitats for aquatic animals that require still or slowly moving, rather than rushing, water. They also expand forest openings, contributing to forest diversity by creating new habitats both for wildlife and for trees and other plants that require ample sunlight. When beavers have exhausted the supply of deciduous trees in an area, they commonly pick up stakes, as it were, and move on to a new area. In the absence of their maintenance activities, the stream quickly fills in the old pond, which is invaded by a succession of plant communities. Many of the small pocket meadows lining streams throughout the Northwest owe their origins to beavers.

Two more valuable fur-bearing mammals, the mink and the river otter, are also restricted to riparian habitats. The mink is essentially a large, dark aquatic weasel. It is an excellent swimmer and dens in the banks of streams, ponds, and lakes. Like many other members of the weasel family, the mink is a fierce, irascible predator that defends its territory against all comers. It is the scourge of muskrats, its favorite prey, but it also feeds on fish, snakes, frogs, riparian birds, and small mammals that visit the water's edge. The river otter also dens in burrows dug into riverbanks. With its streamlined body, webbed toes, and long rudderlike tail, it is the finest swimmer among the riparian mammals—good enough that fish are its main diet item. Often roaming far from water, however, the river otter also preys on small mammals and invertebrates. Both the mink and the river otter occur in forested regions throughout the Pacific Northwest.

Among the numerous birds that favor riparian habitats, the bald eagle reigns supreme. Easily recognized by its white head and tail, the bald eagle is found throughout the Pacific Northwest. The greatest concentrations in the conterminous United States occur in western Washington, where large numbers of this endangered species gather in winter to feast on steelhead runs along the major rivers draining the Cascades and Olympics. Oregon also hosts a large population of bald eagles, particularly in the Klamath Basin, on the east side of the Cascades. Altogether, about 200 breeding pairs and 2,000 wintering birds exist in the two states.

Bald eagles build large stick platform nests in the tops of the tallest conifers in proximity to rivers and lakes. Most nests are located within 600 feet of the shoreline, but the closer the better is the rule. Bald eagles are opportunists, feeding on a wide variety of prey, which they obtain in the easiest ways possible. When scavenging is sufficient, that's what they do, patrolling shorelines for dead fish and other edibles. If necessary, however, they will exert themselves to prey upon fish, waterfowl, seabirds, small mammals, and invertebrates. Such versatility, both in diet items and in the manner in which food is obtained, well serve a large predator that in winter requires roughly a pound of food a day. The birds are able to store as much of two pounds of food in their crops, however, and can go as long as two weeks without eating.

It is startling to see a pair of ducks bobbing on a rapid mountain stream, but in the Pacific Northwest this is not an uncommon experience. Harlequin ducks, a specialty of the region, commonly nest among rocks or fallen trees along swift mountain streams. Hooded and common mergansers prefer cavities in trees alongside lakes or rivers. The wood duck is also a cavity nester, but prefers quiet ponds and slowly moving lowland rivers.

If the bald eagle is the most impressive riparian bird, the American dipper, or water ouzel, is unquestionably the most unusual. This small, drab, gray-brown bird, which resembles a fat wren, spends its entire life along rushing mountain streams, where it forages for invertebrates both along the bank and on the stream bottom. Named for its habit of continuously dipping up and down, the dipper is able to walk along stream bottoms. Rock ledges and crevices alongside, or even within, a stream are the dipper's preferred nesting sites.

Aside from meadows, riparian zones are among the few naturally occurring openings in conifer forests. As a result they are among the few places where rapidly growing, sun-loving deciduous trees such as quaking aspens, black cottonwoods, willows, alders, birches, and ashes can hold their own among the conifers. These deciduous corridors attract a number of birds that would rarely be encountered in conifer forests or open steppes without them. Such birds include the willow flycatcher, red-eyed vireo, yellow warbler, northern oriole, and black-headed grosbeak.

Riparian areas, of course, are among the primary habitats for amphibians. Of the 17 species of salamanders found in the Pacific Northwest, nine breed in lakes or streams but feed in terrestrial habitats, often well away from the water. Among the most common and, during their annual migrations to water, conspicuous of these salamanders is the rough-skinned newt, which can be seen in quiet lowland streams or high mountain lakes. When not breeding the newt lives in damp forest litter and among downed wood, where it feeds on a variety of invertebrates. Unlike the rough-skinned newt, the Pacific giant salamander rarely leaves the riparian zone. Breeding in fast, well-oxygenated streams, adult giant salamanders live under logs and stones in moist coastal conifer forests and their inland counterparts, the cedar-hemlock forests of northern Idaho. Growing to more than a foot in length, the Pacific giant salamander is the largest terrestrial salamander in the region, perhaps in the world. It feeds not only on a wide variety of invertebrates, but also on other salamanders, small mammals, and even birds!

The foothill yellow-legged frog occurs along rocky streams in southwestern Oregon and northwestern California, rarely wandering far from water. The Cascade frog is found near lakes and streams in the Cascades and Olympics to elevations as high as 9,000 feet. This is the small frog most often encountered by campers along the shores of high lakes.

The tailed frog requires clear, cold, fast-moving streams. Endemic to forested areas of the Pacific Northwest, the tailed frog is a member of a primitive family, the bell toads, whose only other members live in New Zealand. The tailed frog differs anatomically from true frogs in several ways. These include the presence of ribs, an extra vertebra, and the stubby tail for which it is named, a primitive "penis" of sorts, all of which are lacking in true frogs. The tailed frog is the only frog or toad of any sort in which fertilization occurs within the female. The tail of the male is actually an extension of the cloaca. Grasping the female from behind, the male inserts this organ into the female, where it remains for up to 30 hours. Its string of eggs is attached to the underside of rocks in swift-moving streams. The tadpole has an oral disk like a suction cup that enables it to remain firmly attached to rocks in fast currents.

The small Pacific treefrog is the most common and widespread frog in the region. Although it breeds in shallow, quiet water, usually with sedges, rushes, or other emergent vegetation, this small terrestrial frog spends most of its time foraging for invertebrates among forest shrubbery, logs, and other woody debris. During dry spells it will seek refuge in rock crevices, in tree cavities, beneath loose bark, and in similar cool, damp places. In spring, when these pint-sized amphibians return to the water to breed, the nocturnal choruses of the males fill the woods.

Reptiles are uncommon in the cool, damp region west of the Cascades, particularly north of the Columbia River. The most common reptiles are garter snakes, a genus that has specialized in cool habitats and whose members are either aquatic or prefer damp habitats. Three species of garter snakes occur widely in the Pacific Northwest, two of which, the western terrestrial garter snake and the common garter snake, both represented by several distinct subspecies, regularly occur along streams, lakes, and other bodies of water.

APPENDIX A

Scientific Names

Scientific names have three main advantages over common ones. First, they are more precise. Each scientific name designates one and only one species, whereas the same common name may be applied to totally unrelated species. For example, Douglas-fir (*Pseudotsuga menziesii*) is unrelated to Pacific silver fir (*Abies amabilis*). Similarly, the western meadowlark (*Sturnella neglecta*) and horned lark (*Eremophila alpestris*) belong to entirely different genera and families. Second, scientific names indicate the relationships among organisms in a systematic way, while common names are, at best, haphazard in this regard. For example, the scientific names for coyote (*Canis latrans*) and wolf (*Canis lupus*) clearly indicate their close kinship (i.e., both belong to the genus *Canis*, along with the domestic dog), while the common names do not. The same holds true for quaking aspen (*Populus tremuloides*) and black cottonwood (*Populus trichocarpa*). Third, scientific names are accepted internationally. For instance, when birders in England refer to having sighted a great diver, their counterparts in the United States may not realize that the bird referred to is the one they call the common loon. Ornithologists on both sides of the Atlantic, however, know the bird by its scientific name, *Gavia immer*.

A scientific name consists of two parts. The first name, which is always capitalized, designates the genus to which an organism belongs. The second name, which is usually in lower case, designates the species. Normally, both names are italicized. A species is usually defined as a population of interbreeding organisms—anything from amoebas to apes—that share a common gene pool. Thus all human beings belong to the same species. Species belonging to the same genus generally cannot interbreed but are thought to have evolved from a common ancestor. Since evolution is an ongoing process, however, different species may be more or less like one another, depending on how long their respective populations have been genetically separated. Two species that have only recently diverged from a common ancestor (certain willows, for example) may still be mutually fertile to some degree and thereby able, at least on occasion, to produce hybrid offspring. At the same time, within a single species there are often divergent populations that differ in one or more ways but that still retain mutual fertility. The dark-eyed junco, for example, includes a number of geographic "races," which look rather different but which interbreed where their ranges overlap.

Readers will notice that some scientific names include a third name; e.g., *Symphoricarpos racemosa* var. *arborescens*. This is the scientific name of the coast red elderberry. The third part of the name indicates that this common shrub is not a species unto itself but a variety of a species that also includes other distinct forms. For example, *Symphoricarpos racemosa* var. *melanocarpa* designates the black elderberry, a variety of the same species whose fruit is dark blue rather than red. Similarly, zoologists have divided certain variable species into a number of distinctive geographic races known as subspecies. Thus, as their scientific names suggest but their common names obscure, the black-tailed deer (*Odocoileus hemionus columbianus*) of the coastal region and mule deer (*Odocoileus hemionus hemionus*) of the interior are considered to be geographic races, or subspecies, of a single species. The distinction between a variety and a subspecies is of great interest to taxonomists, the biologists who classify life forms, but need not concern us here. Subspecific or varietal names are included in this book only for the handful of species for whom such usage is a convention.

Scientific names used in this book are drawn from the following sources:

Plants: *Flora of the Pacific Northwest* by C. Leo Hitchcock and Arthur Cronquist (Seattle: University of Washington Press, 1973).

Mammals: *Revised Checklist of North American Mammals*

North of Mexico by Jones, Carter, and Genoways (Lubbock, Texas: Texas Tech University, 1979).

Birds: *Checklist of North American Birds*, 6th ed. and supplements by the American Ornithologists Union (Baltimore, 1983).

Reptiles and Amphibians: *Amphibians & Reptiles of the Pacific Northwest* by Ronald A. Nussbaum, Edmund D. Brodie, Jr., and Robert M. Storm (Moscow, Idaho: The University Press of Idaho, 1983).

Plants

Agoseris, false	*Microseris troximoides*
Alaska-cedar	*Chamaecyparis nootkaensis*
Alder, mountain	*Alnus incana*
Alder, red	*Alnus rubra*
Alder, Sitka	*Alnus sinuata*
Alder, slide	See Alder, Sitka
Alder, white	*Alnus rhombifolia*
Alders	*Alnus* species
Alkaligrass	*Puccinellia pumila*
Arborvitae	*Thuja* species
Arnica, broadleaf	*Arnica latifolia*
Arnica, heartleaf	*Arnica cordifolia*
Arnicas	*Arnica* species
Arrowgrass	*Triglochin maritimum*
Ash, mountain	See Mountain-ash
Ash, Oregon	*Fraxinus latifolia*
Aspen, quaking	*Populus tremuloides*
Aster, alpine	*Aster alpigenus*
Aster, Cascade	*Aster ledophyllus*
Aster, western	*Aster occidentalis*
Asters	*Aster* species
Avens, large-leaved	*Geum macrophyllum*
Avens, mountain	*Dryas octopetala*
Azalea, Cascade	*Rhododendron albiflorum*
Azaleas	*Rhododendron* species
Baldcypresses	*Taxodium* species
Balsamroot, arrowleaf	*Balsamorhiza saggittata*

Balsamroots	*Balsamorhiza* species
Baneberry, western red	*Actaea rubra*
Bead lily	See Queen's cup
Beargrass	*Xerophyllum tenax*
Bedstraws	*Galium* species
Beeches	*Fagus* species
Bell, yellow	*Fritillaria pudica*
Bellflower, round-leaved	*Campanula rotundifolia*
Bellflowers	*Campanula* species
Bentgrass, creeping	*Agrostis alba* var. *palustris*
Bilberries	*Vaccinium* species
Birch, bog	*Betula glandulosa*
Birch, paper	*Betula papyrifera*
Birches	*Betula* species
Bistort, mountain	*Polygonum bistortoides*
Bitterbrush, antelope	*Purshia tridentata*
Blackberry, Pacific	*Rubus ursinus*
Bladderworts	*Utricularia* species
Bleeding heart, western	*Dicentra formosa*
Blueberries	*Vaccinium* species
Blueberry, delicious	*Vaccinium deliciosum*
Blue blossom	*Ceanothus thyrsiflorus*
Blue-eyed Mary, small-flowered	*Collinsia parviflora*
Bluegrass, alkali	*Poa juncifolia*
Bluegrass, alpine	*Poa alpina*
Bluegrass, Cusick's	*Poa cusickii*
Bluegrass, Kentucky	*Poa pratensis*
Bluegrass, Sandberg's	*Poa sandbergii*
Brake, rock	*Cryptogramma crispa*
Bramble, dwarf	*Rubus lasiococcus*
Bramble, strawberry	*Rubus pedatus*
Brodiaea, Douglas'	*Brodiaea douglasii*
Buckbrush	*Ceanothus cuneatus*
Buckeyes	*Aesculus* species
Buckthorn, California	*Aesculus californica*
Buckwheats, wild	*Eriogonum* species
Buffaloberry	*Shepherdia canadensis*
Bulrush, hardstem	*Scirpus acutus*
Bulrush, softstem	*Scirpus validus*
Bulrushes	*Scirpus* species
Bunchberry	*Cornus canadensis*

Buttercup, creeping	*Ranunculus repens*
Buttercup, subalpine	*Ranunculus eschscholtzii*
Butterweeds	*Senecio* species
Cascara	*Rhamnus purshiana*
Casebearer, larch	*Coleophora laricella*
Cattail, common	*Typha latifolia*
Cattails	*Typha* species
Ceanothus, redstem	*Ceanothus sanguineus*
Ceanothuses	*Ceanothus* species
Cedar, Alaska	See Alaska-cedar
Cedar, incense	See Incense-cedar
Cedar, Port Orford	See Port-Orford-Cedar
Cedar, yellow	See Alaska-cedar
Cheatgrass, downy	*Bromus tectorum*
Cherry, bitter	*Prunus emarginata*
Cherry, mazzard	*Prunus avium*
Chestnuts	*Castanea* species
Chinquapin, golden	*Castanopsis chrysophylla*
Cinquefoil, fanleaf	*Potentilla flabellifolia*
Cinquefoil, shrubby	*Potentilla fruticosa*
Cinquefoil, slender	*Potentilla gracilis*
Cinquefoil, snowbed	*Potentilla nivea*
Cinquefoils	*Potentilla* species
Clintonia, red	*Clintonia andrewsiana*
Clover, marsh	*Trifolium wormskjoldii*
Clubmosses	*Lycopodium* species
Coffeeberry, California	*Rhamnus californica*
Coltsfoot	*Petastites frigidus*
Columbine, red	*Aquilegia formosa*
Copper bush	*Cladothamnus pyroliflorus*
Corn-lily	See False-hellebores
Cottonwood, black	*Populus trichocarpa*
Crabapple, Pacific	*Pyrus fusca*
Cranberries	*Vaccinium* species
Cranberry, bog	*Vaccinium oxycoccus*
Cranberry, cultivated	*Vaccinium macrocarpon*
Cranberry, high bush	*Viburnum edule*
Creambush	See Ocean spray
Crowberry	*Empetrum nigrum*
Currants	*Ribes* species
Cutgrass, rice	*Leersia oryzoides*

Cycads	*Cycas* species
Cypress, Baker's	*Cupressus bakerii*
Daisy, wandering	*Erigeron peregrinus*
Danthonia, California	*Danthonia californica*
Deerbrush	*Ceanothus integerrimus*
Devil's club	*Oplopanax horridum*
Dogtooth-violet	See Lily, avalanche
Dogwood, flowering	*Cornus floridanus*
Dogwood, Pacific	*Cornus nuttallii*
Dogwood, red osier	See Osier, red
Douglas-fir	*Pseudotsuga menziesii*
Douglas-fir, coastal	*Pseudotsuga menziesii* var. *menziesii*
Douglas-fir, Rocky Mountain	*Pseudotsuga menziesii* var. *glauca*
Douglasia, red	*Douglasia laevigata*
Dropseed, sand	*Sporobolus cryptandrus*
Duckweeds	*Lemma* species
Eelgrass	*Zostera marina*
Elderberry, coast red	*Sambucus racemosa* var. *arborescens*
Elms	*Ulmus* species
Everlasting, pearly	*Anaphalis margaritacea*
Fairybell, Smith's	*Disporum smithii*
False-hellebore, green	*Veratrum viride*
False-hellebore, white	*Veratrum californicum*
False-hellebores	*Veratrum* species
Fern, bracken	*Pteridium aquilinum*
Fern, deer	*Blechnum spicant*
Fern, lady	*Athyrium filix-femina*
Fern, licorice	*Polypodium glycyrrhiza*
Fern, mountain lady	*Athyrium distentifolium*
Fern, northern maidenhair	*Adiantum pedantum*
Fern, sword	*Polystichum munitum*
Fern, wood	*Dryopteris austriaca*
Fescue, green	*Festuca viridula*
Fescue, Idaho	*Festuca idahoensis*
Fescue, sheep	*Festuca ovina*
Fir, balsam	*Abies balsamifera*
Fir, Douglas	See Douglas-fir

Fir, grand	*Abies grandis*
Fir, noble	*Abies procera*
Fir, Pacific silver	*Abies amabilis*
Fir, Shasta red	*Abies magnifica* var. *shastensis*
Fir, red	*Abies magnifica*
Fir, subalpine	*Abies lasiocarpa*
Fir, white	*Abies concolor*
Fireweed	*Epilobium angustifolium*
Fleabane, golden	*Erigeron aureus*
Fleabane, shaggy	*Erigeron pumilus* var. *intermedius*
Foamflower, coolwort	*Tiarella trifoliata* var. *unifoliata*
Foamflower, trefoil	*Tiarella trifoliata* var. *trifoliata*
Foxtail, water	*Alopecurus geniculatus*
Fungus, Indian paint	*Echinodontium tinctorium*
Gentians	*Gentiana* species
Gilia, scarlet	*Gilia aggregata*
Gilia, small-flowered	*Gilia minutiflora*
Gingko	*Gingko biloba*
Goldenrod	*Solidago canadensis*
Goldenrod, dwarf	*Solidago spathulata*
Goldenweed, Bloomer's	*Haplopappus bloomeri*
Gooseberries	*Ribes* species
Goosefoots	*Chenopodiaceae* species
Grape, Oregon	See Oregon-grape
Grass, reed canary	*Phalaria arundinacea*
Greasewood	*Sarcobatus vermiculatus*
Groundsel, arrowhead	*Senecio triangularis*
Gum plant	*Grindelia integrifolia*
Hairgrass, tufted	*Deschampsia caespitosa*
Hardhack	*Spiraea douglasii*
Hawkweed, white-flowered	*Hieracium albiflorum*
Hawthorn, black	*Cratageus douglasii*
Hazelnut, California	*Corylus cornuta* var. *californica*
Heather, mountain	See Mountain-heather
Heaths	*Ericaceae* species
Hedgenettle, Cooley's	*Stachys cooleyae*
Hemlock, mountain	*Tsuga mertensiana*

Hemlock, western	*Tsuga heterophylla*
Holly, English	*Ilex aquifolium*
Honeysuckle, blue fly	*Lonicera caerulea*
Honeysuckle, purple	*Lonicera conjugalis*
Hopsage, spiny	*Atriplex spinosa*
Horsebrush, gray	*Tetradymia canescens*
Huckleberries	*Vaccinium* species
Huckleberry, Alaska	*Vaccinium alaskense*
Huckleberry, big	*Vaccinium membranaceum*
Huckleberry, Cascade	*Vaccinium deliciosum*
Huckleberry, dwarf	*Vaccinium caespitosum*
Huckleberry, evergreen	*Vaccinium ovatum*
Huckleberry, fool's	See Menziesia
Huckleberry, ovalleaf	*Vaccinium ovalifolium*
Huckleberry, red	*Vaccinium parvifolium*
Incense-cedar	*Calocedrus decurrens*
Indian-teas	*Ledum* species
Inside-out flower	*Vancouveria hexandra*
Iris, western	*Iris missouriensis*
Isothecium	*Isothecium stoloniferum*
Jaumea	*Jaumea carnosa*
Junegrass, prairie	*Koeleria cristata*
Juniper, common	*Juniperus communis*
Juniper, Rocky Mountain	*Juniperus scopulorum*
Juniper, western	*Juniperus occidentalis*
Kinnikinnick	*Arctostaphylos uva-ursi*
Knotweeds	*Polygonum* species
Labrador-tea	*Ledum glandulosum*
Labrador-tea, bog	*Ledum groenlandicum*
Lady's tresses	*Spiranthes romanzoffia*
Larch, alpine	*Larix lyallii*
Larch, western	*Larix occidentalis*
Larkspurs	*Delphinium* species
Laurel, alpine	*Kalmia microphylla*
Laurel, California	*Umbellularia californica*
Laurel, mountain	*Kalmia microphylla*
Laurel, swamp	*Kalmia occidentalis*

Lilies, mariposa | *Calochortus* species
Lily, avalanche | *Erythronium montanum*
Lily, glacier | *Erythronium grandiflorum*
Lily of the valley, false | *Maianthemum dilatatum*

Locoweeds | *Astragalus* species
Lousewort, coil-beaked | *Pedicularis contorta*
Lovage, Gray's | *Ligusticum grayi*
Lupine, alpine | *Lupinus lepidus* var. *lepidus*
Lupine, broadleaf | *Lupinus latifolia*
Lupine, silky | *Lupinus sericeus*
Lupine, velvet | *Lupinus leucophyllus*
Lupines | *Lupinus* species

Madrone, Pacific | *Arbutus menziesii*
Madrones | *Arbutus* species
Mannagrasses | *Glyceria* species
Manzanita, greenleaf | *Arctostaphylos patula*
Manzanita, hoary | *Arctostaphylos canescens*
Manzanita, pinemat | *Arctostaphylos nevadensis*
Manzanita, whiteleaf | *Arctostaphylos viscida*
Manzanitas | *Arctostaphylos* species
Maple, bigleaf | *Acer macrophyllum*
Maple, Rocky Mountain | *Acer glabra*
Maple, sugar | *Acer saccharum*
Maple, vine | *Acer circinatum*
Marsh-marigold, elkslip | *Caltha leptosepala*
Marsh-marigold, twinflower | *Caltha biflora*
Marsh-marigolds | *Caltha* species
Menziesia | *Menziesia ferruginea*
Microsteris, slender | *Microsteris gracilis*
Milkwort | *Glaux maritima*
Mistletoe, dwarf | *Arceuthobium* species
Mitrewort, starry | *Mitella stauropetala*
Mitreworts | *Mitella* species
Monkeyflower, Lewis' | *Mimulus lewisii*
Monkeyflower, subalpine | *Mimulus tilingii*
Monkeyflowers | *Mimulus* species
Moss, mountain fern | *Hylocomium splendens*
Moss, sphagnum | *Sphagnum* species
Moss-campion | *Silene acaulis*

Mountain-ash, European	*Sorbus aucuparia*
Mountain-ashes	*Sorbus* species
Mountain balm	*Ceanothus velutinus*
Mountain-heather, Alaska	*Cassiope stelleriana*
Mountain-heather, club-moss	*Cassiope lycopoidioides*
Mountain-heather, four-angled	*Cassiope tetragona*
Mountain-heather, red	*Phyllodoce empetriformis*
Mountain-heather, white	*Cassiope mertensiana*
Mountain-heather, yellow	*Phyllodoce glanduliflora*
Mountain lover	*Pachistima myrsinites*
Mountain-mahogany, birchleaf	*Cercocarpus betuloides*
Mountain-mahogany, curl-leaf	*Cercocarpus ledifolius*
Mousetail	*Myosurus aristatus*
Mustard, tansy	*Descurainia pinnata*
Myrtle, Oregon	See Laurel, California
Needle-and-thread	*Stipa comata*
Needlegrass, Columbia	*Stipa occidentalis* var. *minor*
Needlegrasses	*Stipa* species
Nettle, stinging	*Urtica dioica*
Ninebark, mallow	*Physocarpus malvaceus*
Nutmeg, California	*Torreya californica*
Oak, California black	*Quercus kelloggii*
Oak, canyon live	*Quercus chrysolepis*
Oak, coast live	*Quercus agrifolia*
Oak, Garry	See Oak, Oregon white
Oak, huckleberry	*Quercus vaccinifolia*
Oak, Oregon white	*Quercus garryana*
Oak, poison	See Poison-oak
Oak, Sadler	*Quercus sadleriana*
Ocean spray	*Holodiscus discolor*
Old man's beard	*Geum triflorum*
Onion, Olympic	*Allium crenulatum*
Orache	*Atriplex patula*
Orchids, bog	*Habernaria* species
Oregon-grape, creeping	*Berberis repens*
Oregon-grape, low	*Berberis nervosa*

Osier, red	*Cornus stolonifera*
Osoberry	*Oemleria cerasmiformis*
Owl's clover, paintbrush	*Orthocarpus castillejoides*
Paintbrushes	*Castilleja* species
Parsley, desert	*Lomatium* species
Parsnip, cow	*Heracleum lanatum*
Partridgefoot	*Luetkea pectinata*
Pasqueflower, western	*Anemone occidentalis*
Pasqueflowers	*Anemone* species
Penstemon, Davidson's	*Penstemon davidsonii*
Penstemon, little	*Penstemon procerus*
Penstemons	*Penstemon* species
Phlox, spreading	*Phlox diffusa*
Pickleweed	*Salicornia virginica*
Pine, bishop	*Pinus muricata*
Pine, foxtail	*Pinus balfouriana*
Pine, jack	*Pinus banksiana*
Pine, Jeffrey	*Pinus jeffreyi*
Pine, knobcone	*Pinus attenuata*
Pine, limber	*Pinus flexilis*
Pine, lodgepole	*Pinus contorta* vars. *latifolia* and *murrayana*
Pine, ponderosa	*Pinus ponderosa*
Pine, prince's	*Chimaphila umbellata*
Pine, shore	*Pinus contorta* var. *contorta*
Pine, sugar	*Pinus lambertiana*
Pine, western white	*Pinus monticola*
Pine, western yellow	See Pine, ponderosa
Pine, whitebark	*Pinus albicaulis*
Pinegrass	*Calamagrostis rubescens*
Pitcher plant, California	*Darlingtonia californica*
Plantain, rattlesnake	*Goodyera oblongifolia*
Plantain, seaside	*Plantago maritima*
Plum, Indian	See Osoberry
Poison-oak	*Rhus diversiloba*
Pond-lily	*Nuphar polysepalum*
Pondweeds	*Potamogeton* species
Poplar, balsam	*Populus balsamifera*
Poplars	*Populus* species
Port-Orford-cedar	*Chamaecyparis lawsoniana*
Prairie star	*Lithophragma bulbifera*

Pussypaws	*Spraguea umbellata*
Pussytoes, alpine	*Antennaria alpina*
Pussytoes, woolly	*Antennaria lanata*
Pyrolas	*Pyrola* species
Queen's cup bead lily	*Clintonia uniflora*
Quillworts	*Isoetes* species
Rabbitbrush, gray	*Chrysothamnus nauseosus*
Rabbitbrush, tall green	*Chrysothamnus viscidiflorus*
Rabbitbrushes	*Chrysothamnus* species
Redcedar, western	*Thuja plicata*
Redwood, coast	*Sequoia sempervirens*
Redwood, dawn	*Metasequoia* species
Rhododendron, Pacific	*Rhododendron macrophyllum*
Rhododendrons	*Rhododendron* species
Rose, Nootka	*Rosa nutkana*
Rose, woods	*Rosa woodsii*
Roses, wild	*Rosa* species
Rush, Baltic	*Juncus balticus*
Rush, soft	*Juncus effusus*
Rushes, true	*Juncus* species
Rust, white pine blister	*Cronartium ribicola*
Rye, tall wild	*Elymus cinerea*
Rye, wild	*Elymus caput-medusae*
Sagebrush, big	*Artemisia tridentata*
Sagebrush, low	*Artemisia arbuscula*
Sagebrush, mountain	*Artemisia tridentata*
	var. *vaseyana*
Sagebrush, silver	*Artemisia cana*
Sagebrush, spiny	*Artemisia spinesecens*
Sagebrush, stiff	*Artemisia rigida*
Sagebrush, threetip	*Artemisia tripartita*
Salal	*Gaultheria shallon*
Salmonberry	*Rubus parviflorus*
Saltgrass	*Distichlis spicata*
Saltsage	*Atriplex nuttallii*
Sandspurries	*Spergularia* species
Sandwort, arctic	*Arenaria obtusiloba*
Sandworts	*Arenaria* species
Sawwort, American	*Saussurea americana*

Saxifrage, Oregon	*Saxifraga oregana*
Saxifrages	*Saxifraga* species
Sedge, beaked	*Carex rostrata*
Sedge, black	*Carex nigricans*
Sedge, elk	*Carex geyeri*
Sedge, Holm's Rocky Mountain	*Carex scopulorum*
Sedge, Lyngbye's	*Carex lyngbyei*
Sedge, showy	*Carex spectabilis*
Sedge, Sitka	*Carex sitchensis*
Sedge, slough	*Carex obnupta*
Sedge, water	*Carex aquatilis*
Sedge, woodrush	*Carex luzulina*
Sedges, true	*Carex* species
Sequoia, giant	*Sequoiadendron giganteum*
Serviceberries	*Amelanchier* species
Serviceberry, western	*Amelanchier alnifolia*
Shadscale	*Atriplex canescens*
Sheepfat	*Atriplex confertifolia*
Shooting star, Jeffrey's	*Dodecatheon jeffreyi*
Shooting stars	*Dodecatheon* species
Sibbaldia	*Sibbaldia procumbens*
Silktassel, Fremont's	*Garrya fremontii*
Silverweed, Pacific	*Potentilla pacifica*
Skunk-cabbage	*Lysichitum americanum*
Sloughgrass	*Beckmannia syzigachne*
Snapdragons	*Maurandya* species
Snowberry, common	*Symphoricarpos albus*
Snowberry, creeping	*Gaultheria hispidula*
Solomon's plume, starry	*Smilacina stellata*
Solomon's seal, false	*Smilacina racemosa*
Sorrel, wood	*Oxalis oregana*
Spike-rushes	*Eleocharis* species
Spiraea, white	*Spiraea betulifolia*
Spring beauty, western	*Claytonia lanceolata*
Spruce, Brewer's	*Picea breweriana*
Spruce, Engelmann	*Picea engelmannii*
Spruce, Sitka	*Picea sitchensis*
Spruce, white	*Picea glauca*
Squawbush	*Rhus trilobata*
Squaw carpet	*Ceanothus prostratus*
Stickseed, western	*Lappula redowski*

Stonecrops	*Sedum* species
Sundew, round-leaved	*Drosera rotundifolia*
Sundews	*Drosera* species
Sunflower, little	*Helianthella uniflora* var. *douglasii*
Sweet Gale	*Myrica gale*
Tamarack	*Larix laricina*
Tanbark Oak	See Tanoak
Tanoak	*Lithocarpus densiflora*
Tea, Labrador	See Labrador-tea
Thimbleberry	*Rubus spectabilis*
Three-square	*Scirpus americanus*
Toothwort, California	*Dentaria californica*
Trail plant	*Adenocaulon bicolor*
Trillium, western	*Trillium ovatum*
Trisetum, spike	*Trisetum spicatum*
Tule	See Bulrush, hardstem
Twinflower	*Linnaea borealis*
Valerian, Sitka	*Valeriana sitchensis*
Vanilla leaf	*Achlys triphylla*
Violet, evergreen	*Viola sempervirens*
Violet, wood	*Viola glabella*
Walnuts	*Juglans* species
Wapato	*Sagittaria latifolia*
Water-lily, white	*Nymphaea odorata*
Water-milfoil, European	*Myriophyllum spicatum*
Water-milfoils	*Myriophyllum* species
Water-parsley	*Oenanthe sarmentosa*
Water-plantain	*Alisma plantago-aquatica*
Waxmyrtles	*Myrica* species
Wheatgrass, bluebunch	*Agropyron spicatum*
Wheat, Indian	*Plantago patagonica*
Whitecedar, northern	*Thuja occidentalis*
White pine blister rust	*Cronartium ribicola*
Whitlow-grass, spring	*Draba verna*
Whortleberry, grouse	*Vaccinium scoparius*
Willow, Pacific	*Salix lasiandra*
Willow, Scouler's	*Salix scouleriana*
Willow, Sitka	*Salix sitchensis*

Willowherb, alpine	*Epilobium alpinum*
Willowherb, red	*Epilobium latifolia*
Willowherb, small-flowered	*Epilobium minutum*
Willows	*Salix* species
Winter fat	*Eurotia lanata*
Wintergreen, one-sided	*Pyrola secunda*
Wintergreens	*Gaultheria* species
Wormwood, three-forked	*Artemisia trifurcata*
Wormwoods	*Artemisia* species
Yarrow	*Achillea millefolium*
Yerba santa	*Eriodictyon californicum*
Yew, Western	*Taxus brevifolia*
Youth-on-age	*Tolmiea menziesii*

Animals

Ant, carpenter	*Camponotus laevigatus*
Badger, American	*Taxidea taxus*
Bear, Alaskan brown	See Bear, grizzly
Bear, black	*Ursus americanus*
Bear, grizzly	*Ursus arctos*
Beaver	*Castor canadensis*
Beetle, Douglas-fir	*Dendroctonus pseudotsugae*
Beaver, Mountain	See Mountain-beaver
Beetle, mountain pine	*Dendroctonus ponderosae*
Blackbird, red-winged	*Agelaius phoeniceus*
Blackbird, yellow-headed	*Xanthocephalus xanthocephalus*
Bluebird, mountain	*Sialia currucoides*
Bluebird, western	*Sialia mexicana*
Bobcat	*Felis rufus*
Budworm, spruce	*Choristoneura occidentalis*
Bullfrog	*Rana catesbiana*
Bushtit	*Psaltriparus minimus*
Caribou	*Rangifer tarandus*
Casebearer, larch	*Coleophora laricella*
Chat, yellow-breasted	*Icteria virens*

Chickadees	*Parus* species
Chickaree	See Squirrel, Douglas'
Chipmunk, yellow pine	*Eutamias amoenas*
Chipmunks	*Euitamias* species
Cougar	See Lion, mountain
Coyote	*Canis latrans*
Creeper, brown	*Certhia americana*
Crow, American	*Corvus brachyrhynchos*
Deer, mule	*Odocoileus hemionus hemionus*
Deer, black-tailed	*Odocoileus hemionus columbianus*
Dipper, American	*Cinclus mexicanus*
Duck, harlequin	*Histrionicus histrionicus*
Duck, ruddy	*Oxyura jamaicensis*
Duck, wood	*Aix sponsa*
Eagle, bald	*Haliaeetus leucocephalus*
Eagle, golden	*Aquila chrysaetos*
Egret, great	*Casmerodius albus*
Elk	*Cervis elaphus*
Elk, Roosevelt	*Cervis elaphus rooseveltii*
Ermine	*Mustela erminea*
Falcon, peregrine	*Falco peregrinus*
Finch, Cassin's	*Carpodacus cassinnii*
Finch, house	*Carpodacus mexicanus*
Fisher	*Martes pennanti*
Flicker, northern	*Colaptes auratus*
Flycatcher, alder	*Empidonax alnorum*
Flycatcher, gray	*Empidonax wrightii*
Flycatcher, Hammond's	*Empidonax hammondii*
Flycatcher, olive-sided	*Contopus borealis*
Flycatcher, willow	*Empidonax traillii*
Fox, gray	*Urocyon cinereoargenteus*
Fox, red	*Vulpes vulpes*
Frog, Cascade	*Rana cascadae*
Frog, foothill yellow-legged	*Rana boylei*
Frog, red-legged	*Rana aurora*

Frog, spotted	*Rana pretiosa*
Frog, tailed	*Ascaphus truei*
Gadwall	*Anas strepera*
Goat, mountain	*Oreamnos americanus*
Goldeneye, Barrow's	*Bucephala islandica*
Goose, snow	*Chen caerulescens*
Gopher, northern pocket	*Thomomys talpoides*
Gopher, western pocket	*Thomomys mazama*
Gophers, pocket	*Thomomys* species
Goshawk, northern	*Accipiter gentilis*
Grosbeak, black-headed	*Pheucticus melanocephalus*
Grosbeak, evening	*Coccothraustes vespertinus*
Grosbeak, pine	*Pinicola enucleator*
Grouse, blue	*Dendragapus obscurus*
Grouse, sage	*Centrocercus urophasianus*
Hare, snowshoe	*Lepus americanus*
Harrier, northern	*Circus cyanaeus*
Hawk, Cooper's	*Accipiter cooperii*
Hawk, red-tailed	*Buteo jamaicensis*
Hawk, sharp-shinned	*Accipiter striatus*
Heron, great blue	*Ardea herodias*
Hummingbird, Allen's	*Selasphorus sasin*
Hummingbird, Anna's	*Calypte anna*
Hummingbird, calliope	*Stellula calliope*
Hummingbird, rufous	*Selasphorus rufus*
Jackrabbit, black-tailed	*Lepus californicus*
Jackrabbits	*Lepus* species
Jay, gray	*Perisoreus canadensis*
Jay, scrub	*Aphelocoma coerulescens*
Jay, Steller's	*Cyanocitta stelleri*
Junco, dark-eyed	*Junco hyemalis*
Lark, horned	*Eremophila alpestris*
Lion, mountain	*Felis concolor*
Lizard, alligator	*Elgaria* species
Lizard, leopard	*Gambeli wislizenii*
Lizard, Mohave black-collared	*Crotaphytus bicinctores*

Lizard, short-horned	*Phrysonoma douglasii*
Lynx	*Felis canadensis*
Magpie, black-tailed	*Pica pica*
Mallard	*Anas platyrhynchos*
Marmot, hoary	*Marmota caligata*
Marmot, Olympic	*Marmota olympus*
Marmot, yellow-bellied	*Marmota flaviventris*
Marmots	*Marmota* species
Marten	*Martes americana*
Meadowlark, western	*Sturnella neglecta*
Merganser, common	*Mergus merganser*
Merganser, hooded	*Lophodytes cucullatus*
Mice, meadow	See Voles
Mink	*Mustela vison*
Moles	*Scapanus* species
Moose	*Alces alces*
Moth, Douglas-fir tussock	*Orgyia pseudotsugata*
Mountain-beaver	*Aplodontia rufa*
Mouse, deer	*Peromyscus maniculatus*
Mouse, Great Basin pocket	*Perognathus parvus*
Muskrat	*Ondatra zibethicus*
Newt, rough-skinned	*Taricha granulosa*
Nutcracker, Clark's	*Nucifraga columbiana*
Nuthatch, red-breasted	*Sitta canadensis*
Nuthatch, white-breasted	*Sitta carolinensis*
Nuthatches	*Sitta* species
Oriole, northern	*Icterus galbula*
Osprey	*Pandion haliaetus*
Otter, river	*Lutra canadensis*
Ouzel, water	See Dipper, American
Owl, burrowing	*Athene cunicularia*
Owl, great horned	*Bubo virginianus*
Owl, northern pygmy	*Glaucidium gnoma*
Owl, northern saw-whet	*Aegolius acadicus*
Owl, spotted	*Strix occidentalis*
Pigeons, band-tailed	*Columba fasciata*
Pika	*Ochotona princeps*
Pintail, northern	*Anas acuta*

Pipit, water	*Anthus spinoletta*
Plovers	*Charadrus* species
Porcupine	*Erethizon dorsatum*
Pronghorn	*Antilocapra americana*
Ptarmigan, rock	*Lagopus mutus*
Ptarmigan, white-tailed	*Lagopus leucurus*
Ptarmigan, willow	*Lagopus lagopus*
Puma	See Lion, mountain
Quail, California	*Callipepla californica*
Quail, mountain	*Oreortyx pictus*
Raccoon	*Procyon lotor*
Rail, Virginia	*Rallis limicola*
Rat, black	*Rattus rattus*
Rat, Ord's kangaroo	*Dipodomys ordii*
Rattlesnake, Pacific	*Crotalus viridis*
Raven, common	*Corvus corax*
Ringtail	*Bassariscus astutus*
Robin, American	*Turdus migratorius*
Salamander, Pacific giant	*Dicamptodon ensatus*
Salamanders, mole	*Ambystoma* species
Salmon	*Oncorhynchus* species
Salmon, chinook	*Oncorhynchus tshawytscha*
Sapsucker, red-breasted	*Sphyrapicus ruber*
Sapsucker, Williamson's	*Sphyrapicus thyroides*
Sapsucker, yellow-bellied	*Sphyrapicus varius*
Seal, harbor	*Phoca vitulina*
Shad	*Alosa sapidissima*
Sheep, bighorn	*Ovis canadensis*
Shoveler, northern	*Anas clypeata*
Shrew, Trowbridge	*Sorex trowbridgii*
Shrew, vagrant	*Sorex vagrans*
Shrews	*Sorex* species
Skink, western	*Eumeces skiltonianus*
Skunk, spotted	*Spilogale putorius*
Snake, common garter	*Thamnophis sirtalis*
Snake, western terrestrial garter	*Thamnophis elegans*
Sora	*Porzana carolina*
Sparrow, fox	*Passerella iliaca*

Sparrow, lark	*Chondestes grammacus*
Sparrow, sage	*Amphispiza belli*
Sparrow, song	*Melospiza melodia*
Squirrel, Belding's	*Spermophilus beldingi*
Squirrel, Columbian ground	*Spermophilus columbianus*
Squirrel, Douglas'	*Tamiasciurus douglasii*
Squirrel, golden-mantled ground	*Spermophilus lateralis*
Squirrel, golden-mantled ground	*Spermophilus saturatus*
Squirrel, northern flying	*Glaucomys sabrinus*
Squirrel, red	*Tamiasciurus hudsonicus*
Squirrel, Townsend's ground	*Spermophilus townsendii*
Squirrel, Washington ground	*Spermophilus washingtonii*
Squirrel, western gray	*Sciurus griseus*
Steelhead	*Salmo gairdneri*
Sturgeon	*Acipenser* species
Swallow tree	*Tachycineta bicolor*
Swallow, violet-green	*Tachycineta thalassina*
Swifts	*Apodidae*
Tanager, western	*Piranga ludoviciana*
Teal, blue-winged	*Anas discors*
Teal, cinnamon	*Anas cyanoptera*
Teal, green-winged	*Anas crecca*
Thrasher, sage	*Oreoscoptes montanus*
Thrush, hermit	*Catharus guttatus*
Thrush, varied	*Ixoreus naevius*
Toad, Great Basin spadefoot	*Spea intermontana*
Towhee, green-tailed	*Pipilo chlorurus*
Towhee, rufous-sided	*Pipilo erythrophthalmus*
Treefrog, Pacific	*Hyla regilla*
Vireo, red-eyed	*Vireo olivaceus*
Vireo, warbling	*Vireo gilvus*
Vole, heather	*Phenacomys intermedius*
Vole, long-tailed	*Microtis longicaudus*
Vole, Oregon	*Microtis oreganus*
Vole, red tree	*Arborimus longicaudus*

Voles	*Microtis* species
Voles, red-backed	*Clethrionomys* species
Warbler, black-throated gray	*Dendroica nigrescens*
Warbler, orange-crowned	*Vermivora celata*
Warbler, Townsend's	*Dendroica townsendii*
Warbler, yellow	*Dendroica petechia*
Warbler, yellow-rumped	*Dendroica coronata*
Weasels	*Mustela* species
Wigeon, American	*Anas americana*
Wildcat	See Bobcat
Wolverine	*Gulo gulo*
Woodpecker, acorn	*Melanerpes formicivorus*
Woodpecker, black-backed	*Picoides arcticus*
Woodpecker, downy	*Picoides pubescens*
Woodpecker, hairy	*Picoides villosus*
Woodpecker, Lewis'	*Melanerpes lewis*
Woodpecker, pileated	*Dryocopus pileatus*
Woodpecker, three-toed	*Picoides tridactylus*
Woodrat, bushy-tailed	*Neotoma cinerea*
Wren, Bewick's	*Thryomanes bewickii*
Wren, house	*Troglodytes aedon*
Wren, marsh	*Cistothorus palustris*
Wren, rock	*Salpinctes obsoletus*
Wren, winter	*Troglodytes troglodytes*

APPENDIX B

Suggested Reading

General

Arno, Stephen F. and Ramona Hammerly. *Timberline: Alpine and Arctic Forest Frontiers*. Seattle: The Mountaineers, 1984.

Barbour, Michael G. and Jack Major, eds. *Terrestrial Vegetation of California*. New York: John Wiley and Sons, 1977.

Barrett, John W. *Regional Silviculture of the United States*, 2nd ed. New York: John Wiley and Sons, 1980.

Brown, E. Reade, ed. *Management of Wildlife in Forests of Western Oregon and Washington*. Washington, D.C.: USDA, Forest Service, 1985.

Daubenmire, Rexford. *Forest Vegetation of Eastern Washington and Northern Idaho*, Technical Bulletin 60. Pullman, Washington: Washington Agriculture Experimental Station, 1970.

———. *Steppe Vegetation of Washington*, Technical Bulletin 62. Pullman, Washington: Washington Agriculture Experimental Station, 1962.

Franklin, Jerry F., Kermit Cromack, Jr., William Denison, Arthur McKee, Chris Maser, James Sedell, Fred Swanson, and Glen Juday. *Ecological Characteristics of Old-Growth, Douglas-Fir Forests*, General Technical Report PNW-118. Portland, Oregon: USDA, Forest Service, Pacific Northwest Forest and Range Experiment Station, 1981.

Franklin, Jerry F. and C. T. Dyrness. *Natural Vegetation of Oregon and Washington*, General Technical Report PNW-8. Portland, Oregon: USDA, Forest Service, Pacific Northwest Forest and Range Experiment Station, 1973.

Highsmith, Richard M., Jr., and A. Jon Kimerling, eds. *Atlas of the Pacific Northwest*, 6th ed. Corvallis: Oregon State University Press, 1979.

Kirk, Ruth. *The Olympic Rain Forest*. Seattle: University of Washington Press, 1966.

Kozloff, Eugene N. *Plants and Animals of the Pacific Northwest*. Seattle: University of Washington Press, 1976.

Maser, Chris and James M. Trappe, eds. *The Seen and Unseen World of the Fallen Tree*, General Technical Report PNW-164. Portland, Oregon: USDA, Forest Service, Pacific Northwest Forest and Range Experiment Station, 1984.

Price, Larry W. *Mountains & Man*. Berkeley: University of California Press, 1981.

Ransom, J. R., ed. *Harper & Row's Complete Field Guide to North American Wildlife, Western Edition*. New York: Harper & Row, 1981.

Schaffer, Jeffrey P. *Crater Lake and Vicinity*. Berkeley: Wilderness Press, 1983.

———. *Lassen Volcanic National Park and Vicinity*. Berkeley: Wilderness Press, 1981.

Schwartz, Susan B. *Cascade Companion*. Seattle: Pacific Search Press, 1976.

———. *Nature in the Northwest: An Introduction to the Ecology of the Northwestern United States from the Rockies to the Pacific*. Englewood Cliffs, New Jersey: Prentice-Hall, 1983.

Thomas, Jack Ward, ed. *Wildlife Habitats in Managed Forests, the Blue Mountains of Oregon and Washington*, Agriculture Handbook No. 53. Washington, D.C.: USDA, Forest Service, 1979.

Wallace, David Rains. *The Klamath Knot*. San Francisco: Sierra Club Books, 1983.

Waring, R. H. and J. F. Franklin. "Evergreen Coniferous Forests of the Pacific Northwest" in *Science*, Vol. 204, 29 June 1979, pp. 1380–86.

Whitney, Stephen R. *A Field Guide to the Cascades and Olympics*. Seattle: The Mountaineers, 1983.

———. *Western Forests*. New York: Alfred A. Knopf, 1985.

Yocom, Charles and Vinson Brown. *Wildlife and Plants of the Cascades*. Healdsburg, California: Naturegraph Publishers, 1971.

Zwinger, Ann H. and Beatrice E. Willard. *Land Above the Trees: A Guide to American Alpine Tundra*. New York: Harper & Row, 1977.

Plants in General

Atkinson, Scott and Fred Sharpe. *Wild Plants of the San Juan Islands*. Seattle: The Mountaineers, 1985.

Gilkey, H. M. and L. R. J. Dennis. *Handbook of Northwestern Plants*. Corvallis: Oregon State University, 1967.

Hitchcock, C. L. and Arthur Cronquist. *Flora of the Pacific Northwest*. Seattle: University of Washington Press, 1973.

Hitchcock, C. L., Arthur Cronquist, Marion Ownbey, and J. W. Thompson. *Vascular Plants of the Pacific Northwest*, 5 vols. Seattle: University of Washington Press, 1955–1969.

Little, Elbert J., Jr. *Atlas of U.S. Trees*, vols. 1 and 3. Miscellaneous Publications 1146 and 1314. Washington, D.C.: USDA, Forest Service, 1971.

Munz, Philip A. and David D. Keck. *A California Flora and Supplement*. Berkeley: University of California Press, 1973.

Peck, M. E. *A Manual of the Higher Plants of Oregon*. Portland, Oregon: Binford & Mort, 1961.

Thompson, Steven and Mary Thompson. *Huckleberry Country: Wild Food Plants of the Pacific Northwest*. Berkeley: Wilderness Press, 1977.

Underhill, J. E. *Wild Berries of the Pacific Northwest*. Seattle: Superior Publishing Company, 1974.

Whittlesey, Rhoda. *Familiar Friends: Northwest Plants*. Portland, Oregon: Rose Press, 1985.

Wildflowers

Clark, Lewis J. *Wildflowers of the Pacific Northwest from Alaska to Northern California*. Sidney, British Columbia: Grays Publishing Ltd., 1976.

Craighead, John J., Frank C. Craighead, Jr., and Ray J. Davis. *A Field Guide to Rocky Mountain Wildflowers*. Boston: Houghton Mifflin Company, 1963.

Haskin, Leslie H. *Wildflowers of the Pacific Coast*. Portland, Oregon: Binford & Mort Publishers, 1959.

Horn, Elizabeth L. *Wildflowers of the Cascades*. Portland, Oregon: The Touchstone Press, 1972.

Larrison, Earl J., G. W. Patrick. W. H. Baker, and J. A. Yaich. *Washington Wildflowers*. Seattle: Seattle Audubon Society, 1974.

Manning, Harvey. *Mountain Wildflowers*. Seattle: The Mountaineers, 1979.

Niehaus, Theodore F. and Charles L. Ripper. *A Field Guide to Pacific States Wildflowers*. Boston: Houghton Mifflin Company, 1976.

Rickett, Harold W. *Wildflowers of the United States, Vol. 5: The Northwestern States*. New York: McGraw-Hill Book Company, 1970.

Spellenberry, Richard. *The Audubon Society Field Guide to North American Wildflowers: Western Region*. New York: Alfred A. Knopf, 1972.

Taylor, Ronald J. *Rocky Mountain Wildflowers*, 2nd ed. Seattle: The Mountaineers, 1986.

Taylor, Ronald J. and George W. Douglas. *Mountain Wild Flowers of the Pacific Northwest*. Portland, Oregon: Binford & Mort, 1975.

Trees

Arno, Stephen F. and Ramona P. Hammerly. *Northwest Trees*. Seattle: The Mountaineers, 1977.

Brockman, C. Frank. *Trees of North America*. New York: Golden Press, 1968.

Garman, Eric H. *Pocket Guide to the Trees and Shrubs of British Columbia*, 3rd rev. ed. Victoria, B.C.: British Columbia Forest Service, 1963.

Hosie, R. C. *Native Trees of Canada*, 8th ed. Don Mills, Ontario: Fitzhenry and Whiteside, Ltd., 1979.

Little, Elbert J., Jr. *The Audubon Society Field Guide to North American Trees: Western Region*. New York: Alfred A. Knopf, 1980.

Lyons, C. P. *Trees, Shrubs, and Flowers to Know in Washington*. Toronto, Ontario: J. M. Dent and Sons, 1956.

McMinn, Howard E. and Evelyn Maino. *An Illustrated Manual of Pacific Coast Trees*. Berkeley: University of California Press, 1967.

Sudworth, George. *Forest Trees of the Pacific Coast*. Reprint. New York: Dover Publications, 1967.

Watts, Tom. *Pacific Coast Tree Finder*. Berkeley, California: Nature Study Guild.

Ferns, Mosses, and Mushrooms

Harthill, Marion P. and Irene O'Connor. *Common Mosses of the Pacific Coast*. Healdsburg, California: Naturegraph Publishers, 1975.

Keator, Glenn and Ruth M. Atkinson. *Pacific Coast Fern Finder*. Berkeley, California: Nature Study Guild, 1981.

Lincoff, Gary H. *The Audubon Society Field Guide to North American Mushrooms*. New York: Alfred A. Knopf, 1981.

McKenny, Margaret (revised by Daniel E. Stuntz). *The Savory Wild Mushroom*. Seattle: University of Washington Press, 1971.

Taylor, T. M. C. *Pacific Northwest Ferns and Their Allies*. Toronto, Ontario: University of Toronto Press, 1970.

Mammals

Bailey, Vernon. *The Mammals and Life Zones of Oregon*. Washington, D.C.: United States Department of Agriculture, 1936.

Banfield, Alexander W. F. *The Mammals of Canada*. Toronto, Ontario: University of Toronto Press, 1974.

Burt, William H. and Richard P. Grossenheider. *A Guide to the Mammals*, 2nd ed. Boston: Houghton Mifflin, 1964.

Cowan, Ian Mctaggart and Charles J. Guiguet. *The Mammals of British Columbia*, 3rd ed. Victoria, B.C.: British Columbia Provincial Museum, 1965.

Dalquest, Walter W., *Mammals of Washington*, 2 vols. Lawrence: University of Kansas Publications, Museum of Natural History, 1948.

Halfpenny, James. *A Field Guide to Mammal Tracking in Western America*. Boulder, Colorado: Johnson Books, 1986.

Ingles, Lloyd. *Mammals of the Pacific States*. Stanford, California: Stanford University Press, 1965.

Kritzman, Ellen B. *Little Animals of the Pacific Northwest*. Seattle: Pacific Search Press, 1977.

Larrison, Earl J. *Mammals of the Northwest: Washington, Oregon, Idaho, and British Columbia*. Seattle: Seattle Audubon Society, 1976.

Maser, Chris, B. R. Mate, Jerry F. Franklin, and C. T. Dyrness. *Natural History of Oregon Coast Mammals*, General Technical Report PNW-133. Portland, Oregon: USDA, Forest Service, Pacific Northwest Forest and Range Experiment Station, 1981.

Murie, Olaus J. *A Field Guide to Animal Tracks*. Boston: Houghton Mifflin Company, 1974.

Pandell, Karen and Chris Stall. *Animal Tracks of the Pacific Northwest*. Seattle: The Mountaineers, 1981.

Van Gelder, Richard G. *Mammals of the National Parks*. Baltimore: The Johns Hopkins University Press, 1982.

Whitaker, John O., Jr. *The Audubon Society Field Guide to North American Mammals*. New York: Alfred A. Knopf, 1980.

Birds

Alcorn, G. D. *Northwestern Birds: Distribution and Eggs*. Tacoma, Washington: Western Media, 1978.

Farrand, John Jr. *An Audubon Handbook: Western Birds*. New York: McGraw-Hill Book Company, 1988.

Farrand, John, Jr., ed. *The Audubon Society Master Guide to Birding* (3 vols.), I. *Loons to Sandpipers*, II. *Gulls to Dippers*, III. *Old World Warblers to Sparrows*. New York: Alfred A. Knopf, 1983.

Gabrielson, I. N. and S. G. Jewett. *Birds of Oregon*. Corvallis: Oregon State College, 1940.

Godfrey, W. E. *The Birds of Canada*. Ottawa, Ontario: The National Museum of Canada, 1966.

Hoffmann, Ralph. *Birds of the Pacific States*. Boston: Houghton Mifflin Company, 1927.

Jewitt, Stangley G., Walter P. Taylor, William T. Shaw, and John W. Aldrich. *Birds of Washington State*. Seattle: University of Washington, 1953.

Larrison, Earl J. *Birds of the Pacific Northwest*. Moscow, Idaho: The University Press of Idaho, 1981.

Lewis, Mark G. and Fred A. Sharpe. *Birding in the San Juan Islands*. Seattle: The Mountaineers, 1987.

National Geographic Society. *Field Guide to the Birds of North America*. Washington, D.C.: National Geographic Society, 1983.

Nehls, Harry B. *Familiar Birds of the Northwest*. Portland, Oregon: Portland Audubon Society, 1981.

Peterson, Roger Tory. *A Field Guide to Western Birds*. Boston: Houghton Mifflin Company, 1961.

Robbins, Chandler S., Betel Bruun, and Herbert S. Zim. *Birds of North America*, rev. ed. New York: Golden Press, 1983.

Small, Arnold. *The Birds of California*. New York: Winchester Press, 1974.

Udvardy, M. D. F. *The Audubon Society Field Guide to North American Birds: Western Region*. New York: Alfred A. Knopf, 1977.

Amphibians and Reptiles

Behler, John L. *The Audubon Society Field Guide to North American Reptiles and Amphibians*. New York: Alfred A. Knopf, 1979.

Carl, G. C. *The Amphibians of British Columbia*. Victoria, B.C.: British Columbia Provincial Museum, 1966.

————. *The Reptiles of British Columbia*, 2nd ed. Victoria, B.C.: British Columbia Provincial Museum, 1968.

Nussbaum, Ronald A., Edmund D. Brodie, Jr., and Robert M. Storm. *Amphibians & Reptiles of the Pacific Northwest*. Moscow, Idaho: The University Press of Idaho, 1983.

Smith, Hobart M. and Edmund D. Brodie, Jr. *Reptiles of North America*. New York: Golden Press, 1982.

Stebbins, Robert C. *A Field Guide to Western Reptiles and Amphibians*. Boston: Houghton Mifflin Company, 1966.

Butterflies and Other Insects

Borror, Donald J., and Richard E. White. *A Field Guide to Insects*. Boston: Houghton Mifflin Company, 1970.

Christensen, James R. *A Field Guide to Butterflies of the Pacific Northwest*. Moscow, Idaho: The University Press of Idaho, 1981.

Dorfeld, Ernst J. *The Butterflies of Oregon*. Forest Grove, Oregon: Timber Press, 1980.

Milne, Lorus and Margery Milne. *The Audubon Society Field Guide to North American Insects & Spiders*. New York: Alfred A. Knopf, 1980.

Neill, W. A. and D. J. Hepburn. *Butterflies Afield in the Pacific Northwest*. Seattle: Pacific Search Press, 1976.

Pyle, Robert Michael. *The Audubon Society Field Guide to North American Butterflies*. New York: Alfred A. Knopf, 1981.

Pyle, Robert Michael. *Watching Washington Butterflies*. Seattle: Seattle Audubon Society, 1974.

Geology

Alt, David D. and D. W. Hyndman. *Roadside Geology of Montana*. Missoula, Montana: Mountain Press Publishing Company, 1986.

———. *Roadside Geology of Northern California*. Missoula, Montana: Mountain Press Publishing Company, 1975.

———. *Roadside Geology of Oregon*. Missoula, Montana: Mountain Press Publishing Company, 1978.

———. *Roadside Geology of Washington*. Missoula, Montana: Mountain Press Publishing Company, 1984.

Baldwin, Ewart M. *Geology of Oregon*, rev. ed. Dubuque, Iowa: Kendall-Hunt Publishing Company, 1976.

Downing, John. *The Coast of Puget Sound: Its Processes and Development*. Seattle: Washington Sea Grant Program, 1983.

Easterbrook, Don J. and David A. Rahm. *Landforms of Washington: The Geologic Environment*. Bellingham, Washington: Union Printing Company, 1970.

Harris, Stephen L. *Fire and Ice: The Cascade Volcanos*. Seattle: The Mountaineers, 1976, rev. ed., 1980.

McKee, Bates. *Cascadia: The Geologic Evolution of the Pacific Northwest*. New York: McGraw Hill Book Company, 1972.

Tabor, Ronald W. *Guide to Geology of the Pacific Northwest*. Seattle: University of Washington Press, 1975.

Page numbers in italics refer to charts or illustrations.

ology of, 24, 25; glaciation in, 43;
heath shrub communities in, 226;
Inland Forest Zones, 147–166;
Insular Range, 5; Northwest
coastal forest in, 89, 92, 99, 113–
114; in Pacific Border Province,
5; in Rocky Mountains Province,
17–18; subalpine forest in, 168,
169, 172, 173, 174, 176–177,
179, 188, 190. *See also* Coast
Mountains
Buckbrush, 123–124
Buckthorn, California, 123
Bullfrogs, 286
Bulrushes, 278, 283–284
Bunchgrass Steppe Zone, 255–
259
Burrowing animals, 264–267

Caldera, formation of, 32–33
California: Alaska-cedar in, 172; in
Cascade–Coast Mountains Province, 11; climate in, 38, 39; geology of, 24–25, 27; North Coast
Range, 4, 7, 132, 136; in Pacific
Border Province, 4, 6–7; subalpine forest in, 168, 169, 172, 173,
175–176, 179, 188, 189; timberline in, 184; wetlands in, 271. *See
also* Californian zones
Californian zones, 64–67, 118–
146; climate in, 132–133; Coast
Redwood Zone, 4, 64, 125–129;
fires in, 134; geology of, 135–136;
Interior Valley Zone, 118–124;
mesic habitat in, 143–144; Mixed
Evergreen Zone, 64–65, 132–
138; rock types in, 133, 135–136;
shrubs in, 137, 140, 143–144,
145–146; Sierran Mixed Conifer
Zone, 65, 138–146; understory
in, 139–140, 143–144; wildlife
in, 192–211
Canopy, 78
Cariboo Mountains, 17
"Cascade cement," 42, 170
Cascade–Coast Mountains Province, 8–11
Cascade Range: alpine communities in, 223, 226, 227–228; Californian zone, 124, 138–140, 144;

climate in, 35–39, 42, 46–47;
distribution of, 173; geology of
20–22, 24–28, 30–33; glaciation
in, 30–31, 43; High Cascades
32, 33, 173; Inland Forest Zones
147, 151, 154–155; North Cascades, 10–11, 173; parklands in
215–219, 222; pumice flats in
221–222; Southern Cascades, 11
144; steppe in, 246, 248, 258–
259; subalpine forest in, 168
174–178, 188, 190; subalpine
woodlands in, 182; volcanic ac
tivity in, 31–33; Western Cascades, 26–27
Cattails, 283
Ceanothus, 84
Chaparral, 4, 122–123; in Californian zone, 122–123, 137, 144; fire
and, 122–123; in Interior Valley
Zone, 65
Cheatgrass, 256–257
Chehalis River Valley, 38, 41
Chinooks, 43, 44
Chinquapin, 107
Chipmunks, 193
Chugach Range, 30
Clark Fork River, 29
Clark's nutcracker, 189, 232–233
Clearcutting, 87–88; habitat and,
211; loss of diversity from, 88; of
redwoods, 131–132; succession
after, 116–117, 195–197
Clearwater Mountains, 17
Cliffs, 238–243; in steppes, 267–
268
Climate, 35–48; in Californian
zone, 132–133; conifers and, 73,
76–77; cushion plants and, 221;
deciduous woodlands and, 76;
elevation and, 46–48; in Inland
Forest Zones, 147–148; jet
stream and, 38–39; microclimates, 51; in Northwest coastal
forest, 91–92; soil and, 53; in
steppe region, 246–247, 251;
timberline and, 182–186; vegetation and, 50–51
Climax vegetation, 60–61; in
Northwest coastal forest, 98, 99;
seral vegetation vs., 82–83; in

erance of, *80*; in Californian zone, 132, 135, 138, 139; distribution of, 66, 99–100, 139, 150, 151–152; as fire dependent, 82; in Inland Forest Zones, 151–154, 155; in Northwest coastal forest, 90, 99–102; Rocky Mountain vs. coastal, 100, 152; western hemlock and, 99

Drowned-river estuaries, 274

Ducks, 15, 286, 296

Duckweed, 285

Eagle, bald, 281, 296

Earthquakes, 19, 20

Ecotones, 58, 182

"Edge effect," 58

Edge habitat, 193–194; in steppe region, 267; at timberline, 229

Edlerberry, coast red, 95, 106, 108

Elevation, climate and, 46–48

Elfinwood. *See* Krummholz trees

Elk, 193, 202, 233

Elkhorn Mountains, 14

Emergent plants, 284–285

Enchantment Lakes region, 188

Epiphytes, 112

Ericads, 107–108

Erythronium montanum (Avalanche lily), 219, *220*

Estuaries, 273–275

Evergreens, conifers as, 73

Fairweather Range, glaciation in, 30

False-hellebore, green (*Veratrum viridis*), 217

Fault-block ranges, 16

Faults, 20

Fell-field communities, 227–228

Fens, 181, 288–291

Ferns: in Californian zone, 131, 135; common sword (*Polystichum munitum*), *110*, 110–111; deer, 109; lady, 110–111; in Northwest coastal forest, 105, 108, 109–111

Fescue, 222; Idaho, 249, 256

Fiords, 31, 273, 274

Fir: age, size, and relative tolerance of, *80*; grand (*Abies gran-*

dis), *80*, 141, 154–156; Inland Fir Zone, 66, 151–155; noble, *80*, 114–115; Pacific silver, *80*, 113–114, 171; Pacific Silver Fir Zone, 67; Shasta red, *80*, 144–146; Shasta Red Fir Zone, 67, 175–176; subalpine (*Abies lasiocarpa*), *80*, 176–179, *177*; Subalpine Fir/Engelmann Spruce Zone, 68, 168, 177–181; white, *80*, 138, 139, 140–141. *See also* Douglas-fir

Fire: chaparral and, 122–123; climate and, 46, 81–82; Douglas-fir and, 101, 152–153; Inland Forest Zone and, 157–159; knobcone pine and, 137; lodgepole pine and, 159; noble fir and, 114; oak woodlands and, 118–119; plant succession after, 112–113; policy of suppressing, 84; Port-Orfordcedar and, 138; red alder and, 103; redwoods and, 128–129; sagebrush and, 254; subalpine fir and, 179; succession after, 81–84, 195–197; western larch and, 156, 161; western white pine and, 156; white fir and, 140–141; wildlife habitat and, 59–60

Fishers, 208

Flagging, 186

Flathead Lake (Montana), 28

Floating plants, 285

Floods, 43; Spokane, 29

Floodplain wetlands, 271–272, 292

Flowers. *See* Wildflowers

Fog, 38, 91–92, 127

Forbs, 249–250

Forests: in fire aftermath, 59–60; insect damage in, 163–164; layers of vegetation in, 77–79; in logging aftermath, 59, 61; in physiographic provinces, 3–18; role of woody debris in, 86–87; tree ages, dimensions, and relative tolerances, *80*; wildlife habitat in, 86–87. *See also* Conifers, Conifer forests; Deciduous woodlands; *specific trees*

Fraser Plateau Province, 12

Volcanic rocks, 22–24, 26–27; soils and, 53
Volcanoes: alpine vegetation on, 223; in Columbia Basin Province, 15; in North Cascades, 10–11. *See also* Saint Helens, Mount
Voles, 207, 233, 234, 282

Wallowa Mountains, 14, 222, 259
Wallula Gap, 29
Wapato (Indian potato), 284–285
Washington: in Cascade–Coast Mountains Province, 10–11; climate in, 36–46; in Columbia Basin Province, 12–14; estuaries in, 273, 274; geology of, 22–28; glacial features of, 30–31; Inland Forest Zones in, 147–166; Northwest coastal forest in, 89–90, 98, 99, 113–116; in Pacific Border Province, 3–8; riparian woodlands in, 293; in Rocky Mountains Province, 17–18; steppe in, 244–249, 255, 258, 259, 261, 269; subalpine forest in, 168–174, 177–191; timberline in, 184; vegetation zones of, 62–63; wetlands in, 271, 273
Waterfowl, 15, 286, 296
Water-lilies, 285
Water ouzels, 297
Wenatchee region, steppe in, 259
Western Cascades, 26–27
Western hemlock series, 156–157
Western Hemlock Zone, 63–64, 90, 96–98
Western Juniper Zone, 49, 66, 248, 260–261
Wetlands, 15, 270–298; freshwater marshes, 282–288; salt marshes, 270, 271, 273–282; types of, 288; vegetation in, 272–273; wildlife in, 286–288; wooded, 288–298
Wheatgrass, bluebunch (*Agropyron spicatum*), 249, 255–258
White pine blister rust, 163
Wildflowers: in alpine communities, 225–228; in Californian zones, 131, 135, 139, 146; in In-

land Forest Zones, 151, 157; in steppe region, 250, 258; in subalpine forest, 175, 180; in subalpine parklands, 213–214
Wildlife: in alpine habitat, 229–243; on cliffs and talus, 238–243; in conifer forests, 192–211, 205; downed timber and, 86–87; in estuaries, 275; fire suppression and, 84; in freshwater marshes, 286–288; in plant communities, 50, 55–57; plant communities and, 50, 57–61; in riparian woodlands, 293–298; in salt marshes, 273, 280–282; in snags, 200; in steppe region, 261–269; succession and, 195–197; understory as, 202–206. *See also* Edge habitat
Willamette Valley, 3–4, 7–8; climate in, 41–42, 46–47; geology of, 27, 29; oak woodlands in, 118–120; Spokane floods and, 29
Willapa Hills, 6, 26
Winds, 43, 46, 47; in timberline areas, 185–186; vegetation and, 52–53
Winter: alpine wildlife in, 230, 231; storms in, 38–39
Wolverines, 237
Woodlands, 49; in Basin and Range Province, 16; subalpine, 182. *See also* Deciduous woodlands; Riparian woodlands
Woodpeckers, acorn, 120
Woodrats, 241
Wood sorrel (*Oxalis oregana*), 131
Wrangell Range, 30
Wrens, rock, 268
Wrens, winter, 204

Xeric habit, 143–144

Yellowstone National Park, 15, 33–34
Yew: family, 71; western yew, 105
Yolla Bolly Mountains, 6

Zootic climax associations, 248